FLORIDA'S PAST

Volume 3

T0204858

7/96

Dear Dad,
Have a Wonderful
birthday!
Love
Lisa xxx ooo

Useppa Island is surrounded by the world's greatest tarpon fishing grounds. In this 1890s photo, Edward vom Hofe, inventor of the star-drag reel, shows off his 210-pound tarpon caught in Captiva Pass. See p. 188. (DR. JAMES INGRAM COLLECTION)

Florida's Past

Past

Volume 3

People and Events
That Shaped the State

Gene M. Burnett

Pineapple Press, Inc.
Sarasota, Florida

Pineapple Press, Inc. P.O. Box 3899
Sarasota, Florida 34230

LIBRARY OF CONGRESS CATALOGING IN PUBLICATION DATA
(Revised for vol. 3)
Burnett, Gene M., 1928–1991
Florida's past.

First edition—Vol. 2. t.p. verso.
Vol. 2 published in Sarasota, Fla.
Originally published in Florida Trend since 1972.
Includes bibliographical references and index.
1. Florida—History. 2. Florida—Biography.
1. Title.
F311.5.B87 1986 975.9 86-15048

First paperback edition
10 9 8 7 6 5 4 3 2 1

Printing by Edwards Brothers, Lillington, N.C.

Photographs in this book are from the Florida State Archives except where noted.

CONTENTS

ACKNOWLEDGMENTS

Inasmuch as the third volume is but the final series of a single consecutive effort, I would entreat the reader—those at least who have read the first two volumes—to consider the acknowledgments in the earlier works inclusively with this volume. In fact, space considerations would only meanly allot the proper expressions of gratitude and indebtedness the author feels toward the many individuals who rendered aid and assistance, palpably or intangibly, to the creation of the total work.

However, for this particular volume, I must express grateful thanks to Clubhouse Publishers, Inc., of Sarasota, and to Pam Daniel, able editor of *Sarasota* magazine, for permission to reprint the three articles on Mrs. Potter Palmer, the Scotch colonists, and the Sarasota vigilantes. A hearty thanks to Judy Johnson for her incisive copyediting and to Millicent Hampton Shepherd for her photoediting and general shepherding.

A true acknowledgment is that without any one or all of these groups or individuals, the three books would have been, at best, only the lesser for it.

To the memory of
LeRoy Collins
a fellow historian,
but one who made Florida history
and was that history himself.

INTRODUCTION

With this third and final volume on Florida's past, there comes a wistful tug of separation, a pulling away, a feeling not unlike the end of harvest after a fruitful season. But there is also the sanguine satisfaction of a finished task, completion. The work of years passes out of you and now sustains its own viability; whatever merit it possesses must surely be defined by the final arbiter, the reader. This is as it should be.

Despite the sometimes thorny passages and the frustrations of creative composition, I have enjoyed the making of it and have been more than gratified by the response forthcoming. I regard it all as a token and a gift, a restoration and a sharing of what we have been and of what we are still all about. And this is to ask enough.

Gene M. Burnett

F LORIDA'S

P AST

Volume 3

The lines have fallen to me in pleasant places;
indeed my heritage is beautiful to me.

Psalm 136:21 (NAS)

Achievers and Pioneers

1.
The Florida Birth of
Hitler's Buzz-Bombs

The first guided missiles, flown in Arcadia, were often comical Rube Goldberg contraptions.

The most terrifying weapon launched against the Allies in World War II was the V-2 guided missile, or "flying bomb." Coming in faster than the speed of sound, it gave no warning before its near ton of explosives obliterated a factory complex or an entire city block. Fortunately, its debut in the fall of 1944 came too late to save the crumbling Nazi Reich.

Few are aware today that the prototype of the guided missile had its birth in the era of World War I, not World War II, and not in Germany, but at Florida's Carlstrom Field, the Army air base in the small rural town of Arcadia.

Of course, none of the farmers, cowboys, and general citizenry found anything too terrifying about this earliest version of a pilotless bomber. Indeed, it more nearly resembled one of Rube Goldberg's less inspired creations, and the efforts of its developers to get it to do something (such as fly to a target and drop its payload on it) had freakish and sometimes comical results. At best the weapon might have distracted a few cows grazing around the placid Peace River Valley country.

With America's entry into WWI in April 1917, military planners in Washington began a search for new weapons, particularly ones that would expend machines rather than men. Interest in a guided missile had developed much earlier as a result of research by Elmer Sperry, inventor of the gyrocompass. His son, Lawrence Sperry, was already engaged in U.S. naval research in this area.

The Army finally came up with a plan for a small pilotless and expendable airplane, one that could carry about 300 pounds of explosives, fly 50 miles or more under its own controls, and bomb a target with reasonable accuracy. To undertake this project, the Army in December 1917 picked C.F. Kettering of Dayton, Ohio, inventor of the electric self-starter ignition for automobiles and vice president and head of research for General Motors.

An industrialist-engineer of philosophic bent, Kettering once mused: "We find that in research a certain amount of intelligent ignorance is essential to

5

progress; for, if you know too much, you won't try the thing." Whether Kettering had too little of the former or too much of the latter is not certain, but the Kettering "Bug," as the missile came to be called, seemed plagued with bugs from the start.

Variously called a "flying bomb," "robot bomb," and "aerial torpedo," it was regarded more as a loose cannon than a guided missile after its initial tests. In the first unofficial test, the little plane took off as planned, climbed steeply to 150 feet, then whip-stalled, turned, and dove straight toward the spectators below; they scattered to safety as it crashed. Another test saw the Bug launched successfully, but then it climbed to an unplanned 12,000 feet, circled the field a few times, then disappeared behind a cloud patch. Said a disgusted Kettering, "Let the thing stay up there." He then went home to bed while other officials chased the plane by car and discovered the crash site 21 miles away. But another torpedo launched perfectly, flew at its preset altitude, dove on the target 500 yards away and missed it by less than 50 feet.

Despite these erratic test results, the Army was encouraged enough to order a limited production of the missile. One enthusiastic observer, Colonel H.H "Hap" Arnold (later head of the U.S. Air Force in WWII), hurried over to France in October 1918 to inform General John J. Pershing of this "exciting" new weapon. A flu attack delayed Arnold, and he arrived at the front only to hear the guns celebrating Armistice Day, November 11.

But this missile project continued apace. Some of the Bug's problems derived from Kettering himself. He insisted that the weapon be produced quickly, simply, and cheaply, even at the expense of technical sophistication. Known for years as "Boss" Kettering, he could be overbearing, even in areas where his technical knowledge was limited. He argued at length with Orville Wright (of Kitty Hawk fame), whose company was in charge of the missile's biplane body design, and with Ford Motor Company's Ralph de Palma, auto racer and builder, who was in charge of its engine. A certain professional pique also made Kettering balk at using Sperry's gyrocompass even though the instrument was essential to the missile's directional control. Sperry generously provided the gyro drawings and let his son, Lawrence, consult on its use.

Kettering did come up with an ingenious way to use the vacuum from the engine's crankcase to operate the controls. He also devised a small airscrew on the wing that drove a mileage counter for distance control. At a preselected range the counter would hit zero, cut off the ignition, and send the nose-heavy craft toward the target.

The Bug's Rube Goldberg image seemed evident in the muslin and brown paper that covered its two 15-foot wings, the steel tubing used for structural support, the simple pasteboard over the control surfaces, the slotted gas pipes used for a launching track, and the carrier made from the discarded frames of railroad handcars. The design was for lightness, keeping the missile's weight at 300 pounds; it would carry a 300-pound warhead.

On September 4, 1919, 12 flying bombs were completed and shipped to Carlstrom Field at Arcadia for their big day in the Florida sun. Though they were excluded from the secrecy-shrouded testings, Arcadians shared the excitement as top officials of the U.S. Army and Navy and the British Air Corps gathered to observe the first official tests of the new weapon. But only the amazement itself seemed formidable—the tests were humiliating.

A young First Lieutenant, Jimmy Doolittle (the Tokyo bomber of WWII), recorded the fiasco for the Air Service Test Board. Here is a sampling of his comments, beginning with the first flight on September 26: "The tail rose until the torpedo slid off the car and nosed into the ground." "The torpedo took off in a zoom, climbed to 200 feet, fell off and crashed." "Torpedo flew 1-3/4 miles and crashed due to motor failure." "Torpedo flew two miles and wings came off." "The last torpedo, constructed from salvaged parts of previous wrecks, flew about 16 miles. It was approximately on its course, the proper altitude was adhered to and the crash was caused by motor trouble." With some understatement, Doolittle concluded: "The motor is not sufficiently reliable to permit the torpedo flying over friendly troops."

Despite these dismal results, much had been learned from the Florida tests, and when the military relieved Kettering of the project soon after and turned it over to the Navy, Lawrence Sperry would perfect the Navy's version of the Bug. More daring and imaginative (he would even strap himself to the missile's fuselage to study it while in flight) and more technically creative, Sperry hit upon the solution for missile accuracy: remote control by radio in conjunction with the gyroscopic pneumatic controls. His triumph came on June 29, 1922, when the Sperry aerial torpedo hit a 30-mile target twice, a 60-mile target three times, and a 90-mile target once.

Much earlier, Kettering himself had declared that he cared no more for "the Bug Job" since it drained too heavily on GM's research talents.

The Bug was never used by the Allies as a weapon in World War II. The U.S. government decided to put its resources into development of the B-17 Flying Fortress bomber, which played an instrumental role in winning the war. But early research on a flying bomb proved vital after the war in the development of missile technology and, ultimately, in the manned exploration of space.

2.

Key Marco: The Treasure and the Scandal

Ethnologist Frank Cushing uncovered Florida's "lost" civilization, but his efforts met intrigue and scandal.

It was one of the greatest archaeological finds of the 19th century, yielding up from the steamy, brine-soaked muck and marl of Florida's Key Marco the relics of a "lost" civilization.

But the man who disinterred this exotic treasure, the Smithsonian Institution's gifted ethnologist, Frank Hamilton Cushing, would consequently find himself mired in another kind of muck—a muck of calumny and controversy that, amazingly, would linger for almost a century. It still might linger today but for the investigative diligence of Florida archaeologist Marion S. Gilliland, who dug deeply into the past for records, letters, diaries, and notes—much of it hitherto unknown—to re-create the 1896 Marco expedition and its infamous aftermath. In her recently published *Key Marco's Buried Treasure*, she tells an intriguing story that conclusively restores the integrity of both Cushing and his extraordinary Florida discovery.

Cushing's superior at the Smithsonian's Bureau of Ethnology, Major J.W. Powell, picked him to head the Pepper-Hearst expedition, named for Dr. William Pepper, head of the University of Pennsylvania's archaeology department and Cushing's personal physician, and Phoebe Hearst, wife of the noted publisher. It was jointly sponsored by the Smithsonian and the university; each would share in future artifact collections.

Despite lifelong ill health, Cushing, 38, had earned professional distinction with his artistic imagination and genius at interpretative scientific skills. His recent Zuni-Hemenway expedition, a six-year stay with the Zuni Indians in Arizona, had produced major archaeological studies and artifacts.

The Pepper-Hearst expedition arose from Captain W.D. Collier's accidental discovery in 1895 of unusual Indian artifacts on his Marco Island settlement and Cushing's subsequent survey of the area. Cushing's 14-person team included his wife, Emily, and a perceptive young lawyer, artist, and photographer, Wells Moses Sawyer, whose notes, photos, and paintings rescued for posterity glimpses of the more perishable artifacts. After some delay at Tarpon Springs, Florida, where they made Indian mound excavations, the team arrived at Marco in late February, 1896, and set to work at once. Within days, an excited Cushing wrote to Pepper: "My discoveries have been literally startling. The entire collection will be unique and almost priceless if we keep on this way."

What Cushing uncovered at Marco was "a degree of culture hitherto undreamed of" among earlier American people, dating from about 750 to 1513 A.D. The Calusa Indians, who doubtless had migrated from Central America, had developed a well-knit community (up to 10,000 people) and were primarily sea-dwellers inhabiting the countless islands off the southwest Florida coast. They constructed huge island shell mounds, engineered networks of canals, lagoons, and fish ponds, and, their artifacts revealed, achieved an advanced technology of craftsmanship unparalleled among early cultures. Their tools, carvings, and paintings often were equal in quality to the finest Egyptian antiquities. One ingenious carving tool, made from the teeth of the leopard shark, enabled the sea-dwellers to carve wood with a delicate precision equal to the best modern Swiss carvers. Their shell paintings and their carvings and paintings of animal figureheads, statuettes, and tablets ranked them, Cushing noted, among "the brainiest" of early peoples. Incredibly in that tropic climate, the blend of briny muck and tannic acid from surrounding mangrove trees had preserved the relics in "mint" condition over centuries. However, in the absence then of modern sugar solution or polyethylene glycol, barely one-fourth of the specimens survived exposure to air. Even so, when the work ended in May, 1896, 11 barrels and 59 boxes of them were shipped to Washington. The unique Marco collection became the topic of the day in scientific circles as well as in general public interest. But it would soon draw interest of a less salutary nature.

William Dinwiddie, a Smithsonian photographer, examined the collection one day and made a startling accusation against Cushing—fraud. Dinwiddie singled out a shell painting depicting a costumed Indian dancer and claimed that Cushing had altered the shell's line drawing with common India ink. He took his accusation to the *New York Herald* whose editors soon informed Smithsonian officials that they were preparing a story on the "fraud." Dinwiddie then searched out other Cushing detractors such as bureau ethnologist F.W. Hodge, Cushing's assistant on the Zuni-Hemenway expedition. Hodge still claimed he had seen Cushing "manufacture" a Zuni artifact, a shell-inlaid "jeweled frog." (Cushing earlier explained that he had merely restored some loose shell fragments on the frog.) Cushing had once soundly castigated Hodge for mishandling Hemenway business accounts. Another Hemenway staffer joining Dinwiddie was Mrs. M.C. Stevenson, who had begrudged Cushing's informal relations

with the Zunis (he was made an honorary tribesman). Hodge even persuaded—
for a time at least—anthropologist Dr. J.W. Fewkes that the frog was a fraud.
By now, Dinwiddie had churned up such a climate of suspicion toward Cushing
that total strangers were entering the fray—such as a tall, attractive blonde who
one day called on a Smithsonian official to inform him that she was writing an
article charging Cushing with immoral conduct and fraud. But this was the last
anyone ever saw or heard of either the nameless lady or her manuscript.

Meanwhile, a stunned Cushing was demanding an investigation of "a
conspiracy" to create a "scientific scandal," but Smithsonian officials were more
concerned that such a probe might lend official dignity to "utterly unfounded
accusations." Major Powell even reexamined the disputed shell and determined
that its paint pigment was identical to pigments on the other artifacts. Finally, a
number of eminent specialists were called in to examine the entire collection;
they were "uniformly satisfied" of its authenticity. The bureau then fired
Dinwiddie for his "unjustifiable conduct and utterances" and also informed the
Herald that publication of such charges would bring "immediate legal action."
The *Herald* earlier had joined Dinwiddie and his cohorts in political efforts to
get a Congressional probe, but nothing official ever came of this maneuver. The
newspaper now spiked its "Cushing story," but, sometime later, it hired
Dinwiddie as its Sunday editor.

Remarkably, Cushing bore little if any personal ill will toward his maligners

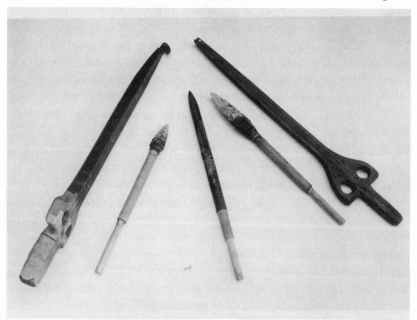

*For delicate carving, the tooth of the leopard shark, shown here, offered a cutting edge
which surpassed any other primitive implement employed by the American Indian. The
best Swiss carver of today could scarcely give it a better finish.*

during this lengthy ordeal. (He was even concerned about getting the unemployed Dinwiddie a job.) During this period Cushing was also suffering from chronic health ailments and the straitened finances resulting from supporting both his home and his field work. He was under much pressure to publish his full expedition report (which he never completed). Then in 1898 a grievous blow came with the deaths of his parents, a brother, and his close friend Dr. Pepper. Cushing himself died at 42 on April 10, 1900.

Unfortunately, Cushing's detractors would keep the fraud controversy fueled long after his death. In retrospect, it seems unimaginable that such an ignominious pall should be cast over Cushing's achievements for nearly a century.

During the controversy, the distinguished anthropologist Franz Boas, concerned for its effect on the welfare of science itself, wrote to Smithsonian anthropologist W.J. McGee in 1897 urging "radical action" to quell the rumors, gossip, and contentions, and adding: "I have always considered him [Cushing] one of the frankest, most generous, open-hearted and honorable men whom it was my good fortune to meet. His greatest enemy is, I take it, his genius."

Thus it seems beneficently ironic, even if tragically posthumous, that thanks to the efforts of a latter-day colleague and admirer, Ms. Gilliland, Cushing's genius would become not his enemy but his redeemer.

3.
The Romance of a "Heavenly" Railroad

The world's shortest railroad prospered Lake Worth settlers,
but a mighty rail mogul sidetracked it.

It was called the "Celestial Railroad," and back in the 1890s it did indeed seem
to hold out heavenly prospects to folks in the little port village of Juno at the
northern tip of Lake Worth.

It was probably the smallest railroad in the world, but that fact in no way
belied its importance. It was a narrow-gauge line that ran all 7.5 miles from
Juno, through the wilderness way stations of Venus and Mars, to Jupiter on the
Atlantic. It also was the southernmost railroad in the country and made Juno the
terminus for all passenger and freight traffic, north- and southbound, between
Jacksonville and Miami. It was the pride of the several hundred settlers in the
Lake Worth region—Lantana, Palm Beach, Hypoluxo Island. And to Junoans
it was a glimmering lodestar, the little train that could—and would—make Juno
a thriving capital of commerce for southeast Florida.

The line's uniqueness had already caught some national and international
attention. In fact, that's how it got its name. Travel writer Julian Ralph, writing
in *Harper's* magazine in March, 1893, first dubbed it the "celestial railroad." A
British visitor used the moniker again in a *Chamber's Journal* story. Lake
Worthians liked it; it stuck.

But a formidable figure looming out of the north eventually would cast a
giant shadow down Florida's east coast, a shadow that would engulf and doom
both Juno's dream of bustling cityhood and the little railroad itself.

In those days, Dade County, with only 861 souls plus 134 Indians, sprawled
all the way up nearly to Jupiter. Both passengers and freight, from either coastal
steamboats at Jupiter or the steamer *Lake Worth* on the lake, were shunted over
the rough trail between the two ports by "bull trains" (ox wagons). The "barefoot
mailman" walked the 60 miles south to Miami, Coconut Grove, and Lemon
City, and the "fiddling mailman"—John Clemenson—played a fiddle as he
walked beside his wagon between Jupiter and Juno.

But 1889 was a landmark year for Juno. Disaffected citizens of the lake country wrested the county seat of Dade from Miami in a bitter election and moved it to Juno, where citizens promptly erected a small but sturdy two-story courthouse, Dade's first. Soon afterward, the Jacksonville, Tampa, and Key West Railroad, of Jacksonville, took over the "bull trains" and the Jacksonville Transportation Company (steamers) and announced plans to build the Jupiter and Lake Worth Railway. Jubilant lake-area citizens eagerly paid $7,500 to own a piece of the J. & L.W. and by late June an engine with a freight-passenger car and a flat car was ready to roll. Rail officials hosted nearly 100 excited Lake Worthians for a free train ride to Jupiter and a festive Fourth of July picnic.

The little railway was an instant success, and by 1891 it would have two full passenger coaches and three freight cars. Of course, with no competition in the area, the Jacksonville company was able to levy some rather stiff rates. One-way passenger fare for the 30-minute trip was 75 cents; freight charges were 20 cents per 100 pounds, with wharfage additional. But the new line was bringing a steady stream of both settlers and tourists. Juno itself hummed with activity. New building was going up. The town soon had its first newspaper when Guy Metcalf brought his Tropical Sun down from Melbourne, and its first lawyer and later judge, C.C. Chillingworth, who swapped the county legal counsel for office space in the new courthouse. As Juno prospered, land prices in the vicinity rose to a high of $75 an acre.

Ironically, the two little way stations north of Juno would remain just that, untouched by the flush lake times. Mars was only an unsettled clearing along the railroad right of way. Venus's population consisted of one J.B. Wells and his two cats, and despite the prodigious efforts of Wells to sell his "embryo city," there were just no takers.

Relations between Junoans and the company itself were often strained. Citizens were exasperated with its often erratic one-trip-a-day schedule and especially its cramped and stuffy wharfside station house into which was packed freight, passengers, and ticket and telegraph offices. Metcalf's *Sun* scorned the "shabby, unpainted, unsightly" building and exhorted rail officials, unsuccessfully, to expand the station house and spruce it up.

But rail employees — conductors, wharf agents, and others — often made up the difference by performing extra services and small favors. The Celestial itself was a difference. The engine was vintage 19th century, complete with cowcatcher and funnel stack, and its genial engineer, Blus Rice, operated it with the informal caprice of the frontier it served. At the Juno wharf, children scrambled in play over the engine, and at Jupiter, incoming steamboat visitors were greeted by Rice with a train-whistle rendition of "Dixie." The train also hauled settlers to picnics, dances, and civic events that weren't always on the schedule. Rice always carried along a hunting dog in his cab and often would stop along the wilderness right-of-way to let passengers off to bag a turkey or deer. When Rice married Juno's Rosa Clark, the little engine was decked out by citizens with flowers and evergreen for the occasion. This was clearly no Amtrak special.

But the golden skies over Juno were soon to turn leaden when, in March, 1893, a distinguished-looking gentleman in a black cutaway gazed across Lake Worth toward the exotic skyline of coconut palms on Palm Beach and liked what he saw. Henry M. Flagler, oil magnate-cum-railroad developer, wasted no time. Within the year, he had picked up options on huge land tracts on both sides of the lake; he would build the resort of Palm Beach for his friends and the town of West Palm Beach "for his help." The J. & L.W. was soon reaping fantastic earnings hauling lumber to build Flagler's Royal Poinciana Hotel on Palm Beach. But bad management and a touch of avarice on the part of the J. & L.W.'s parent line were about to seal the fate of the Celestial Railroad and of Juno itself.

When Flagler offered to buy the Celestial from the debt-ridden J.T. & K.W., the latter asked such an exorbitant price that the outraged developer balked. Instead—to the mortification of Junoans—he bridged the Loxahatchee River westward, completely bypassing Jupiter and Juno when he brought his railroad into West Palm Beach in March, 1894. He also dug a canal north of Juno for ocean-lake steamer traffic.

Thereafter, both railroad and town languished in economic decline, and in June, 1896, the Celestial's rolling stock was sold at public auction in Jacksonville. The sadness of the Celestial's passing was recalled by Dora Doster Utz who, as a girl, used to play on its locomotive: "The jungles and the underbrush were fast claiming the right-of-way, and the sorrowful call of the Mourning Dove seemed to be sounding a requiem to its passing."

Miami in 1899 won back the county seat, and, soon after, a forest fire destroyed Juno. In the 1930s, Judge Chillingworth discovered the brick foundation of the old courthouse, and area citizens erected a monument to the Celestial and Juno. It was embedded with a bronze medallion and adorning figurines, but in later years vandals would steal both medallion and figurines. Then, in the 1940s, a road department machine at work on the highway near the site knocked over the monument, and it lay there as so much rubble thereafter.

Today, except for a few treasured railroad spikes and two old photos of the Celestial engine (one of them discovered in the Library of Congress), the demise of both railroad and Juno seems complete.

4.
Springtime for a Resort Queen

One of Florida's earliest resort hotels near Daytona gets a modern facelift.

Once a dazzling queen among the world's grand hotels in the great Gilded Age, then a gradually fading beauty, maintaining herself in genteel poverty as she deftly dodged the poorhouse and the wrecking ball, the historic Ormond Hotel of Ormond Beach today has had her antiquated image bobbed. She is coming on with the vigor of a modern Young Miss who has swapped her ballroom slippers for tennis shoes and the "now" look.

The 90-year-old grand dame of hostelries—a massive wooden structure that is one of the world's few still existing—no longer hosts the economic titans, celebrities, and royalty of that glittering Diamond Jim Brady era, when John D. Rockefeller, Sr., dueled at golf with the Prince of Wales, and Winton, Olds, Vanderbilt, the Marriotts, and the Chevrolets were sporting around to make that hard-packed silvery beach the birthplace of auto speed.

Her long, tall doors are now wide open to the common gentry, both young and old, for a night, a week, a season, or year-round. The John Quincy Does will find themselves accorded the same treatment once reserved solely for the John Jacob Astors. (The prices are apt to be more modest, too.) Moreover, many ancient rooms in the huge edifice are seeing modern plumbing for the first time; air-conditioning replaces quaint ceiling fans; huge clothes closets are being accommodated to kitchenettes; the grand ballroom now serves as a chapel and will also be used as a banquet room; and, across the street, the new Racquet Club is hosting international tennis teams on its eight hard courts.

The regeneration of the Ormond, now a corporation, is being sparked by its enthusiastic young manager, W.J. (Bill) Wetherell, the son of one of its two owners, Thomas J. Wetherell and T.T. Cobb, who bought the hotel in the late 1950s. Wetherell developed a fondness for the grand old structure even as a high school teenager when he had to slap fresh paint on her weathered, aging joints and facades for 50 cents an hour. "We've spent about $600,000 over the last five years on renovation alone," he noted. This includes new carpeting and lighting, new fire escapes and an ultra-fireproof sprinkler system, air-conditioning, and, beneath her sprawling foundations, huge, solid steel I-beams to reinforce the already solid supporting wooden beams. Wetherell observed of the latter: "That original cypress wood is still so hard you can barely drive a nail into it."

The hotel still hosts a large number of the elderly and retirees, seasonally and year-round, but through a planned diversification of activities and interests, Wetherell reports that the Ormond is now bringing in business it has never had before—scores of young people and sports enthusiasts as well as those tourists who might otherwise drop off at the Holiday or the Ramada. The great five-story structure, which rambles leisurely over its original 12-acre site overlooking the scenic Halifax River, sill provides easy access to the famous Ormond Beach, about a three-minute stroll down Granada Avenue. However, one need not even leave the great building to seek exercise; its 11 miles of corridors and sprawling broad open verandas and breezeways provide balmy sea winds and tropical vistas enough for any restless ambler.

And yet the modern spirit of rejuvenation for this vintage piece of history does not detract from, nor overshadow, its romantic and opulent heydays. Rather it seems to blend the now and the yore into a continuity that retains the distinctive features of both.

The hotel began as an impossible brainstorm by two men who came to the small Ormond settlement in the late 1870s, James D. Price, of Kentucky, and John Anderson, of Maine. They believed the area would make a good site for a tourist hotel even though the jungle strip, as settlers jeeringly reminded them, had no river bridge and was 50 miles from the nearest railroad. With the aid of a wealthy financier friend, Stephen V. White, who had recovered his health during a Florida winter visit, they were in business. With mules and men they set to the task, and the new Ormond Hotel opened its doors on January 1, 1888. Shortly after, a railroad came through and a bridge spanned the Halifax. Among the first visitors from New York's social set were the wife of the late President U.S. Grant and Mrs. Henry Ward Beecher. And when multi-millionaire Henry Flagler visited the hotel in its third season, he saw its potential as a link in a chain of luxury hotels he hoped to plant from St. Augustine on down Florida's coast. He bought the Ormond in 1890 for $112,000.

The tycoon spared no expense to outdo even his magnificent Ponce de Leon in St. Augustine. He added huge new wings, a swimming pool, a casino, a dormitory and laundry, a beach pavilion, and a river pier, plus three water-powered Otis elevators. The railroad bridge was restructured so that wealthy nabobs could sidle their private Pullman railroad cars right up to the hotel's west entrance. Costly rugs and carpets and crystal chandeliers decorated the grand and spacious lobby and corridors, the dining room sparkled with the finest silver, china, crystalware and linens; and the grand ballroom was banked with plants and exotic flowers. Activities included sailing, swimming, fishing, a seven-hole golf course, and a medieval tournament each year when men garbed themselves as knights and jousted over the spacious lawns while indulging in a week of merrymaking. Flagler imported entertainment celebrities to perform for the wealthy visitors during the long winter season, and, in the early 1900s, auto racing replaced bicycling as the ultimate playboy sport.

The Astors, Vanderbilts, Fords, and other gilded titans mixed fun and games with Europe's counts, dukes, and assorted nobility, and what came to be known as "Millionaire's Colony" flourished unabatedly for more than 30 years. Rockefeller occupied a whole specially-built wing of the hotel's second floor for his entourage but later, in a personal tiff with Flagler, left the Ormond and moved across the street where he had bought a mansion, The Casements, in which he remained until his death in 1937. The Casements is still preserved today. But in the decade of World War I, Flagler who had already pushed his railroad empire farther south, began to haul his golden reveler hordes to luxury playgrounds at Palm Beach and Miami.

The Ormond gradually lost its fabulous clientele during the 1920s and became popular mainly as a convention center. Up through the '30s and '40s, it struggled to keep its doors open through a succession of owners. It alternated as a nightclub, a hotel management school, and a retirement home for ministers and missionaries, barely keeping a step ahead of bankruptcy until Wetherell and Cobb purchased it in 1957.

Today, the great structure has come through a successful post-operative stage in its adjustment to the late 20th century. Young Wetherell has found diversification—in both activities and clientele—to be the key to that adjustment, and, so far, it is successfully proving out.

For example, it no longer sports the crude auto machines of those early racing buffs, but it does host an annual Antique Car Show each November, which draws even greater crowds than those that once lined the dunes at Daytona.

Another annual event that has met with success is the colorful Halifax Art Festival each fall, when the spacious grounds and verandas are studded with the bright creative efforts of a host of state and national talent.

The new Ormond Hotel Racquet Club across the street, little more than a year old, is drawing tennis buffs, young and old, from all over the country and Europe as well. The club has hired Bill Farmer, 56-year-old teaching pro, as its director, aided by a younger pro, Bill Lefko, 29, who hold clinics on the eight courts for everyone from tots to oldsters. Club plans for the future include a swimming pool, four more courts, a new locker room, and air-conditioned indoor racquetball courts.

The hotel's 380-plus rooms are being modernized rapidly, and the huge dining room now serves its guests cafeteria-style, with modestly priced buffet luncheons open to the public.

By combining the hotel's functions in a manner to draw both residents and tourists, the hotel has traded its seasonal image—and consequent economic slumps—for flourishing year-round trade. Its 130 permanent guests, mostly retirees, now mix in with the activities of winter guests and transients and, where once "winter used to be our only season," Wetherell has found the summer business more than doubling over last summer.

Many planned activities keep both resident and visitor occupied, such as musical programs, parties, sight-seeing trips to area attractions like Disney World, physical fitness classes, and even accredited college courses.

Thus a grand old girl of world-famous hostelries is kicking over the traces as she pushes sprightly toward her second century. Still retaining her quaint 1900s atmosphere, furnishings, and baubles, she is swapping circumstance and pomp for the populist ways of the day and recovering, in the process, her once youthful spirit as well as economic well-being. Wetherell, therefore, feels certain she is in good shape for at least another 50 years, "maybe even more"—a revived and thriving page out of Florida history.

5.
St. Pete's Visionary Town Planner

Journalist Straub peered into the far future and laid out St. Petersburg accordingly.

The City of St. Petersburg enjoys the distinction of being one of the few cities in the world that planned its downtown development many decades before the term "city planner" ever entered the modern lexicon.

Its uniquely developed downtown waterfront and its spacious, well-platted streets are no accident. While most cities in this century permitted their river-, bay-, oceanfronts to become run-down, commercialized eyesores, requiring staggering costs to restore, St. Pete was alone in pioneering a planned development that would benefit all of its citizens some 50 years hence.

Thus it did not merely save future taxpayers millions of dollars, plus a scad of urban woes. It also created a bountiful array of public benefits for all of its citizens—a pier, beach, park, baseball field, activities center, boat basins, airport, and other attractions—nearly all of which are a few minutes' walking distance from downtown. (It is not hard to see why the city received an All-America City award in 1973 from the National Municipal League.)

But not many people are aware that this unusual, far-sighted planning is attributable to the crusading zeal of one single-minded publisher-editor back in the 1900s—a man who took on no few odds and incurred no little wrath in order to preserve that beautiful waterfront for the public's ownership and benefit. However, this newspaper editor, W.L. (William Lincoln) Straub, was willing to make himself "so obnoxious," according to a contemporary, Dudley Haddock, that "city council finally approved his /planning ideas/ in 1908, largely to shut his mouth."

But in addition to preserving the waterfront and having city streets platted for use in 1977 as well as 1907, Straub also employed some deft surgery to sever the peninsula from its domineering "stepmother" across the bay, transforming an orphan-like West Hillsborough County into brand-new Pinellas County and

19

greatly facilitating the town's singular development. But he had to first fight, and then out-maneuver, a formidable Tampa political machine that was not about to part with the lucrative tax revenues that St. Pete paid—and for which it received few benefits in return.

Straub was, according to historian Walter Fuller, "a complete idealist." Although a gentle man who "fought for issues, not against people," he possessed a bulldog tenacity and patience which either wore down or infuriated his foes. But his efforts were generally selfless. As Fuller assesses him: "He never subdivided a piece of land or built a building for profit or started a bank or owned a bulldozer. His only weapon was a pen."

W.L. Straub was born July 14, 1867, in Dowagiac, Michigan. After finishing school at age 16, he went to the Dakota Territory where he edited several newspapers. In the meantime he married Sarah A. Moore, also of Dowagiac, and they had one daughter, Blanche. Already afflicted with a crippled leg from birth, Straub developed severe bronchitis, and doctors told him he had not long to live. But Straub had already wintered in St. Pete in 1898-99 and decided to move his family there permanently in 1900; the climate, sun, and outdoor activities soon restored his health completely.

In 1901, Straub bought the St. Petersburg Weekly Times, a shaky, sometime little paper that had changed hands many times in the previous 17 years. Within a few years, he would turn it into a daily.

The waterfront scene of the village of St. Pete in the 1900s—population over 7,300 souls—was one of the cutthroat competition for steamboat travel and commercial shipping. Railroad tycoon H.B. Plant enjoyed a virtual monopoly with his 3,000-foot railroad and steamboat pier at the present city pier site. When D.F.S. Brantley built a 1500-foot pier and laid some wooden railroad tracks, Plant fumed over his competition and attempted, unsuccessfully, to squeeze Brantley out. Even then, free competitive enterprise, it seemed was more ritual slogan than fact. But when George L. King attempted to build a third pier, Plant found a way to forcibly stop him, and this occasioned an angry mass meeting of citizens to censure the action. Nevertheless, King never got his pier constructed. The rail titan, however, came to loathe the town, especially when he was rebuffed by the citizenry in his attempt to win price concessions to build a waterfront hotel similar to his huge, Moorish Tampa Bay Hotel. He stormed over to Clearwater and built one there.

Meanwhile, Straub, probably one of the earliest environmentalists as well as practical city planners, realized not merely the natural beauty of the waterfront but also its long-range value to the public generally. If there were to be a port, he wanted it to be a city-owned port. Eventually his efforts would secure a federal grant for what would be Bayboro Harbor. But his main concern was in securing the waterfront under public ownership, to prevent its commercial exploitation and allow the public to enjoy its natural attraction and benefits. He first quietly won the backing of a few leading citizens, but they were unable to acquire more than a few northward parcels of frontage.

Finally, he took pen in hand openly and began hammering away with articles and editorials on the critical necessity of the city to keep the waterfront out of private hands. He was attacked from right and left by those with both real and tentative designs on this choice property. But, after several years, his persistence was rewarded as citizens came to recognize the importance of his proposals. However, a vacillating city council still refused to act, and Straub kept a pressure hose of cogent persuasion, factual studies, and at times biting wit, through cartoons and editorials, on the city fathers. Finally, in 1908, they relented.

John Nolen, a world-famous city planner (among the few existing then), was hired for $8,000 to come in and lay out some blueprints. This was a great sum in the 1900s, but few cities ever got such value received. Nolen not only designated a variety of present and future usages of the waterfront and city park systems but also laid down the orderly gridwork of 100-foot city streets, with 20-foot alleys running through every block. The overall plan was unusually bold and futuristic for its day, but Straub kept a sharp editorial pen pointed at the council table until it was adopted.

Nevertheless, if St. Pete were to have complete freedom to forge ahead with its growth and development, Straub saw an even more formidable task before him. For years, West Hillsborough County (St. Pete, Clearwater, Largo) had been the stunted step-child of Tampa and East Hillsborough. Somehow, most of the taxes the peninsula towns sent over to Tampa never returned in the form of roads, schools, or other services, and its one "token" commissioner had little voice on the Hillsborough commission. Moreover, the tax burden seemed somehow disproportionate with peninsula residents paying $6.34 per head to East Hillsborough's $4.37 per head. But the powerful political and commercial interests of the Tampa area held sway, both locally and in the legislature. They were not about to surrender this tax revenue, and Tampa itself feared that an independent St. Pete would pose a serious competitive threat to its own bustling port.

But Straub plunged into the battle in earnest, opening first fire with a factual "bill of particulars" and an eloquent editorial, published in 1907, entitled: "A Declaration of Independence" (from Hillsborough). He carefully researched and tabulated the great tax inequities and the almost negligible funds received for roads, bridges, and schools. As if to punctuate his campaign at the time, a major bridge in Seminole collapsed for lack of maintenance and dumped a mule team and its driver into the bayou. However, Straub kept to a low-key, sober, factual analysis of taxation, roads, and schools, and he stressed the benefits of division to St. Pete and other peninsula towns: better government at less cost. He stressed the isolation of St. Pete from the east. The sole mode of travel from St. Pete to Tampa was 160 miles and a full day by train, going north to Trilby, then south to Lakeland, and finally west to Tampa. He struck a particular sore spot when he showed how Tampa's high crime rate absorbed such a large tax expenditure.

E.D. Lambright of the Tampa *Tribune* and D.B. McKay of the Tampa *Times* lashed at Straub with a barrage of vitriolic editorials. Meanwhile, the potent Hillsborough legislative delegation was able to block successive bills for county division in both the 1907 and 1909 sessions. But Straub finally hit upon a unique plan to get a full airing of the facts before all of the state's legislators and let them decide the bill on its merits.

A year prior to the 1911 session, Straub got permission to put the entire legislature on the St. Pete *Times*'s mailing list; for the next 10 months, he was able to apprise each lawmaker, with cool understatement and an objective appraisal of the facts, of the peninsula's right to its own county. Meanwhile, he lulled the Tampa political machine into the belief that St. Pete had all but given

St. Petersburg's municipal pier at the turn of the century. (FLORIDA TREND)

up in its fight for division. Therefore, the Hillsborough delegation was both shocked and angry when it arrived for the 1911 session to find a stone wall of legislative opinion favoring the division. Even so, the bill creating Pinellas County had to trip and stumble through the entire session before it was finally signed into law by Governor Albert Gilchrist.

But Straub had triumphed. The divorce decree became final on January 1, 1912, and a new Pinellas County was born. If the "craggy-faced, gentle crusader," as Fuller described him "patient, wise, skilled but unobtrusive," had done nothing more, these two great accomplishments for future generations might easily have been accounted sufficient for a lifetime. The city's almost five miles of public-owned waterfront, from Coffee Pot Bayou north to Lassing Park on the south, have proved of lasting value to millions of visitors as well as local citizens for over half a century. Few cities in the world can boast a similar achievement.

But Straub's devotion to these two great achievements was too often exerted at the expense of the paper's solvency, and he was forced to sell it in 1912 to another enterprising newspaperman, Paul Poynter. However, the latter wisely retained Straub as editor, and, except for a brief period as Postmaster of St. Pete, Straub served as editor-in-chief until his death in 1939. Later that year, the city belatedly named a waterfront park for Straub, but peers agree that the venerable old journalist couldn't have cared less. In fact, had he been around, he probably would have been the first to squelch the tribute.

6.
Miami's Heritage:
A Doctor Remembered

Miami preservationists link a small-town doctor to that city's heritage.

If a concerned band of people in Dade County have their way, Miami's sleek skylines and urban glut are not going to crush out totally the historic and architectural memoirs of that town's pioneering yesteryear.

The Dade Heritage Trust, a historical site preservation group, has plunked down, right in the midst of downtown's high-rise jungle, a rustic piece of early Miami—the original office and surgery quarters of a pioneer citizen who was the city's first physician in residence, Dr. James M. Jackson, Jr., (for whom Jackson Memorial Hospital is named). And, if the glaring facade of glass and concrete and the hustle aura of the magic city today seem, at times, to coldly impersonalize and intra-alienate the town, Trust members believe that this "roots" memorial will revitalize an old-fashioned sense of personal community, as well as honor those who staked their modest means on its future. If so, the doctor's story is a fortuitous symbol.

Fortuitous in that, upon arrival in the spring of 1896, Dr. Jackson took one look at the little settlement's cluster of unpainted buildings and shacks and tents, its muddy dirt streets specked here and there with jags of coral rock, and its generally dreary aspect, and promptly fled the scene. Or tried to. But there was no return boat scheduled for several days, and he had to lay over.

Seeing no future in his North Florida hometown of Bronson, the young doctor had tentatively accepted a post as surgeon for Henry Flagler's Florida East Coast Railroad, with residence in Miami, the railway's southern terminus. The line was due to reach Miami in a matter of days after Jackson missed the boat, so he decided to wait for it. But in the meantime, he met some of the town's young leaders and was impressed with their enthusiasm for the town's future. "This Miami spirit is a great thing," he wrote his wife. "It is infectious." So infectious that he decided to cast his lot with the village, becoming its first physician. After three years of "camping out" in makeshift quarters, the doctor and his wife, Ethel, now blessed with two daughters (and a son who died in

24

infancy), bought from Mrs. Julia Tuttle a corner lot at Twelfth Street and Avenue B in 1899, and built the spacious home they would occupy for the next 20 years.

Through the years, the doctor would immerse himself in the social, business, and religious affairs of the community. He also nursed the town through epidemics ranging from yellow fever to smallpox. Professionally, he was active statewide. He did a pioneer study on how the health of phosphate mine workers was affected seriously by drinking water laced with phosphate residue. When the State Board of Health was created, he became its local agent and was the first to warn citizens that the dead animals, filth, and garbage they casually tossed into river, bay, or other watercourse would be hazardous to their health. After a number of related fatalities, he secured a law against the practice.

Contemporaries described him as a "keen observer, careful thinker, and man of good judgment" with a "warm, enthusiastic disposition." He kept constantly abreast of his profession's progress, taking annual refresher courses in medicine, in keeping with his belief that a successful physician must be "always a student." He served in many capacities with the Florida Medical Association, including its presidency.

A man of deep religious conviction, the doctor never presumed that he and his colleagues had all, or even a part, of the answers to the mysteries of the human organism. He often acknowledged this mortal dependency, as on one Sunday when he rose in service at his Trinity Methodist Church and asked the congregation to pray for the survival of a young man with a ruptured appendix on whom he was to operate next day. Providentially—at least to the doctor—the man survived the critical surgery.

His acute conscientiousness was illustrated when one day, while operating, a hair from the mustache he had worn for many years fell into the open wound. He promptly shaved the growth and never grew another. His one vice was the cigar, a five-center called *Cinco* (which he dubbed "stinko"). Before entering a home, he would leave his cigar on the porch rail or floor, often forgetting about it. Thus one could almost track him down on his town rounds by tracing cigar butts. Although a conservative dresser, he could readily sacrifice vanity for comfort, as when, in summer, he wore his Panama straw hat with the crown cut out for ventilation. In the city's sultry heat, he would also always wear an ice collar while operating. (He did not know that this habit might one day prove fatal.)

By day, the doctor made his numerous house-call rounds by horse and buggy; but for night calls, he found a bicycle more convenient. Later, in 1907, he would delightedly purchase his first car, a "Ford Motor Company Machine," the Model C.

It was in 1905 that he built the office and surgery building next to his home. When he leased this property in the late teens, the house was barged down the bay a short distance to the historic site it now occupies on Twelfth Terrace.

Throughout his career, the doctor continued to involve himself actively in his community's affairs, particularly its health needs. He sought and received aid from Flagler in laying the town's first sanitary sewer lines. He organized the city's first board of health and saw that its provisions were strictly enforced. He supervised the "pest" houses during periodic epidemics and would later act as a planner and consultant in establishing the large hospital that would later develop into the huge medical complex it is today, and which was later named for him.

In 1923, shortly after recovering from a serious intestinal disorder, the doctor developed bronchopneumonia and had to travel to Baltimore to consult a specialist friend. Soon after, a streptothrix infection set in and the doctor was forced to enter Johns Hopkins Hospital and submit to a series of extremely painful treatments. He was allowed to return home in early 1924, bringing with him Dr. E. Clay Shaw, who continued to give him the painful mercurochrome therapy. The doctor finally decided that the cure was worse than the disease and dismissed Dr. Shaw. On April 2, 1924, he died, at age 58. He attributed the cause of his ailment to the years he had worn the heat-relieving ice collar in surgery.

All Miami mourned the doctor, stores displayed black-creped portraits of him, and Mayor E.C. Romfh proclaimed all businesses to be closed during funeral services. In a eulogy given by Miami's first mayor, John B. Reilly, Dr. Jackson was described simply as "one of the community's greatest friends." Shortly after, the city renamed City Hospital after him.

The Dade Heritage Trust has termed the original office and surgery building, a pine wood structure with red tile roof, as "an excellent example of early 20th century architecture." It is also listed in the National Register of Historic Places; this has enabled the Trust to secure federal funds for its restoration as a medical museum as well as historic site. The surgery facilities display all of the doctor's early medical equipment, from scalpels to X-ray machine. One useful purpose of the building has been to provide one room for headquarters for the Trust. Prior to this, according to Trust spokesperson Mrs. A.C. MacIntyre, "We've been operating out of our homes, cars and borrowed quarters at the Historical Museum for five years, so you can imagine how excited we are to have a home base.

Dr. Jackson had taken much care with the design of the one-story structure, especially in regard to the sultry climate. The ceilings in each room were very high, windows were situated to provide four-way ventilation, and a spacious attic was built at the rear of the building with a centrally-placed dormer window. A simple rectangle in shape, the building has six rooms, plus a kitchen and two baths. Each room has a lofty ceiling and is finished with classical molding. The two large rooms used for surgery have white hexagonal tile walls and floors. Five marble steps lead to the porch which has a wooden balustrade on the north and west sides. Along the east side of the building is a screened wooden porch. The hipped roof is covered with red barrel tile. It is a classic structure of its period, only enhanced by the innovative features added by the doctor.

The building is located in an area along the bayfront, near downtown Miami. It is a fitting and proper place for a community's historical treasure. It is surrounded on four sides primarily by high rises and multi-story commercial buildings and, consequently, provides a sudden, unique, and refreshing visual relief, not unlike coming upon some tiny, weathered, ancient log cabin set down alongside the Fontainbleu in the concrete canyon of Miami Beach.

But the building and site is presently owned by an investors group in an area where growth is pell-mell and burgeoning; for this reason alone, the historic site could easily soon become an endangered species.

But the Dade Heritage Trust is composed of some far-sighted and determined citizens who believe strongly that a city's heritage has no price tag, and that the measure of a community's value is irrevocably linked in continuity to the values of its past—and the values of the earliest pioneers who created that community. It will be interesting to observe how seriously Miami cherishes this past, especially when that perennial Great Tempter—greed in the guise of "progress"—comes knocking at the door again with his Faustian sales pitch.

7.
David Fairchild's Exotic Fairyland

He traveled to strange and faraway places to transplant a treasure of exotic flora in a city's heart.

A stroll through the lush verdure of this tropical rain forest, dappled with brilliant splashes of color from every kind of fruit, flower, and vine, might fill one with astonished wonder.

For the moment, anyone might insist he was in the exotic jungles of Borneo, the Amazon, Sumatra, or Java. But in fact he is only a few short miles from another kind of jungle, the concrete, glass, and asphalt jungle of Miami—a geographic counterpoint that the rain forest would gladly disavow.

Yet here is a wonder of tropical flora, 83 acres of strange and beautiful flowering plants and trees, complete with lakes and rain forest, weaving the splendorous tapestry of Fairchild Tropical Garden, the largest tropical botanical garden in America. Here one sees trees that walk or sing or make noises, trees so thick that families can make homes in their trunks. And most of them bear flowers and fruits of such rare beauty, fragrance, color, and taste as to stimulate and enchant the dullest senses.

Perhaps the real wonder is that this tropical Eden flourishes in such an improbable setting, near bustling metro Miami. But this fact is mostly due to the remarkable efforts of its namesake, David G. Fairchild, America's first pioneer plant explorer.

Fairchild was already one of the country's foremost authorities on foreign plants in 1916 when he and his wife, Marian, daughter of Alexander Graham Bell, settled in Coconut Grove. In 1889, at age 19, the horticulture student had joined the newly created U.S. Department of Agriculture and worked in its foreign-plant section, the aim of which was to collect and introduce into American markets foreign vegetables, fruits, drug plants, grains, and any other useful plants unknown in the United States. But Fairchild's avid curiosity about his studies caused him to chafe at desk work. So when Barbour Lathrop, a benefactor, lifelong friend, and plant enthusiast himself, invited the youth to study the foreign scene firsthand, Fairchild eagerly accepted. For the next eight years, the pair would explore the jungles and mountains of Java, Sumatra, Malaysia, Australia, Southeast Asia, and a number of islands in the Pacific Ocean.

Their journeys took them into primitive and unexplored areas, and they discovered a treasure-house of rare exotica. In Java they found the delicious pineapple-apricot mangosteen and in Borneo, the rare durian, a coconut-size fruit that emitted the foulest odor outside but was "indescribably rich and sweet" inside. Borneo headhunters reportedly would kill for the durian. In Sumatra was the famous shaddock and in Siam the delectable wampi, a citrus fruit. Chinese bird's nest soup was exactly that, they discovered, the ground nest of the swift, made of a tasty mushroomlike substance. Here, too, was the nutritious water chestnut. In Java, where everything from houses to hats is made from bamboo, they found many valuable bamboo varieties. There were apprehensive moments, too, as when a guide escorted them to the Cannibal (Fiji) Islands where native tribes gradually were shedding their practice of eating other humans. Hoping to ensure a safe and impressive reception, the guide introduced Lathrop and Fairchild as the president of the United States and his secretary. Whatever his current dietary habits, the tribal chieftain was properly impressed. The Fijis introduced Fairchild to the valuable taro root.

During this period, Fairchild sent valuable seeds and seedling plants to the department's foreign-plant section, which at the turn of the century was a ferment of activity. Few Americans were aware then that none of their important food plants was native to North America; all of them were imported from abroad or from South America. American food then—especially bread—also was considered poorer in taste and nutrition than most foreign fare. Fairchild, along with scientists in his section, such as Mark Carleton and W.T. Swingle, would help to change U.S. agriculture by introducing Japanese rice, soybean, kudzu, grapes, alfalfa, dates, and some 78,000 other food and ornamental plants.

One of their most spectacular successes was the import of durum wheat from the Black Lands of Russia in the late 1890s. Within two years, the United States produced 60,000 bushels of this rich quality grain; five years later, it produced 20 million bushels.

Fairchild visited South Florida in 1898 and was certain that it was an ideal area for foreign tropical plants, but the department was not receptive to any major projects in such a "backward country." Finally Fairchild decided to live there himself, and when he and his wife, Marian, and three children arrived at Coconut Grove in February 1916, they fell in love with the area and immediately bought property on Old Cutler Road, a tract 200 feet wide and 1,800 feet down to the shore of Biscayne Bay. Its "idyllic" tropical setting, with its old house, stone barn, and scattered small "shacks," resembled a typical Javanese kampong, or village, and so it was called The Kampong.

Over the years Fairchild experimented with varieties of edible fruits—the mango, papaya, and avocado; iron-wooded trees such as the Brazilian jaboticaba, the tree with the cannonballs dangling from trunk strings and its trunk enveloped in rose-pink flowers; the "sausage" tree, its gourd fruit dangling in the shape of sausages; flowers of every color and hue; and rare tropical vines. Fairchild's neighbors included other plant enthusiasts such as naturalist Charles Torrey Simpson, pioneer Mary Brickell, the Deerings of Vizcaya, and palm grower Colonel Robert Montgomery, whose unique palm and cycad collection, with its acreage, was later donated to the Fairchild Garden.

Only after promising to show him a live manatee could Fairchild lure his father-in-law, Alexander Graham Bell, to visit them; bright sunlight hurt Bell's ultrasensitive eyes, and he hated warm weather. Learning of his arrival, the Miami Telephone Company called on Bell to present him with the latest telephone model, offering to install it at once. But Bell politely declined the offer, saying that, although he had invented the telephone, he never used one himself; it intruded on his thoughts.

Fairchild was among the earliest to detect growing threats against Florida's botanical environment and ecosystems. He eagerly joined the fight to eradicate a statewide scourge of citrus canker in the late 1900s. But he did not foresee its reappearance many years later. He also warned of "the destruction and devastation" caused by the blasting out of "that long, ugly straight line of glaring white," the Tamiami Trail, across the "magnificent water landscape" of the Everglades. He often lamented over how a great city (Miami) "threatens to cover the whole shoreline with white, polished dwelling places, in which will live in comfort people who are not much interested in anything that is hard to see."

In the mid-1930s, concerned citizens such as the Montgomerys and historian Marjory Stoneman Douglas were, with Dade County's aid, able to secure enough acreage to forestall this threat on the Fairchild Tropical Garden; scientists, students, and citizens gathered there this past December to celebrate the garden's 50th charter anniversary.

Fairchild died in 1954, at 85, suffering heart failure while walking with Marian through their Kampong garden. But one who had contributed so prolifically and munificently to America's, and Florida's, horticultural progress left his garden knowing that a flourishing portion of his legacy would remain.

8.
When Jacksonville was "Hollywood"

*The town was pioneering the movie industry years before
California's "tinsel town" succeeded it.*

The streets and vacant lots of the city were abuzz with cries of "lights, camera, action," as angry mobs of extras gathered menacingly. Meanwhile, other men rolled off rooftops, leaped from windows, rushed from burning buildings, or held spectacular car chases down a main street.

The city was Jacksonville, the time the early century, and all the din of commotion derived from an exciting new industry that had just come to town—moviemaking. It was a time, moreover, when Florida's then-largest city seemed destined to become the nation's film capital, leaving the tinsel town of Hollywood in the dust. From 1908 to the end of World War I, Jacksonville was being hailed as the Klondike of the movie industry. In the peak year of 1916, more than 100 film companies were in full-time production in the city.

But ultimately, the promise of this glittering celluloid kingdom was dashed on the rocks of provincial demographics. Filmmakers were obliged to pack their bags and head for the West Coast.

From the first successful plot film made in the United States, *The Great Train Robbery* (1903), through the *Many Perils of Pauline*, Americans en masse were fascinated with these grainy, jerky, exaggerated images of heroes, heroines, and villains flickering across the silver screen; movies had become the nation's most popular form of mass entertainment. But nearly all of the major studios were based in New York, where film production was severely curtailed by the cramped, hazy-lit rooftop studios and harsh northern winters. Clearer skies, more space, and a climate for longer shooting sessions seemed essential to meeting the market demand.

As early as 1898, Spanish-American War documentaries had been filmed at Tampa, and in 1905, noted cinematographer Billy Bitzer produced a popular film on the Ormond-Daytona auto races. But not until 1908 did the state get its first studio. Kalem Studios randomly selected Jacksonville to shoot Florida's first film, *A Florida Feud: Or, Lost in the Everglades*. It was a national hit, noted especially for its fine, clear photography. But its demeaning portrayal of poor whites angered some locals, and a seed of local enmity was planted.

Still, the success of other Florida films by Kalem began to lure more major producers—film pioneers such as Lubin, Biograph, Essanay, Gaumont, Thanhouser, and Vitagraph. They found an ideal locale for varied and exotic scenery, a clear sunny climate, civic support, and inexpensive land and labor. Other studios followed, and moviegoers soon were thrilled by films such as *Witch of the Everglades* (about the Seminole Osceola), *The Cracker Bride*, and many others. Actors flocked in, too, among them a portly jobless aspirant called "Babe," who found work in Lubin comedies such as *Plump and Runt*; thus did Oliver Hardy create the prototype for the "Laurel and Hardy" series of later years.

Statewide protest greeted later films, such as *The Wine of Madness* (1913) and *The Toll of the Marshes* (1914), both dealing with Florida real estate swindles and both decried as "libelous, anti-Florida" films, prompting the former to be withdrawn from U.S. exhibit. All-black casts gave jobs to blacks, but most of these films were little more than racist parodies. Nevertheless, white producer Richard Norman used all-black casts for sympathetic portrayals such as *Birth of a Race*, a counter to D.W. Griffith's racist *Birth of a Nation*.

By 1916 Jacksonville surpassed its Hollywood rival in film production, prompting producer David Garrick, nephew of famed stage actor Richard

Actors gather near a Jacksonville theater during the city's moviemaking heydey in the early 1900s.

Garrick and producer of the first technicolor film in that city, *The Gulf Between* (1917), to comment: "There is every reason why [Florida] should be the logical motion picture-producing center" of the United States.

Still, although the industry enjoyed local support from merchant groups, the *Times-Union*, and film-boosting Mayor J.E.T. "Jet" Bowden, opposition to the moviemakers—educational, religious, and other groups—became increasingly vocal. Nor was antagonism lessened by local incidents—a mob scene of 1,380 extras, which almost destroyed two commercial buildings; a hazardous car chase down a main street and off a ferry dock into the river; false alarms that brought out city fire trucks for fire scenes; "bank robberies" shot on the Sabbath. A more telling blow came from fly-by-night "instant" studios that engaged in a series of stock frauds with unwary local investors, thus eventually drying up local financial support for legitimate studios. Then, in a heated mayoral campaign in which filmmaking itself became an issue, movie booster Bowden was roundly defeated.

By the end of World War I, Jacksonville's "film capital" dream lay in pieces. One by one, discouraged filmmakers migrated west to the more hospitable Hollywood. Disillusioned Henry Klutho, whose studio opened in Jacksonville in 1917, recalled: "At that time I was pointed to as a man of vision and ideas for the good of the town. Later I was often told I was a bit of a fool."

During the euphoric land boom years and after, numerous attempts were made to revive Florida filmmaking, but most were abortive, according to *Lights! Camera! Florida!*, the first comprehensive history of Florida filmmaking, written by Richard Alan Nelson under the auspices of the Florida Endowment for the Humanities. Jacksonville tried to recoup its cinematic losses with a proposed Fine Arts City, an extravagant studio complex, but it failed financially. So did Tampa Films, Inc. at Sulphur Springs, co-invested by noted photographer W.C. Burgert, after producing a few minor films. That city's single success was the first "talkie," *Hell Harbor*, starring Latin siren Lupe Velez, done by Tampa's Beecroft studio. "Movie fever" in Miami was so heady that the *Herald* ran a story about a "tip-off" from eminent scientists that a newly discovered "treacherous Arctic current" would soon freeze California's climate, sending filmmakers rushing to Florida. Miami's only successful studio was Fleischer's, the creator of animated cartoons such as *Betty Boop* and *Popeye*.

Today, Florida ranks among the country's most important film centers, with numerous full-length movies, TV shows and advertisements produced in such cities as Orlando and Miami. But in the early part of the century, it was Jacksonville that held the greatest—if fleeting—promise as the nation's movie mecca.

9.
The Stormy Origins of the Phosphate Industry

Ancient bones in the Peace River Valley spawned a maelstrom of conflict between labor and capital.

Antediuvian fossils, the chalky remains of creatures that once roamed in hordes over the ancient Florida plateau, would hardly have seemed destined to provide fertilizers to help feed a hungry world. But that is exactly how things turned out. In fact, Florida's giant phosphate industry had its beginnings with the remains of those animals, and today it provides a third of the world's phosphate requirements and nearly 80% of the nation's.

Born in the Peace River Valley—part of the massive Bone Valley that stretches from Dunnellon south to Arcadia—the industry's early development was anything but peaceful. Mining the mineral was once a crude and primitive task, exacting the severest toll from those who mined it—a condition that later would explode into a bloody clash rocking the state and sending tremors as far as Washington.

Captain J. Francis LeBaron, a surveyor with the U.S. Army Corps of Engineers, first discovered the mineral in pebble form near Arcadia in 1881. In 1885, two Orlandoans found the pebbles in the Peace River bed near Fort Meade. Then, in 1888, south of Arcadia, George Scott attempted to tie his boat up to a river root; the "root" turned out to be a fossilized mammoth tusk. (In 1889, Albertus Vogt would discover hard-rock phosphate near Dunnellon, which, for more than a decade, would be known as a loud and lawless boom town as well as the world's leading center for phosphate production. Gradually, the Dunnellon phosphate vein was depleted just as the southern region burgeoned with discoveries of high-grade ores in the pine lands, especially those in Polk County.)

After Scott's discovery, speculators poured into the Peace River Valley, and land prices shot from $1.50 to $200 an acre. By the 1890s, 10 companies were dredging pebbles up and down the river near Arcadia and as far north as Bartow. At first, laborers pried the rock lumps loose with picks and crowbars, hand-loading them onto barges, which later took them to the gulf for ship-loading. Later this arduous method was replaced with stream dredges and centrifugal pumps that could suck up 40 tons of pebbles a day. But the discovery of the rich pine land deposits virtually phased out river-mining by 1908. Early in this century, most ore was exported to Europe to restore its worn-out farmlands. But by 1911, the U.S. domestic market had exceeded export demand, and the industry grew quickly to keep pace with a growing market at home.

By World War I there were 17 phosphate companies operating in Polk County. While vast fortunes had literally come overnight to some 80 mine owners, most of them northern-based absentees, the mine laborers (the majority of whom were black) lived in what can only be called an oppressive form of serfdom. In 1907 a laborer in the mines drew $1.50 for a grueling 12-hour day; 12 years later, he drew only $2.50 for a similar day. He lived in a company town, and bought his groceries at the company store at prices set by the company. He lived in a small, company-owned, wood-box house, which he was allowed only to rent—the company didn't allow workers to own their houses. The laborers' plight did not go unnoticed, however. Investigations by the U.S. War Labor Board revealed that workers were being "held in a virtual state of peonage."

At the time, the workers were being represented by the International Union of Mine, Mill, & Smelter Workers, and were seeking an eight-hour day and a 37-cents-an-hour minimum pay. The Labor Board charged Hillsborough and Polk companies with gross exploitation after its investigation, and recommended a short workday and the right of collective bargaining.

But Peter O. Knight, the industry's counsel and a wealthy and powerful

Work was hard for phosphate miners. A strong human back moved the tons of overburden and scooped up the valuable phosphate. (FLORIDA TREND)

West Coast political boss, refused to enter into the arbitration process and denounced the workers as "Bolsheviki." In April 1919, 3,500 workers at Prairie, Nichols, and Tiger Bay mines walked out, followed by workers in 14 other companies. They were supported by a sympathy strike of railroad workers who refused to haul the phosphate from the mines. A confrontation was inevitable.

The first clash came when mine operators imported "scab" labor from Georgia and asked armed strikebreakers and "guards" to accompany the outsiders. One striker was fatally stabbed; soon after a strikebreaker was shot and killed. Trigger-happy guards fatally shot a black child being carried by its mother and then killed a storekeeper at random.

A 46-car armed convoy escorting imported labor was ambushed near Mulberry; a strikebreaker and a deputy sheriff were killed. The violent incidents spiraled until Governor Sidney Catts called out the National Guard and removed Polk Sheriff John Logan for "siding" with the operators and failing to quell the violence, which he personally accused Knight of "inciting." In turn, Knight enlisted powerful business interests, including much of the state's press, to lash out at the "Bolsheviki" workers and at the governor.

But the workers were drawing support. While area churches and the Tampa Labor Temple opened their doors to worker families, the Lakeland *Star* and legislators like Senator Doyle Carlton and Polk Representative Samuel Williams spoke on their behalf. The governor attempted, with success, to get federal mediation. Finally, a permanent court injunction against the workers effectively broke the strike. Later strikes and minor clashes (none of which would match the violence of 1919) would finally help bring collective bargaining to the mine fields.

In the wake of changes in the phosphate industry toward modernization, new mining techniques developed. Old steam shovels were replaced in 1920 first with diesel, then electric, draglines that could move 700 cubic yards of ore, called overburden, an hour. In 1946, the Bigger Digger, which literally "walked" on compression feet, boasted a 21-cubic-yard bucket, but it is dwarfed today by huge machines with 45- to 65-cubic-yard buckets.

The industry had other problems, too. It was forced to spend millions to clean up air and water pollution as well as to reclaim thousands of acres already mined for use as pasture or recreation and building sites.

In 1981, the phosphate industry's 100th anniversary, phosphate is the state's third-largest industry and, directly or indirectly, accounts for more than 80,000 jobs in Florida. From its primitive and even violent beginnings, a vital international industry has successfully struggled to reach modern industrial maturity.

10.
Mr. "Jiggs" Opens the Swamp Country

The comic strip character's namesake was a real-life roadbuilder in Okeechobee land.

He put a road over one of the most "impossible" swamp-choked terrains in Florida, from West Palm Beach to Okeechobee City, bringing in 1924 the first highway linkup to the state's west coast.

And he did it faster than you could say—well, corned beef and cabbage. Because, although his name was W.J. "Fingy" Conners, most people could only think of him as Jiggs, of the famous George McManus comic strip characters, Maggie and Jiggs, in "Bringing Up Father." Reliable but unofficial sources swore he was the real-life model for Jiggs, who was born of a star-crossed romance. McManus would not—probably could not—confirm it. On query, Conners would only smile and say nothing—but he never denied it.

At all events, the 52-mile toll road was certainly an engineering feat, and, when a jubilant throng of 15,000 gathered for the ribbon-cutting festivities in Okeechobee City on July 4, 1924, "Fingy," alias "Jiggs," was hailed by Governor Gary Hardee as "The Great Developer," a peer of Henry Plant and Henry Flagler. Others even compared Fingy to Appius Claudius, Charlemagne, and St. Patrick. Fingy, in response, could only call it the kind of "damn fool thing" that had made him a millionaire in the first place.

But in that era of manic grandiosity, the 1920s Florida Land Boom, the highway was surely a fit subject for gushing. And authorities agreed that Conners had done for the Lake Okeechobee region what no one had done before—he had brought Ford's "Tin Lizzie" to the lakeshore and had advanced the area's development by 25 years.

But Fingy Conners himself seemed to fit like a native son into the rough and primitive Okeechobeeland of that day. Historians A.J. and Kathryn Hanna said his "fighting record" surpassed that of legendary Sheriff "Pogy Bill" Collins; his boldness made John Ashley of the notorious Ashley gang "look anemic," his Everglades vision exceeded that of even Governor Napoleon Broward; he invested more in the region than Richard Bolles; and his language had the salt and color of a Lake Okeechobee catfisherman.

As for his "Jiggs" role, the Hannas' research, to them, seemed certain. "The likeness—physical and otherwise—between Fingy and Jiggs is startling," they noted. And, they said, he had the kind of appeal that had put Jiggs into more than 750 papers worldwide, in 27 different languages, from the 1920s to the 1950s. Okeechobee historian Lawrence Will reported that a young Buffalo, New York, artist (McManus) fell in love and sought to marry millionaire Conners' daughter. Conners didn't object, but his society-minded spouse, finding McManus shy of Social Register connections, squelched the romance. In revenge, McManus created the shrewish "Maggie," whom the harried Jiggs was forever eluding to sneak off to Dinty Moore's saloon for corned beef and cabbage or a peaceful poker game. And Fingy was a ringer for Jiggs, right down to his corned beef-and-cabbage diet.

Fingy Conners began his career as a cabin boy on the Great Lakes and then fought and scrapped his way to leadership over the Buffalo dockworkers. (A hand injury in one such fight accounts for the nickname Fingy.) He then made a meteoric rise in maritime and other interests and was soon a young multimillionaire. Whereupon he and "socialite" Maggie came to Palm Beach where he proceeded to spend his money as hard as he had earned it.

Then, in 1917, at a dinner celebrating the opening of the West Palm Beach Canal to Lake Okeechobee, Conners' interest in the Everglades region was

Even the Tamiami Trail, shown here in 1927, was a primitive route when Conners built his highway through the Florida Swamps.

sparked, and he took a tour through the canal. He immediately invested a large sum for two large tracts east of the lake, naming one of them Connersville, and tried to make them "showcase" farms. But his agricultural methods were limited and ineffective and both projects failed. Next, he bought up over 12,000 acres northward along the east lakeshore for about $700,000 and then purchased most of Okeechobee City and its vast farm tracts nearby.

To attract buyers into these vast holdings, he proposed building a paved road to the lakeshore, citing the region as "the greatest place on earth, unlimited opportunities for development . . . nothing like it on earth."

The legislature apparently agreed, for it took them only two hours and 20 minutes to enact a law authorizing Conners to build a toll road 19 miles along the West Palm Beach Canal, from Twenty Mile Bend to the lake, and then 33 miles around the lakeshore to Okeechobee City. It would be the first south-central connection with state roads leading to Tampa and St. Petersburg.

In the fall of 1923, Conners met a trouble-shooting engineer, R.Y. Patterson (who was later vice president of the U.S. Sugar Corporation in Clewiston), and hired him at once. But the $2 million project looked formidable if not forbidding—and Conners wanted it done as fast as possible.

Patterson's challenge was to try to build a highway on soft muck over a normally inaccessible route where foundation and drainage conditions were unknown. But he was up to it. For the east-west route, he excavated the canal bottom for wet marl. Rocks compressed muck to half its five-foot depth; on this he laid the 24-foot roadbed. For the lakeshore route—much of it under water—he threw up a tight mix of sand and muck, then spread over it a deep layer of crusher-run rock, a high-grade lime rock from the St. Lucie canal, and topped it with an oil application. To haul the rock from the canal, three-foot gauge rails were laid on the center of the roadbed, and side tracks were put down every two miles, with telephones that could connect to eight locomotives. This enabled the dispatcher to keep operations running round-the-clock. This triple-frenetic pace saw the last rock dumped on June 23, 1924; the remarkable feat took only eight months.

Engineering News-Record declared the Conners Highway as one of the 14 outstanding engineering achievements in North America for 1924. The area was jubilant—and so was Fingy. A celebration was in order and it duly took place in Okeechobee City the following July 4th. Airplanes performed stunts over West Palm Beach, dropping 30,000 leaflets publicizing the ribbon-cutting. Okeechobee City was festooned with decorations while cowboys, Indians, and celebrities were joined by a caravan of 2,000 cars coming in on the new road. "The barriers of America's last frontier . . . fell here today," declared the *Palm*

Beach Post, mixed with other statewide press accolades. For Fingy himself, it was his "happiest day."

Needless to say, the road prospered with a daily average toll take of over $2,000. Fingy also cleaned up by selling lakeshore and farm land—with sales of up to a million dollars a month the first year, following a nationwide promotional campaign. He would thereby handily survive the boom's bust in 1926; most of his land would be sold by the time he died in October 5, 1929.

The region prospered, too, and folks around the lake would long remember the wonderful "damn-fool thing" he did for them—at least they would every time they glanced at the comic strips and saw Fingy's redoubtable alter ego—Jiggs himself.

11.
Winter Park:
A Fantasy-cum-Reality

Ill health brought Loring Chase to Florida; his fertile fantasy created a cultural mecca.

Winter Park, that quaint, posh and artsy exception to burgeoning Orlando next door, almost missed its birth date years ago because its founder, Loring A. Chase, wasn't in the mood for town-building at the time. A prosperous Chicago realtor, Chase suffered from bronchitis; so in February, 1881, he came to Florida, "not looking for real estate, but health," he brusquely informed a Florida friend.

But the friend persisted, and Chase finally assented to a buggy-ride tour of "the loveliest spot" in Orange County. As they rode over the high, fertile land with its tall, graceful pines and then around the shore of lakes Osceola, Virginia, Killarney, and Maitland, Chase's realtor instinct overcame him. The wild, virgin beauty of the era incited him to fantasize "not a castle in the air but a town, never thinking it would materialize."

It did take some fantasy, since the only civilized traces left in the area were several windowless homesteader cabins and a wood platform overlooking "two faint streaks of iron, over which a box car went slowly once a day between Sanford and Orlando." Sanford was little more than a general store, while Orlando, which had just been incorporated, had barely 200 souls. The railroad was H.B. Plant's.

Fantasy indeed, Chase shrugged, as he prepared to board a steamer for Jacksonville. But at the last minute, an old friend, railroad scion Oliver Chapman, turned up. Chase lingered and was happily surprised to find that his friend was enthused about his "dream town." The next thing they knew, they were laying out $13,000 for a 600-acre tract adjoining the four lakes. On August 29, 1881, they named it Winter Park.

"With commendable zeal, they [Chase and Chapman] have had the town most advantageously platted for artistic beauty and convenience." said an area newspaper at the time. Curving thoroughfares encircled special sites for churches, schools, parks, and a hotel. The railroad would run through a 10-acre

41

park, planted with tropical fruit and flowers, in the town's center. Two broad boulevards, along one of which 1,000 budded orange trees were planted, connected the four lakes.

Understandably, the first building erected was a railroad depot; the next, a lodging house. Chase spent most winter months either in Jacksonville, meeting and inviting wealthy northern visitors to an "idyllic" resort, or waiting with Chapman at the depot, greeting and personally escorting each visitor. His success was measured somewhat by the response of General Henry Sanford, who privately fumed that Chase "was diverting many prospective settlers" from his own town of Sanford.

And divert he did. Before long several new houses went up. Then came a lumbermill, wagon factory, cabinet shop, and combination general store–post office with a town hall on its second floor. Within three years, a hardware store, blacksmith, telegraph station, school, and church were added. Plant also had pushed his railroad to Tampa. By now, there were 63 new houses within a mile of the depot. The newcomers included not only wealthy businessmen but such a host of professional people that one resident advised a prospective visitor: "Don't be afraid to address anybody you meet as doctor or professor, for you will hit it right about eleven times out of eight."

While his town began to thrive, Chase focused his "enthusiasm, persistence, and persuasion" toward a major goal. The Florida Congregational Association had plans to build a Christian college, and five sites were contending for it—Mount Dora, Jacksonville, Daytona, Orange City, and Winter Park. Bells pealed, and the whole town celebrated when, On April 18, 1885, the FCA voted for Winter Park. Cash, stocks, and land had been pledged previously, but the decision was capped when A.W. Rollins, for whom the college gratefully was named, made a bottom-line gift of $50,000. The coed school would be the first and oldest institution of higher learning in Florida.

Another major event was wealthy merchant F. B. Knowles' completion of the Seminole Hotel, with its plush 150 rooms, easily the largest south of Jacksonville. When it opened January 1, 1886, bonfires blazed as 2,000 visitors crowded its corridors, awaiting a lavish banquet preceding a grand ball. In its first three months, 2,300 guests would register (with many turned away). It quickly became a famous resort in the state, attracting such diverse luminaries as presidents Arthur and Cleveland, Edwards Pierrepont, Hamilton Disston, the Duke of Sutherland, George Pullman, and George Westinghouse. The great hotel burned down in 1902 but was soon replaced and continued to rival Palm Beach as a resort site for affluent northerners.

Today Winter Park retains its original charm and beauty. Its center is still

Rollins College, with its distinctive Spanish and Mediterranean architecture. Its European-style shopping area, Park Avenue, boasts more than 120 shops and art galleries. In addition, more than 300,000 people are drawn annually to its Sidewalk Arts Festival in March and its Bach Festival in February. It remains a favorite Florida mecca for writers, artists, educators, and professionals of all kinds.

12.
From Swamp to
Florida Showplace

*Out of a dense morass of swamp and cypress came a major
Florida showplace, Cypress Gardens.*

It did seem the quixotic "impossible dream," especially in the early days of the Great Depression. But Dick Pope, Sr., had a vision.

At a time when concern focused more on bread and jobs than flowers, he dreamed of transforming 16 acres of wild, wooded swampland on the edge of Lake Louise near Winter Haven into a beautiful semi-tropical garden. The skeptics hooted derisively. Newspaper columnists called him the "swami of the swamp," "the Barnum of botany," "maestro of the muck." Even the Winter Haven town council became edgy, first backing the project, then withdrawing support.

But Dick Pope, Sr., had the tenacious zeal and ebullient confidence of a born salesman and promoter. He and his "green thumb" wife, Julie, kept at their arduous toil in the hot, steamy muck and jungle growth—cutting and hacking, digging canals, planting flowers, landscaping, paving paths—for four long years, single-mindedly ignoring detractors.

And even when Cypress Gardens officially opened on January 2, 1936, few dreamed that the park would expand over years into 223 acres and become a world-famous attraction drawing millions of visitors. Not many people foresaw that the Gardens would be publicized year after year on the pages and film of the national media or that Pope's former detractors would later dub him "Mr. Florida," the number one promoter of Florida tourism.

Early in life, Pope displayed a singular grit and initiative. He used to hang around his father's real estate office, first in Lake Wales, then in Winter Haven. One day, when his father was off on a business trip, the ten-year-old child sold a house to a young couple. By the time his father returned, Pope remembers, "we already had the deal settled."

Prospering in real estate until the 1920s boom busted, Pope then read an ad seeking a publicity man for the Johnson Seahorse Outboard Motor Company in Chicago. Pope and his brother, Malcolm had long been boat racing enthusiasts, so Pope drove north with his wife and son, Dick, Jr. At major city stops en route, he sent telegrams to Johnson's saying: "Your problems are solved. Don't do anything until I get there." They didn't, and he was hired. His success with the Johnson company enabled him to open his own advertising offices later, with clients like Jantzen Swimwear and Gulf Oil.

The long icy winters, however, made the family yearn for sunny Florida. When Pope read of a South Carolina man who opened his private garden to the public at 25 cents admission, something clicked. The family was soon headed home to Winter Haven, which at that time was isolated four miles off a newly constructed state highway. Pope believed that a beautiful garden would draw visitors to the town. "But I was the only one who thought so," he recalls.

The young couple, aided in the backbreaking creation of the attraction by citrus pioneer John Snively, Jr., opened the Gardens on January 2, 1936. Even the skeptics were impressed with the sprawling scene of lush and colorful botanical gardens. Central Florida had its first tourist attraction.

Pope had few funds to spare for the national publicity he knew would be essential to the park's success, so he devised an ingenious formula he called "OPM2"—"our photographic material times other people's money." The combination of profuse and brilliant floral color, greenery, and water beneath towering, ancient cypress trees did indeed give the Gardens a unique photogenic aura. Under a blitz of mailings and personal persuasion, it was not long before a major picture magazine, *Life*, was dubbing the Gardens "a photographer's paradise." Meanwhile Pope was organizing races and regattas on Lake Louise, promoting Johnson Outboards and the Gardens.

During World War II, Pope was off to the army, but his wife proved ever resourceful. The family had long been water ski enthusiasts (Pope is said to be the first to make a ski jump over a ramp and was the first to kite fly behind a boat). Soldiers often visited the Gardens from nearby bases; one day in 1943, a soldier, observing the lake skiers, asked if they had a ski show. No, Julie Pope answered, but we're going to. She then rounded up her son and daughter and their friends and devised an impromptu ski routine. It soon became the popular attraction that would make Cypress Gardens "The Water Ski Capital of the World."

After his army service, Pope decided to enhance the Gardens' photogenic images with pretty girls. In addition to the antebellum Southern belles gracing the landscape, he brought in water ski beauty queens and other professionals to perform graceful and daring feats. Since then, the Cypress Gardens Water Ski Revue has been the longest-running entertainment production in the world— well over 56,000 performances.

The four daily shows feature holders of world ski jump records in gravity-defying feats. Among the thrills are the Aquamaids' water ballet, which they perform on swivel skis, and their famous human pyramid ending with the topmost skier standing 18 feet above the water. Helmeted rampmasters zoom up the ramp at 70 mph, becoming airborne as their skis twirl in the "helicopter spin." In another act, a skier is harnessed to the Delta Wing Kite and towed into the air where, at 500 feet, he releases the rope and soars free to a stand-up landing on the beach. This repertoire of precision skill and daring is all under the able instruction of Phil Baier and Nancy Zara.

But the park's attractions are not only the trees and skies, nor the 8,000 varieties of exotic greenery and flowers gracing each scenic pathway. An authentic Southern mansion surrounded by magnolia trees and rose gardens houses the Florida Sports Hall of Fame. Honored are such state sports notables as Babe Zaharias, Chris Evert, Bob Griese, and Jack Nicklaus. And not far away is Southern Crossroads, a replicate antebellum village where, along with other acts, a bevy of ducks, the Florida Quackers, do amazing feats on musical instruments.

In the Animal Forest, one can observe in a natural habitat 400-plus exotic and endangered species such as capybaras, the world's largest rodent, and Malaysian tapirs. Included are exotic birds like the scarlet ibis, crown cranes, toucans, African hornbills, and many others. Farther on, the Gator show tests the skills of expert handlers to display the reptiles to their best advantage.

Honoring America's "melting pot" origins are the Gardens of the World, where a 50-foot Holland windmill, Italian Fountains, a Grecian stage, Ireland's Blarney Stone, Oriental Gardens, and Mediterranean Falls are among the salutes to other nations. Then there is a 750-seat Garden Cinema, children's rides, specialty shops, and the 480-seat County Fare restaurant featuring a variety of regional dishes.

The Gardens' latest feature is Kodak Island. This Island in the Sky, a flying saucer-shaped rotating platform camouflaged within a lush floral landscape, slowly rises off the terrain, carrying up to 100 passengers to nearly 16 stories above the Gardens, 200 feet above Lake Louise, for a breathtaking view of the Gardens, lake, and countryside.

Dick Pope was once described as "an exuberant ball of energy in perpetual motion" in his efforts to keep the state before a nation's eyes. The Gardens have been the site for ten Mike Douglas shows, a Johnny Carson special, an MGM movie, and many other TV and film features. It is also the setting for the internationally televised religious program, "Day of Discovery." The Reverend Norman Vincent Peale once even made Pope the subject of a "positive thinking" sermon. And Pope affirms that thinking big and positively is the key to any success. "That and having fun with whatever you're doing. And if it's not fun, to heck with it."

His particular brand of "fun" has drawn more than 30 million people to the park since 1936; it draws an annual average of 1.4 million visitors. Dick, Jr., has noted that continuing surveys reveal that 35 to 40 percent of their guests are repeat visitors. With such an artful combination of natural primeval beauty and spectacular showmanship, it is little wonder that people come back for more.

But only recently the park, under the management of Dick Pope, Jr., has decided to divest itself of many of its extracurricular activities—the Animal Forest and its feature shows, Kodak Island, various novelty features and other highlights—in order to confine itself to its basic botanical gardens theme. But these lush and wondrous gardens, along with the water-skiing, were the original lure for countless thousands of visitors and it seems certain that the popularity of this attraction will continue unabated.

13.
School Marm in
the Woods

She taught both whites and Indians in the Florida backwoods and eventually became one of the state's foremost educators.

She was considered "the first lady" of Fort Lauderdale, but it is unlikely that Ivy Julia Cromartie (Mrs. Frank Stranahan) ever regarded herself in such august terms.

A modest, unassuming woman, she was certainly the town's first school teacher. And, beyond that, she was also a friend and teacher of the beleaguered Seminole Indians, a champion of woman's suffrage, an early conservationist, and a town benefactress generally for over half a century.

But such things were hardly on the mind of the young girl who, in the 1890s, half-walked, half-waded across the wild swampy woods and scrubland of the state with her parents, a sister, and four brothers, from Tampa to the lower east coast. They eventually wound up at little Lemon City, near Miami, and here, after high school graduation, Ivy studied for and passed her teacher's exam.

Fort Lauderdale, then a part of Dade County, had less than 50 inhabitants when it petitioned the Dade School Board for a school of its own. They replied: "Build a schoolhouse and gather at least nine pupils and we'll send you a teacher." Together, the settlers helped E.T. King, a pioneer farmer and a skilled builder (inventor of the hollow sand construction block), build a one-room schoolhouse in a wild woodland south of New River. Finally, in October, 1899, petite, blue-eyed 18-year-old Ivy Cromartie stepped off the train, exclaimed in wonder at "a perfectly beautiful place," and began teaching grades one through eight, while boarding at the King family home.

In 1900, long before it was swabbed over with concrete, steel, and asphalt, the New River area had a pristine wilderness beauty that enchanted Ivy as she walked the three miles to school each day. She paused often to pick wild fruit or flowers or just to watch wild turkey, quail, deer, and exotic birds in their natural setting. Before long, the area postmaster and trading store owner, Frank

Stranahan, began courting her. He often took her fishing up the New River, which then was profusely lined with wild ferns and lilies and "crystal clear, very like an aquarium. One had to be very quiet to catch one of the trout, or a snapper or bream," she recalled. In fact, the teeming fish and wild game, plus large home vegetable gardens, provided settlers with virtually all the food they needed.

Frank and Ivy were married in August, 1900, and Stranahan commissioned King to build his bride a roomy, two-story home on the river, a building later known as The Pioneer House—and still in sound condition as late as the 1970s.

But Ivy soon left the schoolhouse to take on a less "official" teaching challenge. Every few weeks, a colorful spectacle graced the river as a flotilla of Seminole Indians, their cypress dugout canoes packed with families, camping gear, and the hides and pelts of deer, coon, alligator, otter, and other game to sell Stranahan, tied up at his trading post. The Seminoles had learned to trust Stranahan for his meticulous fairness—and personal friendship—to them; but they were uncertain about his new bride. The bitter ancestral memories of dishonored treaties and truces and three bloody wars had taught them to deeply distrust the white man—his government, education, missionaries, or his "talk papers." But Ivy was determined to teach these children and put them on a solid footing with that "outside world." With fruits, cookies, and kindness, she slowly overcame their wary diffidence and soon she had them laughing and playing

Ivy Stranahan's first classes at the schoolhouse in the woods.

inside the big house, trying on her Merry Widow hats and shoes and posing before mirrors.

Although millions are spent for education today, Ivy had neither funds nor supplies. Her classrooms were a car running board or a tree log, and her texts were the Sunday School lessons and colorful picture cards that the Presbyterian Church agreed to send her. Aside from reading and writing English, she sought to teach them that government could be their friend, but "this was the most difficult," she related. On teaching Christianity: "I made tremendous efforts to only teach of Jesus and his works," excluding all denominational positions. "The children learned quickly and, in turn, taught their parents." They began to call her Watchie-Esta/Hutrie, "White Mother," and, over many years, she gradually earned from the tribal leaders a deep respect and trust, especially when she represented them before government agents. During the 1920s land boom, when developers turned greedy eyes toward a vast beautiful tract proposed for an Indian Reservation near Dania, she persuaded the tribes to move there, convincing them that "It's your home, your land. If you don't take it, someone else will." For her lifelong efforts to help them achieve social equality and economic independence, she drew from the Seminoles their highest honors and tributes. In 1968, the U.S. Department of the Interior also gave her its highest citation award for "a lifetime of unselfish and devoted service" to the Seminoles.

But this versatile lady had other causes, too. She long fought for women's voting rights and was state president of the Woman's Suffrage League until the 19th amendment was ratified. As a member of the Audubon Society, she joined with an older woman, Mrs. Kirk Munroe, of Coconut Grove, to stop the widespread slaughter of Florida's birds, especially the beautiful egret whose delicate lacy feathers for women's hats brought fortunes to illegal South Florida poachers. The outspoken Mrs. Munroe, Ivy recalled, confronted, and embarrassed, many a fashionable matron in resort hotels, telling them killing birds was against the law and to "take those bird feathers off your hat." Mrs. Stranahan once risked personal threats when she exposed a cache of egret plumes near Miami. State troopers raided the site and recovered $35,000 in feathers. No threat materialized.

In the community itself, the Stranahans deeded land sites for numerous public and private buildings and served on many civic improvement projects. For 10 years, on the city zoning-planning board, Mrs. Stranahan fought to save some of the town's natural beauty, zeroing in especially on developers, filling stations, and sign boards. "They never seem to know where to stop," she noted, prophetically enough.

In the aftermath of the Florida land boom bust and the great hurricane of

1926, the entire town was bankrupted, and many citizens began losing their homes at courthouse tax auctions. Mrs. Stranahan at once threw her efforts, locally and statewide, behind a bill, by local State Representative Dwight L. Rogers, for a $5,000 homestead exemption. The bill passed and won final referendum approval in 1934. It would spare thousands of Florida families' homes during the Great Depression.

When she died at the age of 90, in 1971, this pioneer woman had won many honors, including the proclamation of "Mrs. Frank Stranahan Day" by former Governor Claude Kirk. But her fondest memories always remained with the idyllic wilderness beauty of another, earlier hometown, and especially with the bronze-hued children of a forgotten nation who learned to love and honor the "white mother" who remembered them.

14.
The Count of
Tampa Bay

*Count Philippe foreswore Napoleonic
pomp to carve out a pioneering future
in Old Tampa Bay.*

He had come a long way—from chief naval surgeon for Emperor Napoleon Bonaparte to the shores of Old Tampa Bay where he became the first settler of what is now Pinellas County.

Misfortune seemed to dog his footsteps—imprisonment in war, death of a beautiful young wife, home and lands twice destroyed, Civil War—and yet Dr. (Count) Odet Philippe would thrive into ripe old age and speckle the Tampa Bay area with a host of descendants.

Pirates would first inform the doctor of this "most beautiful body of water" which he would later proclaim as "God's own country." But it took him a while to get there.

Odet Philippe was born in Lyons, France, in 1769, a nephew in the royal family of Louis XVI, who was executed in the French Revolution. At boarding school, Odet and Napoleon Bonaparte became fast friends; the pair journeyed together to Paris for further studies, Bonaparte in military science, Philippe in medicine. A contemporary described Philippe as "a person of joyous, buoyant spirit, noted for his frankness and rugged constitution," plus a brilliant student in sciences, languages, and a talented artist.

When Napoleon became emperor, he appointed Philippe as chief naval surgeon, but the doctor was captured by Lord Nelson at Trafalgar in 1805 and was later interned in the Bahamian Islands. Here he practiced medicine, studied citrus culture, and finally won his freedom in 1808. Migrating to Charleston, South Carolina, he joined the large French Huguenot Colony there and soon prospered as a grower of corn, cotton, and tobacco, and in shipping. He also met and married a beautiful French girl, Dorothée Desmottes, and they had four daughters, the last of whom would cause the wife's death in childbirth. Two years later, he married the children's governess, Marie Fontaine, an attractive woman but one who proved to be an ambitious shrew with "an ungodly temper."

Misfortune struck again when the doctor signed a large note for a friend; the friend defaulted on the note, and Philippe was forced to sell his farm and vessels to pay the debt. Finally, in 1828, he bought a schooner and sailed with his family to Florida to start over. A salt manufacturing business proved too costly, so he next began planting citrus groves along the Indian River. In the 1830s, he also spent part of his time in Key West, where he practiced medicine and had modest success with a cigar-making business.

But still Philippe searched for his "ideal homesite." Then during one of his Bahamian trips to buy seedlings, he was accosted and boarded by the pirate Juan Gomez. Fortunately for Philippe, Gomez and most of his crew were fever-ridden, and, when the doctor successfully treated their ailments, a grateful Gomez presented him with a chest of precious jewels. He also gave Philippe a map on which he had marked Tampa Bay, calling it "the most beautiful body of water in the world, with the possible exception of the Bay of Naples." The Second Seminole Indian War forced the doctor to flee his Indian River settlement; it also made him determined to seek out Tampa Bay for a permanent home.

But meanwhile, during a family vacation trip to Havana, Cuba, Philippe's wife so opposed his settling at Tampa Bay that she threw a violent temper tantrum; the outburst caused a cerebral hemorrhage from which she died.

In 1839, Philippe purchased three lots on Tampa Street near the army post of Fort Brooke. The Indian War had ushered in a business boom, and, before long, the doctor was operating a bowling alley, an oyster saloon, and had interests in real estate, livestock, and a hotel. But he had also found his paradise—fertile soil, mild climate, and ample rainfall—at the headwaters of Old Tampa Bay, near present-day Safety Harbor, where he homesteaded 160 acres of land.

He named his estate St. Helena, after the island to which his boyhood friend, Napoleon, had been exiled, and soon he and his daughters were prospering with groves of grapefruit, oranges, limes, avocados, and bananas. Some historians believe that Philippe's were the first successful citrus groves in Florida; he was also reported to have given some citrus stock to a visiting Methodist preacher named Brown, who later, at his home in north central Florida, produced from it the well-known family of oranges called Parson Brown.

When the mammoth "granddaddy" of all Florida hurricanes struck the west coast of Florida from Sarasota to Pinellas in September, 1845, it first swept the waters of Old Tampa Bay completely out into the channel. Then, as the eerie silence of the hurricane's "eye" passed, Dr. Philippe, watching from the front porch of his shoreline home, was stunned to see a huge tidal wave come roaring back up the bay toward him. With only moments to spare, he managed to get his children and servants atop a nearby 50-foot Indian mound. Huddled securely together against the winds, they watched in dismay as the huge wall of water smashed over their home, ripping it apart. With as much lumber as they could salvage from the wreckage, the doctor later rebuilt the house, but this time on a hill set behind the high mound that had saved their lives. His severely damaged groves were also soon rejuvenated and began to flourish as before.

During this period, his daughters had married, but only one, Melanie, remained with her husband and children at St. Helena with her father. A prospering time was again interrupted when the Civil War broke out and the doctor was forced to remove his family to the Keystone Park community in adjoining Pasco County to escape periodic Union raids. At the war's end, in his nineties and ailing, the doctor returned to St. Helena. Still, with the aid of a loyal servant, Nelson, he was able to get his groves back into production. He would remain alert and active up to the time of his death, in 1869, in his hundredth year.

"This is God's own country," he had often proclaimed to friends and visitors, and here he chose to be buried, on an oak-covered knoll near the site of his original house. Today that site is a popular recreation area, Philippe Park, named in remembrance of the man who once served an emperor but, like Job of old, survived repeated misfortunes to find a peaceful pastoral existence, spawning many descendants and living to a ripe old age in the land he was convinced was "God's own."

15.
Of Rare Birds and Fine Art

Naturalist John James Audubon discovered Florida's early rare bird life and preserved its beauty for posterity.

The great American bird hunter was not overly impressed with Florida when he arrived at St. Augustine in 1831.

He thought the town to be "the poorest hole in the Creation," one that would surely perish were it not for its orange groves and abundant fish. And beyond the town lay only "sand, sand, and sand."

But John James Audubon, then already internationally acclaimed for his naturalist classic, *The Birds of America*, was determined to track down, describe, and paint the elusive water birds of Florida to add to his famous tome. He knew that water fowl, unlike the scores of land birds he had painted, were "the wildest and most distrustful" of birds and hence the most difficult to study. But, he wrote assuringly to his beloved Lucy, "industry and perseverance joined to a sound heart" would more than meet the challenge.

And so, with his long, double-barreled shotgun cradled in his arms and his trusty Newfoundland retriever, Plato, beside him, he set off on his venture. Florida would prove to be a "golden period" for the ornithologist-artist-author-woodsman, and for American natural history as well.

Audubon's passion for studying and drawing birds began early. He already was sketching wildlife when his father shipped him, at age 18, from his native France to America in 1803 to dodge Napoleon's sweeping conscription laws. At the Aubudon-owned farm, Mill Grove, in eastern Pennsylvania, young John spent more time hunting, fishing, and drawing than he did doing his regular studies. He also fell in love with a bright and pretty young English Quaker neighbor, Lucy Bakewell, whom he married in 1808. Two sons, John Wood-house and Victor Gifford, were born (two daughters died in infancy), but the young family often suffered privation. Audubon failed in several Midwest business ventures (minding the woods more often than the store), and the family later moved to New Orleans.

By this time Audubon had a large and distinctive portfolio of drawings. It was in 1820, with Lucy's encouragement, that he set for himself the monumental task of describing and painting all the birds of America and publishing the collection. Lucy went to work as a governess and private-school director; Audubon went off to the frontier wilderness, where the bear and the antelope often provided him with food and clothing, and the Indians taught him the most esoteric of bird calls. There was hardship and hazard. Once he barely escaped quicksand while pursuing a great horned owl, and he nearly fell from a dizzying precipice while feverishly painting a golden eagle.

His collections drew praise and recognition in New York and Philadelphia—but no publisher. And so, again with Lucy's blessings, he sailed for the British Isles in 1826. Here his work found almost instant acclaim from Edinburgh to London. Lords and ladies feted him, and science societies such as the prestigious Royal Society of London gave him membership. His sales of subscriptions (one to King George IV himself) enabled him to contract with the renowned engravers Havell and Son to engrave and publish the work, and in Paris the eminent zoologist, George Cuvier, enthused of the watercolors, "the greatest monument ever erected by art to nature."

Audubon himself, with his Gallic charms and his usual garb of wolf-skin jacket, leather leggings, and boots, seemed to convey a romantic image of the "American frontier woodsman" to his more sedate British admirers. To Lucy, he wrote: "My situation [here] borders on the miraculous." The publication months later of the first edition of *Birds of America* drew rave reviews in both Europe and America, and the somewhat overwhelmed naturalist found himself famous virtually overnight.

Such was his prestige that, by 1831, as he prepared for his long-anticipated Florida expedition, the U.S. Navy (in perhaps the first federal science-arts endowment) provided Audubon and his assistants with a revenue cutter for transportation.

As he roamed from oak forests to cypress swamps to seashore in the St. Johns River region, Audubon quickly revised his dour first impressions of the state, and his hunt proved rewarding. He was elated to bag "two of the finest specimens" of the wary brown pelican. He also found the rarely seen caracara, or Brazilian eagle, the herring gull, American coot, sanderling, glossy ibis, yellow red-poll warbler, cayenne tern, ruddy duck, schinz's sandpiper, orange-crowned warbler, and others, all destined for the *Birds* volumes.

The singular art of Audubon's bird portraits lay in their vivid animation and lifelike poses. Lying concealed sometimes for hours, studying each species in habit and habitat, he was an accurate and succinct observer, and this lent a scientific intensity to his paintings. He disdained the portrayal of birds in "stiff, unmeaning profiles," much as he scorned "closet naturalists" (museum scientists) who dabbled with dead skins trying to form them into "tidy systems." Much earlier, he had invented a method for inserting wires into freshly killed specimens by which to plant them in varied "action" poses—in flight, feeding, playing, fighting, courting, defending the nest. His art emphasized behavior, action, the bird in life.

His winter sojourn in upper east Florida was followed in the spring of 1832 with a trip to the Florida Keys. It was here that Audubon found his feathered Elysium. The flocks of new and different species sighted on arrival at Indian Key in April filled him with "uncontrollable delight." But days later, on a trip to remote Sandy Island off Cape Sable, the flocks became massive clouds that "so astonished us that we could . . . scarcely believe our eyes." In less than three weeks here, Audubon had painted such elusive species as the double-crested cormorant, roseate tern, great godwit, rose-colored curlew, purple heron, white ibis, flamingo, gallinule, pipery fly-catcher (or gray kingbird), white-crowned pigeon and reddish egret.

At Key West, physician friend and naturalist Dr. Benjamin Strobel found it hard to keep up with Audubon, whom he called "the most enthusiastic and indefatigable man I ever knew." Indeed, a typical Audubon workday found him rising at 3 A.M. to wait undetected for his quarry, observe, shoot, then move on, often pushing his bark for miles over mudflats under a burning sun amid tormenting mosquito hordes to another habitat. The afternoon was spent rapidly painting his specimens, a necessity since the natural coloring of a bird begins fading within hours of its death. Then evenings were spent writing up his bird notes and daily journal.

Aside from his prized find, the great white heron, and the shearwater, or dusky petrel (both named for Audubon), he also recorded the mangrove cuckoo, frigate pelican, Key West quail-doves (pigeons), white-tailed tropic bird, blue-headed quail-dove, and that rare tiny hummingbird, the black-throated mango. On a brief trip to the Dry Tortugas, he drew the sooty tern, noddy tern, and brown booby.

Florida was a crowning achievement for the *Birds* books. The four-volume final edition consists of 435 plates containing 1,065 life-size bird portraits, with textual description. Printed on double-elephant (29½ by 39½ inches) hand-made paper, it sold in the United States then for $1,000. (In 1983, many of the original plates sold at auction for sums totaling $1.7 million.) He later published a similar work on quadrupeds.

It is perhaps fitting that Audubon is the progenitor of modern conservation movements. His gift was to record for posterity the freshness and abundance of a continent while it was still in pristine condition. But even then the slaughter of birds and other wildlife by trappers, eggers, and other human predators led him to warn: "In less than half a century these wonderful nurseries will be entirely destroyed, unless some kind government will interfere to stop the shameful destruction. Nature herself seems perishing."

16.
The Arabian Nights of Glenn Curtiss

Aeronautical whiz Glenn Curtiss caught the boom fever and shucked his cow pastures for town-building.

There were more than a few would-be city builders who shoveled and dredged about in Florida's golden sandbox during the land boom of the roaring '20s.

And more than a few of them fell on bad times when the bubble burst in 1926. George Merrick (Coral Gables) struggled to operate a Keys fish camp; Carl Fisher (Miami Beach) died broke and alcoholic; Addison Mizner (Boca Raton) lived hand-to-mouth and died on a paper pyre of litigation; debt-ridden D.P. "Doc" Davis (Davis Islands) died mysteriously on a Europe-bound liner at sea, either a homicide or suicide (he could hardly have squirmed through a ship's porthole "accidentally," as often reported).

But one of the more successful of these developers had no thought of town-building when he came to Florida. Aviation pioneer and inventor Glenn Curtiss was content with dairy farming and operating a flying school north of Miami. But the multimillionaire airplane manufacturer was caught up in the vortex of the frenzied boom years almost in spite of himself. He ended up creating three Dade County towns, one of which was among the most lavish of fantasy creations, a "dream of Araby," Opa-locka.

Curtiss' dazzling career, from making bicycles and motorcycles to engines and airplanes, brought him to Florida early. Running his famous motorcycle at the Ormond Beach Speed Carnival in 1907, he became known as the "fastest man in the world" (136.7 miles per hour). Several years later, he was zooming up and down Biscayne Bay in a strange new machine, a "flying boat," forerunner of the seaplanes he would send on the first trans-Atlantic air flight to Europe in 1919. He operated a flying school first on Miami Beach and then over on a pastureland tract north of Miami that he purchased from local cattle and dairy rancher James Bright. This was after he and his wife, Lena, came to Florida in 1916 to build a permanent home.

In those years, Miamians drank canned milk in lieu of the brackish and distasteful city water. Curtiss saw a golden market here for fresh milk and joined in partnership with Bright to expand their dairy business. Purchasing prize bulls and 25 carloads of cows, the partners saw their milk business prosper phenomenally. They began buying land sections at $2 to $3 an acre north and west of Miami and, by 1921, had 120,000 acres. The dairy business soared but soon proved too valuable for its own good.

Curtiss was in New York divesting himself of his huge Curtiss Aeroplane and Motor Corporation (from which he cleared $32 million) when Bright visited him to propose that they break up and sell some of the ranch property for building lots. Scoffed Curtiss: "Jimmy, nobody but you would want to live out there." But he agreed to try it, and the pair formed the Curtiss-Bright Realty Company. Both Curtiss and Bright could scarcely believe what was happening when their lots began selling faster than streets could be laid out. By now hordes of out-of-staters were pouring into South Florida to scoop up a chunk of the sand and the action. In one 10-day period the partners sold $1 million in lots. They soon incorporated the section into the city of Hialeah. Later, Curtiss somewhat regretted allowing formation of the Hialeah Race Track in 1925; it had become a jazzy mecca for gamblers, bootleggers, and gangsters.

Curtiss was fast on his way to a second fortune when the team created the "residential paradise" of Country Club Estates (changed later to Miami Springs). Streets were laid out like winding and curving parkways with a rolling golf course as the centerpiece. When a well sunk on the course produced an abundance of spring-pure water, the partners sold the golf course and its water rights in 1923 to the city of Miami for $1, permanently solving that city's water problems. The cows had long since been relegated to a ranch near Lake Okeechobee.

For the next project, Curtiss wanted to combine unique artistic beauty with expert planning on a tract whose Indian name, Opatishawockalocka, was fractured to Opa-locka. One day when a lady relative was viewing the site with Curtiss, she suddenly exclaimed: "Oh, Glenn, it's like a dream from the Arabian Nights!" Struck by the analogy, Curtiss acquired an illustrated volume of the famous tales, studied it, and finally hired noted architect Bernhardt Muller to lay out the "Baghdad of Dade County." Each section of the town would be simulated on a story from the famous tales.

Noisy bulldozers were soon slashing out streets with names such as Aladdin, Sesame, Caliph, and Sherazed and avenues such as Sinbad, Ali Baba, and Sultan. Sales agents in Curtiss' mosquelike sales center fanned out all over to make every man a sheik, albeit sans harem. The erection of a fantastic six-domed city hall, modeled on the emperor Kosroushah's palace in the tales, set the motif for this oriental splendor rising out of the cow pastures. With the town's domes, minarets, arches, balconies, tile frescoes, and an inner courtyard square with fountain and statuary, future city fathers might easily imagine themselves as grand caliphs. This extravagant mix of Persian and Moorish architecture was all highlighted in pastel shades of pink, ivory, blue, and green.

But there was only a smattering of lot buyers when Opa-locka was incorporated in early 1926. There had been a sharp falloff in South Florida real estate activity, and Curtiss accurately perceived this as an early sign of the boom's collapse. Thus he made tentative plans to put his "dream of Araby" on hold even though the project represented merely a fraction of the millions in boom profits he had set aside. The bust finally did come in September, but associates convinced the aviation mogul that the bust was only temporary and he should finish his "masterpiece." Soon new buildings and homes, with domed garages and minarets, began to speckle the landscape.

Curtiss persuaded Seaboard Air Line Railroad to curve its Miami extension slightly inland to serve the Arabesque station at Opa-locka and, in January 1927, a gala celebration greeted the first train, the Orange Blossom Special, carrying Governor John W. Martin with assorted celebrities and railroad officials. The guests were startled when local sheiks on horseback "raided" the train, waving mock scimitars with threatening shouts and gestures. But all were soon escorted to a grand feast of Middle Eastern culinary fare.

Nevertheless, the economy had not recovered, and the downturn deepened. The few solvent lot buyers still around might momentarily fantasize themselves as grand viziers, dwelling in opulence, but the doomed and spired dwellings seemed a little too exotic for which to lay out hard cash. By late 1927, the "dream city" was coming more to resemble an abandoned Hollywood stage set for a Rudolph Valentino movie. Nor did the boom's soaring land valuation drop with the market. Curtiss was beset with an untenable tax squeeze on his vast holdings. Reluctantly, he made an arrangement with Bright to withdraw from the project, returning to his hometown in Hammondsport, New York.

But he did leave behind as a gift his airport tract, and today Opa-locka has one of the busiest small airports in the country. He also gave an airport site to Miami, embraced today by Miami International Airport.

But all that remains of his Arabian Nights are a few shabby domed garages and the incredible city hall, its pastel colors fading and peeling, its grand domes teetering in disrepair, its frescoed walls defaced with graffiti, almost a fitting symbol of the era that spawned the dream.

17.
Black Star Out of Jacksonville

Native son achiever James Weldon Johnson was lawyer, educator, composer, author, diplomat, and national black leader.

He had a stable and virtually carefree childhood; for a black boy growing up in turbid, post-Civil War Reconstruction Florida, this seemed almost anomalous.

But burgeoning, tourist-bustling Jacksonville was known as "a good town for blacks." Racial lines were loose, informal, and often blurred—unportentous of the harsh and oppressive Jim Crow laws that arose at the century's close. And so James Weldon Johnson, born there in 1871 to James and Helen Louise Johnson, and his younger brother, Rosamond, enjoyed the greenhouse nurturing effects of solid middle-class life in a quiet westside suburb. James was known as "a steady, coolheaded boy"; possibly he derived these qualities from his earthy, practical father, a respected and successful headwaiter at the popular resort hotel, St. James. His artistic, schoolteacher mother acquainted him early with the classics, and he became a voracious reader of everything from *The Pickwick Papers* to *Pilgrim's Progress*. The forceful spirituality of his grandmother would quicken in him awareness of his own spiritual currents.

His childhood was prosaically uneventful, but there were some vivid high points: shaking hands, at age 7, with visiting President U.S. Grant; learning fluent Spanish from a black Cuban student staying at their home; being filled with "worshipful awe" during a local speech by the great advocate, Frederick Douglass; becoming himself a teenage athletic hero with his artful skills as a "shutout" baseball pitcher. But, after all, he would one day deal personally with presidents; his Spanish would equip him for foreign service; his baseball skills would imbue him with a poise and tact that softened the more painful buffetings of Jim Crowism; and, like Douglass, he would himself become a leading national figure in the struggle for black civil rights.

In fact, this educator, lawyer, editor, composer, author, poet, and diplomat would become a sturdy fulcrum for black America's transition in 1916 from the softspoken conformity and accommodation of the Booker T. Washington era to a vigorous militant idealism that targeted no less than full equality.

Graduating from Jacksonville's eight-grade Stanton School, one of the few such for blacks in the South, Johnson was still well prepared for enrollment in an all-black, coed Atlanta University. Yale-oriented in both its faculty and its strict moral and traditional values, the university was recalled by Johnson as an "excellent school" which offered everything from Greek, Latin, and the classics to carpentry. In summers, Johnson taught Georgia's rural black children for a nickel a pupil.

Graduating with honors in 1894, Johnson spurned a chance for a Harvard medical scholarship and accepted an offer to become principal of his native Stanton School; at age 24, he was the youngest school principal in the state. Over several years, with the tacit approval of the white county superintendent, he transformed Stanton into a full 12-year school. In the same period, he took time to found the country's first black local daily newspaper, *The Daily American*. Although it won an enthusiastic response, straitened finances forced its closing within the year. Johnson also studied law part-time under the tutelage of a prominent local white attorney and became the first black admitted to the Florida Bar.

One day in 1900, Johnson's song-writing brother, Rosamond, visiting from New York, agreed to set to music an inspired poem James had written for a school program observing Lincoln's birthday. Neither man dreamed that the song, "Lift Every Voice and Sing," would later be sung in schools and churches nationwide and acquire the reputation of the Negro National Hymn. (Unfortunately, in recent years a bastardized version of the song has appeared, which omits reference to God and is set to a pop tempo.)

On a visit to New York months earlier, James became fascinated by "a world of tremendous artistic potentialities." He soon decided to shelve his legal work, resign Stanton, and work in New York with Rosamond as a composing team along with a friend, Bob Cole. His resolve here was reinforced when he narrowly missed being lynched by an out-of-town white militia mob after being seen in a park with a "white woman," a very light-skinned black journalist interviewing him about the great Jacksonville fire in 1901.

The Johnson brothers prospered as a composing team, with such enduring hits as "Under the Bamboo Tree" and "The Congo Love Song." They also wrote songs for leading actresses like Anna Held, wife of Flo Ziegfeld, Faye Templeton, Lillian Russell, and others and were warmly received on tours in Paris and London.

But Johnson decided on a career change after a campaigning stint for the successful reelection of President Theodore Roosevelt who offered him a post as U.S. Consul at Venezuela in 1906. The Spanish-fluent Johnson accepted and found that his routine consular duties left him ample time to write stories and poems. He also worked on a novel, *The Autobiography of an Ex-Colored Man*, the story of a black man who "passed" the color line by marrying a white woman. It would be published in 1912, and its psychological innovations would exert much influence on black writers in the 1920s. After being promoted next to the consulate post in Nicaragua, Johnson married a longtime girlfriend, the black and attractive Grace Nail. Finally, with a new president (Woodrow Wilson), Johnson resigned his consulate post in 1914.

Back in New York, Johnson became an editor for *The New York Age*, a paper founded in the 1880s by a Jacksonville family friend, T.T. Fortune, a renowned black journalist.

In this era of mob lynchings, disenfranchisement, and rigid Jim Crow laws, black American leadership was divided into two often antagonistic camps: the conforming gradualism and accommodation of Booker T. Washington and the more militant activism of W.E.B. Du Bois. With the death of Washington in 1916, Johnson saw a critical need for transition from passive accommodation to "high courage and idealism." Therefore, in that same year he accepted the post of national field secretary for the recently formed National Association for the Advancement of Colored People, offered to him by NAACP officials J.E. Springarn and Du Bois. Perceiving that the "ultimate and vital" work for civil rights "would have to be done by black America itself," Johnson set at once to work, targeting Southern cities from Richmond to Tampa to set up NAACP branches. His tireless travel and efforts saw growth mushroom from 68 branches nationwide (three in the South) in 1917 to 310 branches in 1919, 131 of them Southern. He also observed a general rejuvenation of black morale, and this emboldened the association to call its first national conference—in deep South Atlanta. At this gathering, Johnson took note of an energetic and idealistic young Atlantan and successfully promoted him as assistant NAACP secretary; Walter White would later become one of the group's most distinctive leaders.

But with a reemergent Ku Klux Klan in the World War I period, racial violence gained impetus. From Chicago to Houston lynchings and mob attacks on blacks accelerated. The nation was appalled by a massacre of unusual savagery in East St. Louis in which thousands of black citizens were burned out of their homes and hundreds brutally killed. Some 10,000 blacks marched down New York's Fifth Avenue in eloquent silence while muffled drums rolled in protest. In another incident, Johnson met personally with President Wilson to stay execution of 63 black soldiers after white-provoked violence in Houston.

After investigation, Wilson halted the execution; the 63 were later freed. Johnson and White were on the scene of almost every racial flare-up and were often ably assisted by the famed attorney Clarence Darrow. During this period, the NAACP won a major case when the U.S. Supreme Court ruled as unconstitutional a Louisville law establishing residential segregation. Elsewhere he worked tirelessly in Congress to pass a federal anti-lynching bill. The bill failed by a narrow margin, prompting from Johnson the observation that "in large measure the race question involves the saving of black America's body and white America's soul."

Remarkably, in this period the activist was also the writer. With publication in 1917 of his powerful *Fifty Years and Other Poems*, his literary reputation was established. He became a singular influence in the "black renaissance" of the 1920s, along with Countee Cullen, Langston Hughes, Zora Neale Hurston, and others. In 1925, he won the Springarn Award for his definitive volume on the origin and cultural impact of American black spirituals. In 1927, his masterwork, *God's Trombones*, was said by one critic to have raised black poetry to its "highest classic elegance." The work, which won him the Harmon Award and Gold Medal, transformed cadences of seven sermons by black Southern preachers into a poetic idiom of unusual imagery and power.

But Johnson remained immersed primarily in civil rights work until his resignation from the NAACP in 1930 to take a chair in literature at Fisk University. In 1933, his now classic autobiography, *Along This Way*, was published, and, in 1934, his last book, *Negro America, What Now?*, appeared. In this work, Johnson urged that blacks never surrender their "spiritual integrity" while employing "coordinated racial action" to achieve full equality and opportunity. "If the Negro is made to fail," he warned, "America fails with him." In this he presciently anticipated the generation of Martin Luther King, Jr., or, as a later critic summarized: "He took the velvet glove approach . . . and adapted it to the ways of militancy and agitation."

In June, 1938, Johnson and his wife, returning home by car from a visit to friends in Maine, ran into a blinding rainstorm and failed to see a speeding train at an unguarded railroad crossing. The impact of the crash killed Johnson at the scene; his severely injured wife later recovered.

Thousands of mourners turned out for the funeral service at Harlem's Salem Methodist Church; condolences poured in from across the country. Noted speakers on the occasion ranged from Walter White to New York Mayor Fiorello La Guardia. But perhaps the most poignant and simple eulogy, one biographer noted, came from an obscure unknown admirer who reflected: "Mister Johnson climbed very high and he lifted us with him."

Villains and
Characters

18.
Bedlam Reigns in an "Ideal" Town

Denys Rolle was going to "reform" London's miscreants in a Florida colony, but his ineptness undid the plan.

It seemed like the worthiest philanthropic experiment. He would recruit "colonists" from 18th-century London's slums and jails—vagabonds, prostitutes, pickpockets, and the poor—transplant them to the banks of Florida's St. Johns River, and there, in penitent sweaty labor, let them build a utopian settlement.

And since it didn't hurt to mix a little profit-making with such lofty benevolence, Denys Rolle, a wealthy young English landowner and member of the Parliament, figured to gain a few thriving prosperous plantations even as he reformed his wayward charges—a little pound sterling recompense for noblesse oblige.

But Rolle, penny-wise and pound-foolish, hardly knowing a palmetto from a corn stalk and imbued with a flighty, arbitrary temperament, soon became so oppressive that his "colonists," not exactly hardy wilderness types anyway, rebelled and turned back to their wicked ways. Thus, Bedlam succeeded Eden in short order.

It began in 1763 when Britain won Florida from Spain, and King George II offered generous land grants to any well-born gentry who would develop the territory. Rolle's "ideal" town scheme met receptive ears at Court, and in 1764 he was on his way to Florida with a grant of 20,000 acres at "any site of his choosing."

But Rolle's "choosiness," along with his priggish and oppressive behavior generally, would soon prove too much for the mild-mannered Royal governor, James Grant, at St. Augustine. Grant no sooner approved a site on the Gulf at St. Marks when Rolle capriciously changed his mind and picked instead a sandy pine barren bluff on the St. Johns River, 22 miles southwest of St. Augustine. Then, when the governor informed him he could not, under land-grant terms, claim both sides of the river, Rolle sailed in a petulant huff back to England where he had the King's Privy Council overrule Grant. Finally, after three years of petty bickering over boundaries—and keeping all other grant claimants waiting in line—Grant approved an "irregular" site, "just to get him [Rolle] off my hands upon any terms."

In 1767, Grant wrote London that all claimants had been served "successfully, except in the case of Mr. Rolle" with whom he had taken "more pains to be as civil as possible," but "his plans are wild and inconsistent...'tis impossible to direct him or put him right."

Rolle's first batch of 49 men and women colonists, already discontented on learning that their benefactor had covertly altered their terms of indentured servitude in transit, were even more chagrined to discover, upon arrival at "Rollestown," that there was not one dwelling to live in. Yet, before building the first cabin, Rolle set them to work grubbing up palmetto roots, generously informing them they could keep half the roots to sell. Realizing that they "couldn't buy a pound of bread at that rate," the colonists refused the job, choosing instead to raise produce. Heated arguments ensued, and a few settlers ran off to St. Augustine. When Rolle retaliated by withholding food rations (already meager) from those remaining, they all fled into town where three Peace Justices heard their complaints. Although Governor Grant censured Rolle for "acts of injustice and oppression," he intervened privately to have the colonists returned, fearing, he said, the precedent of "letting the servants get the better of their masters."

But under Rolle's petty and niggardly management, little productive work came out of the colony. During one of two more trips to London for colonists, most of the 89 men and women aboard simply "vanished" once they hit Charleston. At its peak "Rollestown" would host 200—mostly reluctant—settlers.

During his absences, too, many of Rolle's "pioneers" chose frolicking over farming. The dubious "ladies" fell back into their easy ways, joining the ex-cons and vagabonds in bouts of "drinking, revelry, and licentious behavior." Once one of Rolle's "agents" simply sold all of his boss's cattle and fled to the woods, later joined by other runaways. A disgusted Governor Grant would report: "Rolle could have had two valuable plantations on his estate for the money he spent on two boatloads of settlers."

Rolle meanwhile continued to besiege Grant with complaints about his unwilling workers—even one he had become enamored of. "He [Rolle] insisted upon my taking in charge," sighed Grant, "a young girl of 16 or 18, who he had brought out from England for the second time, because they quarreled and she was going to leave him." Grant reconciled them, but later they quarreled over the price of a gown for her, and she left him for good. At this, Grant recalled,

"Rolle actually applied for a [felony] warrant against the girl's brother," to be tried for his life" on suspicion of stealing a blanket.

In all, Rolle spent some 23,000 pounds on his "experiment," but by the late 1770s, most of his indentured charges had fled "utopia." In despair, Rolle dumped his dream colony and imported about 100 black slaves, and for a while his plantation began to prosper—in turpentine, orange juice, rice, indigo, cattle, and hogs. But the recovery was brief. The American Revolution had forced England to cede Florida back to Spain, in 1783, and plantation grantees were given seven months to get out of the territory.

An embittered Rolle frantically gathered what possessions he could transport and went first to a West Indian island and, finally, back to England.

But, ever brazen and haughty, Rolle demanded indemnification for his Florida losses and, surprisingly, secured enough to retire to his country home in Devonshire. A now somewhat chastened philanthropist, Rolle still probably never discerned that his "philanthropy" had never been predicated on any truly altruistic motives but on a meaner strain of covetousness, a strain that bore the seeds of failure for his "ideal" town even before it began.

19.
The Barker Gang's Last Square-Off

The Barker gang hid out in a lakeside Florida hamlet, but the refuge became a battleground when the FBI showed up.

If folks in the sleepy little central Florida hamlet of Oklawaha had known what the loud crackling of gunfire was all about that early winter dawn, they might have given a little shudder and tugged their blankets harder.

But, after all, their winter visitors, the "Clark" family, had seemed like just folks, shy but friendly. They also spent freely and tipped the local tradesmen generously. In that hard depression time, people were willing to abide by the old "cracker" code of minding one's business. So how were they to know they were playing host to the FBI's "most wanted" scourge, the Karpis-Barker gang—Ma Barker and her boys, Alvin Karpis, and other desperadoes?

Therefore, when more than a dozen FBI agents drove silently into the village that early January 16, 1935, and set up a pre-dawn cordon around the Barker's rented two-story frame cottage on Lake Weir, everyone was surprised—especially the Barkers. And thus began one of the longest, deadliest shootouts in FBI history when an estimated 3,000 rounds of rifle, shotgun, and machine-gun fire shattered the peaceful pastoral setting of lake and hilly woods with a deafening staccato beat. When it was over, the riddled bodies of Ma and her son, Fred, the cottage's sole occupants at the time, lay sprawled on an upper room floor. And it marked, for all purposes, the end of an era, one of the most colorful and notorious in U.S. history.

It was the era of bizarrely individual gangsters and gang leaders, bandits, and killers who terrorized the midwestern United States in the first half of the Great Depression—John Dillinger, Baby Face Nelson, Roger Touhy, Pretty Boy Floyd, Clyde Barrow and Bonnie Parker, and numerous lesser known figures who went on a rampage of payroll and bank robberies, kidnappings, and sporadic mayhem. But soon enough, local and federal lawmen began to mount an all-out state-by-state manhunt for these desperadoes, fanning out into dozens of big cities and small towns in a relentless search. Gradually, they nabbed all of the major figures, who were killed either in desperate shootouts or put behind bars for long terms.

Most authorities agreed that the last of these major operators—the Karpis-Barker gang—was the cleverest, most effective, and most elusive of all the gangs. They would meticulously stake out a small-town bank for weeks ahead, studying the daily habits of the target principals and mapping every getaway route down to the most obscure country back road. Every detail was coordinated. They preplanted "gas drops" at intervals along escape routes in case of a bullet-punctured gas tank from pursuing lawmen. Medicine kits and vials of morphine were carried for any wounded, and, almost always, they fled with two women hostages positioned to ride on each running board of their car. This always discouraged pursuing gunfire. Often they had a second (stolen) car waiting at some predesignated spot. After dividing the loot, they would lay low for a period of time—and then plan another job, usually in a different state.

Characteristically, this era also spawned its share of colorful myths, the most ludicrous of which was the one portrayed in newspaper stories, movies, comic books, and fiction, of Ma Barker as the gang's "mastermind." She had even trained her boys in a "crime school" in Tulsa. In fact, this dull, dumpy, semi-literate little woman from the Ozarks probably couldn't have planned a banana-cart snitch. She was usually sent home, or out to see a movie, when "her boys" were planning some caper. Karpis recalled Ma as "superstitious, gullible, simple, cantankerous...a slightly nutty old queen" whose vaunted cerebral powers were confined to nothing more complex than working jigsaw puzzles or listening to hillbilly radio music. But the boys looked after her devotedly, and she also made a "nearly foolproof cover" as a poor widowed mother and her sons when the gang moved about renting hideaways—which was often. But the myth took hold, largely due to the acute image consciousness of J. Edgar Hoover, G-man director, who wrote that Ma Barker "was the most vicious, dangerous, and resourceful criminal brain" he had yet tangled with. Actually, Hoover had never tangled with any big gang leaders, even Karpis, whom the director later claimed he had personally disarmed and arrested.

Ma Barker had raised her four boys—Arthur "Doc," Lloyd, Herman, and Fred—in a poor section of Tulsa. She was abnormally possessive toward her brood and would zealously alibi for them in their numerous forays into petty crime as teenagers. Later, when the boys took to full-time criminal careers, Pa Barker left Kate Clark Barker and went off to live a "straight" respectable life, as did Lloyd, for the same reasons. The oldest, Herman, was finally shot to death in a Tulsa robbery. Fred and Doc served a few years of prison time for their escapades. Ma continued to "look after her boys"—guarding them especially from their "bad woman" friends with whom they often had to meet separately—

but she rarely even handled a gun, not until that fateful day in Oklawaha when her Fred was direly threatened.

Fred was the brain, Karpis recalled, "efficient, cold and expert...planning jobs to run like clockwork." The two were close friends, but Karpis never forgot his friend's "vicious streak" or that "my great pal Freddie Barker was a natural killer."

The gang had just pulled two successful kidnappings in St. Paul, Minnesota—collecting $100,000 and $200,000, respectively for William Hamm, Jr., of Hamm's Beer, and banker Edward Bremer—when the federal heat became so intense they decided to take a long vacation. Luggage stuffed with clothes and cash, they headed south—to Florida.

In that fall of 1934, they could not have picked a more remote hideaway than the tiny town of Oklawaha, almost midway between Ocala and Leesburg, situated on the old back road highway, U.S. 441, far from major throughways. They rented a two-story frame cottage 50 yards back from the road on Lake Weir and were known as "the Clarks" to townspeople. The village accepted them as "nice, down-home people" and these winter visitors, in turn, spent generously at area stores. They seemed to have a lot of "guests" streaming in and out on visits, but this was uneventful—that is, until the locals were disturbed to learn that some of the "guests" were chasing wild ducks on the lake and shooting them with machine guns. They became truly riled when they heard that Fred and Karpis had killed "Old Joe," a 12-foot alligator who had been for years a sort of area mascot, almost a pet. The two men had towed a live pig behind their motor launch to lure the reptile; the 'gator was later discovered on an island beach, riddled with bullets. The Barkers decided then to cool their antics, confining them to bream and perch fishing. Even so, "Old Joe" was about to get some posthumous revenge.

In Chicago, on January 8, 1935, G-men surrounded an old house and arrested "Doc" Barker and two other gang members without firing a shot. In a search of the house, the federals discovered a map of Florida, with Oklawaha and its area circled in pencil. Agents were dispatched at once to that city and, by discreetly probing around, learned about the incident with "Old Joe." This led to some tallying descriptions of the 62-year-old woman and her sons who had rented a cottage on the lake. They did not have to probe any further.

In pre-dawn darkness the following Wednesday, January 16, 14 G-men, headed by Special Agent E.J. Connelley, and some area lawmen parked their cars some distance away and crept up to the cottage, positioning themselves in a semicircular cordon. As dawn broke, Connelley broke the stillness with a loud command: "Come out and surrender." A deadly silence followed. Finally, two agents walked up to the cottage door and knocked. Behind the door, they heard a gravelly female voice bark: "Who's there and what do you want?" "We're federal agents and we want to speak with your son, Fred Barker," they responded. "Well," she answered, "you'd better send in your Army and Navy and Marines" and, with that, she fired a machine gun burst through the door. The agents scurried for cover, and the battle was on, as G-men returned the fire. Soon a withering hail of rifle and machine-gun fire spattered in a deadly criss-cross between cottage and tree covers, echoing loudly over the lake and through the town. Frightened and excited residents by then had poured out into their yards and onto the highway main street as the roar of gunfire continued without pause through the morning. The arsenal of federal arms and even a few lobs of tear gas had thus far proved ineffective as Ma and Fred sustained an endless spray of return fire from an upstairs room.

Finally, after some four hours, the rain of bullets from upstairs suddenly stopped. The agents stopped. For 45 tense minutes they waited. In this time, Connelley had skirted around to look into a garage-shed near the house where he found a frightened couple huddled near a bunk bed. Willie Woodberry and his wife had been hired earlier by the Barkers to serve as a maid and cook, but neither knew their employers' real identities. The agent then walked with Woodberry onto the porch of the cottage and the handyman was asked to go in and inspect the premises. Moments later, Woodberry shouted from the upstairs window: "They're all dead."

Fred had a machine-gun tattoo across his collarbone and three head wounds; Ma had been slain with several bullets. The G-men soon saw how the pair could sustain such a lengthy fusillade: three Thompson machine guns; three bullet-proof vests; two sawed-off shotguns; two 30-30 rifles, and several handguns. They found four $1,000 bills on Fred and $10,500 in Ma's purse; a later search uncovered $40,000 in cash hidden behind wallboards on the back porch. Karpis and gang member Harry Campbell had left the cottage for Miami only the day before. Connelley himself, heading a stake-out team, would arrest both men in New Orleans the following year. (Karpis would survive to serve 33 years of a life term, mostly at Alcatraz, before winning extradition parole to his native Montreal, Canada, in 1968, at age 62. He would later write a book on his crime career.)

As for the little citrus and resort town of Oklawaha, they had not experienced so much excitement since the great winter freeze of the 1890s, when citrus tree buds and twigs popped and crackled in the icy cold all over the area, sounding almost like gunfire. But the pop and crackle that woke them up that winter morning in 1935 didn't come from orange trees, and today oldtimers will still show you the bullet-splintered trees and tell you exciting stories of the great shootout at the lake and how Fred must have been mighty proud of his Ma, knowing she could, in the end, handle a gun like a true Barker, protecting her boy right down to the bitter finale, as the curtain closed on an infamous era like no other in history.

20.
When Cow Land Was
Another Country

*It was a land of cattle kings, gold doubloons, and wild-riding
cowboys who made the rules as they went along.*

Once upon a time in Florida there existed a region that was virtually another
country, a kingdom unto itself, with its own customs, economy, politics, and
law, and where the coin of the realm was not dollars but gold. This kingdom
sprawled over the vast scrub flats, piney woods, and palmetto thickets from Fort
Meade to Fort Myers, embracing most of Southwest Florida, a land where cattle
was king and the kings of cattle made fortunes. It would thrive for more than a
generation.

And yet the region and era seemed like some picturesque anachronism. It
had emerged in the post-Civil War period when the South—and Florida—
writhed in the impoverishment of defeat. Indeed, many in this kingdom had
recently fled this destitution. The kingdom's boom started about 1865 and
peaked in the late 1800s, the period when the Western part of the United States
was being opened in a similar rough-and-ready spirit.

But the Old West had nothing on Florida's land of cowboys and cattle
barons. The men had free-wheeling spirits, and their laws were often "home-
made," wrought in a blaze of Colts and Winchesters. And the average cowboy
didn't mind living in a crude log hut, on a diet of fried pork, grits, and coffee,
as long as a sack of gold doubloons lay in a dirt-floor corner, ready to be tapped
for the next town spree.

Colorful characters thrived, too. There was legendary cowpoke "Bone"
Mizelle, titanic Judge "Zibe" King, and small wiry Jacob Summerlin, "King of
the Crackers," the man who started the growth of the cattle industry in South
Florida and became a millionaire before age 40. There were the Hendrys,
Hollingsworths, Boggs, Knights, and the Lykes brothers.

The floodtide of gold came from Spanish Cuba, which would import tens
of thousands of cattle from the shipping docks at Punta Rassa, just south of Fort
Myers, over several decades. The gold doubloon quickly became the region's
currency for clerk, shopkeeper, farmer, and schoolteacher, as well as cattleman.

Ironically, most of these cattle were descended from the "vacos" brought over by early Spanish colonists. By the 1840s, great herds of these wild cattle roamed freely over the Southwest Florida plains. The land was replete with tough, sinewy, little "scrubs" of vegetation, a hardy, nourishing food staple which was free for the taking. Jake Summerlin took advantage of the vegetation, gradually building large herds, and when the Civil War broke out, he made a fortune supplying beef to the Rebels.

After the war, other cattlemen moved in to grab their share of the wild herds, and Florida's cattle land empire was born. It was a boom accelerated by the outbreak of Cuban insurrection, prompting Spain to cable Summerlin for "an unlimited supply" of beef; the shrewd Cracker King sent men over the state to buy up as many herds as possible.

Driving the beef to port were the Florida cowboys, mostly ex-Rebel soldiers, ex-blockade runners and ex-guerillas. They could pop their 16-foot cowhide whips with deadly skill, enough to decapitate a snake, gut a hen, or keep a herd moving. Awaiting them at the cattle pens and long loading wharf at Punta Rassa were the Spanish schooners. Spanish buyers would ride up on fancy five-gaited show horses, prancing along to inspect steers and negotiate prices. The bellowing, kicking beasts were then winch-hoisted by their horns from wharf to ship holds. Then sacks of gold doubloons were dragged out for payment. Cattlemen gathered the coins in saddlebags or large cloth sacks. The cowboys were paid with bags of gold and were soon whooping into little Fort Myers village, where they drank the potent Spanish brandy *aguardiente*, gambled, or looked for friendly companionship.

There was no law in the region, but no thievery either. A cowboy could leave a saddlebag of gold on a porch, fencepost, or chair or with a storekeeper or friend, without fear of loss. Summerlin himself would hide his gold in sacks, tin cans, wood boxes, or tied rags, never forgetting whether it was perched on a rafter or beneath his mattress. He later used some of his vast wealth to create and endow, with land and buildings, the Polk County seat of Bartow and Orange County's seat, Orlando.

In contrast to Summerlin, towering Judge Ziba King (6-feet-6) looked every inch a cowpuncher. Literally so. Once, angered by a wild steer that attacked him, he swung a haymaker on the beast, near its heart, killing it instantly. He plowed his gold into banking, citrus, and real estate. He was also a reigning political kingpin and even served terms in both state legislative houses, the better to scrutinize laws that might be "unfriendly" to cattleland. Indeed, the cattle industry long held the whip hand over state lawmakers, even controlling powerful railroad interests. When a train struck a straying cow, the railroads were required to pay for the animal, but they were not permitted to impede the "open range" with fenced-in tracks. In fact, highway-roaming cattle remained unfenced in Florida until Governor Fuller Warren finally rammed fence laws through the Legislature in 1949.

Another thriving cattle business was that of Dr. H.T. Lykes and his seven sons. The two oldest sons, Frederick and Howell, borrowed $20,000 from their father to start their own herds. With the five other brothers, they eventually parlayed their business into a powerful modern-day corporation.

Range wars often enlivened the cattleland scenario. Roaming over such vast fenceless ranges, herds sometimes got "mixed up" (intentionally or otherwise). A Remington rifle, not a court, often decided which steer belonged to whom. The famous cowboy painter Frederic Remington graphically commemorated such battles in his numerous Florida canvases.

But the prevailing attitude toward law among cattleland dwellers was perhaps best illustrated by an incident involving Napoleon Bonaparte "Bone" Mizelle, a cowboy who could outrope, outride, outshoot, and outdrink any cowman in the region, and who was something of a folk hero to settlers in the Peace River Valley. Bone was arrested one day for allegedly stealing a cow, and he was convicted by a court of law. But Valley settlers, aware that many of the big cattle kings were guilty now and then of a cow theft or two, raised a protest. They got up a petition to have Bone pardoned. Authorities were sympathetic but had to point out a technicality; he could not be pardoned until he had served "time." No problem. The good folks dressed Bone up properly and sent him on the train to Raiford. Here an official greeted him, escorted him through the prison buildings, and then gave a dinner for him, at which Bone gave a short speech affirming that he found no fault with the management. Having thus served his "time," he picked up his pardon and left for home.

Such informal meting out of justice might be unfathomable today. But, as noted, the region was, for a colorful period in Florida history, truly "another country."

21.
The Vigilantes of Sara Sota

Prejudice, envy, and avarice led to bloodshed when self-styled
vigilantes stalked early Sarasota.

A little over a century ago, there was much about the land of Sarasota that evoked an almost idyllic pastoral image; its sparkling bay waters literally teemed with fish and shellfish, wild game of every variety throve in its woodlands, and the fertile soil yielded an abundance of produce year-round.

It was still a wilderness community of widely scattered homesteads gathered into areas called Sara Sota, Bee Ridge, Horse and Chaise, Fruitville, and Myakka. The nearest town as such was Manatee, on the Manatee River, and Sarasota County then was part of Manatee County.

Thus from the time in the early 1840s when founding settler Bill Whitaker first built his lonely cabin overlooking the pristine bay, men were drawn to pioneer in the Eden-like semitropic setting. Gradually they trickled in—the Crockers, Webbs, Knights, Currys, Edwardses, Blackburns, Trescas, Reasoners, Redds, and others—especially after the 1862 Homestead Act offered them up to 160 acres at $1.25 per acre if they would build a home and till the land for five years. Other individuals were drawn, too, men not exactly prone to pioneering zeal—Cracker roustabouts, assorted squatters, and maverick opportunists—some outwardly respectable, others openly lawless.

And thus the scene was set for one of the most infamous chapters in Sarasota's history when, in the year 1884, this sprawling frontier community would be shaken to its pine roots by the emergence of a bizarre coterie called the Sara Sota Vigilance Committee, a literal "assassination society" whose brutal crimes would outrage a community and draw national attention and notoriety.

Among the pioneer settlers was Charles E. Abbe, an Illinois native who in 1876 came with his wife, Charlotte, two daughters, Carrie and Nellie, a cousin, Dr. Myron Abbe, and his wife, Carrie, and settled on the bayfront where he built a home and a general store. Abbe was an educated, plainspoken, and enterprising man who would soon own almost 400 acres of prime bayfront land which he hoped to develop. He was also a prolific farmer and cultivated a variety of produce on an inland farm. In August, 1878, he secured the first post office of

Sara Sota, located in his store, and was Postmaster. He was later appointed a
U.S. Commissioner for the federal courts. He often assisted settlers in proving
their homestead claims, and on frequent northern trips he promoted Florida
products at fairs and exhibitions. His daughter, Carrie, volunteered to teach the
area's first school; a dozen pupils attended. Nellie would marry Whitaker's son,
Furman, then a medical student.

In 1881, there were other new arrivals. Alfred and Mary Bidwell, of
Buffalo, New York, purchased bayfront land and opened a small general store
on the bay near Cunliff Lane. Dr. Leo S. Andrews, of Iowa, settled in Bee Ridge;
Georgian Jason L. Alford homesteaded on the bayfront; Dr. Adam W. and
Virginia Hunter arrived, and he went to work for Bidwell in his store. Dr.
Andrews developed a modestly successful practice.

Then, in 1883, a calamity of sorts visited Sara Sota when almost 90 percent
of the present county was removed from any immediate development after
Governor William Bloxham persuaded Philadelphia magnate Hamilton Disston
and his associates to buy 4 million acres of "swamp and overflow" land at 25
cents an acre. The million dollars was critically needed to pay off a pre-Civil
War railroad bonded indebtedness. The sale provoked a storm of bitter protest
from many Sara Sota residents, especially from squatters who had delayed
proving their land claims and now found their homesteads sold out from under
them. Much of the sale also included good land, neither swampy nor overflow-
ing. (In fairness to Bloxham, however, without the sale, both state and citizenry
faced the disastrous prospect of rail bondholders forcing the sale of some 14
million acres of pledged lands.) But it caused bitter feelings to fester throughout
the Sarasota area.

There are occasions when people who have long nurtured personal resent-
ments or hatreds toward others will find in some general calamity a catalyst by
which to express such hostility more overtly. The Disston land sale was just
such a catalyst for a group of men who, for several years or longer, had harbored
deep and harsh feelings toward some of the more prosperous settlers of the area,
especially Abbe. On the night of April 17, 1884, present at a meeting at the home
of Jason Alford were Bidwell, Doctors Hunter and Andrews, Joe Anderson,
Charles Willard, Edmond Bacon, Louis Cato, Chandler Yonge, and several
others. Their talk was later described as "inflammatory." And thus was born the
Sara Sota Vigilance Committee.

The following June 30, the silence of a lonely trail out of Bee Ridge was
shattered with three successive shotgun blasts; a settler named Harrison "Tip"
Riley fell wounded from his saddle. Three men emerged from the palmetto
clumps. One fired at Riley again, a second man slit his throat. A coroner's jury

impanelled by Peace Justice William Bartholomew ruled: "Killed by parties unknown." No further investigation followed. Most of that jury were vigilante members.

But the slaying of Riley would create a tension in the community, one that left people with a vague sense of foreboding. Some had heard rumors of some vigilante group in the area. They would sometimes discuss it in nervous whispers. Then, two days after Christmas, 1884, the tension exploded.

On the morning of December 27, Charles Willard, Ed Bacon, and Dr. Hunter were carousing and drinking moonshine in Bidwell's store. Not far away, Abbe and a visiting friend, Charles Morehouse, were painting a boat near the beach road. Later, Willard and Bacon came along the road and approached Abbe. "Hello, Charlie," Abbe greeted, and then introduced Morehouse. Then, without warning, Willard raised a double-barreled shotgun and fired at Abbe point blank, killing him instantly. After telling Morehouse to "run for his life" (which he did), they took Abbe's body several miles out into the Gulf and dumped it.

News of the cold-blooded murder swept like brushfire throughout the county, inducing mixed passions of outrage, fear, and hate. For months, Sheriff A.S. "Sandy" Watson had been hearing of the vigilante group and gathering names. With an armed posse he set out to arrest them one by one over the next few days. Willard and Alford escaped, but a 10-man posse chased Willard through swamp and forest, as far as Charlotte Harbor and back to Myakka, where the exhausted fugitive surrendered.

Indicted and arrested were Bidwell, Dr. Andrews, Dr. Hunter and his wife, Virginia, Bacon, Willard, Cato, Anderson, and Thomas Dryman. On his trip to jail at the county seat at Pine Level, Bidwell tried to poison himself with morphine, but his escorts worked through the night and saved him.

But the citizens' outrage had reached an explosive point, and there was much talk of a more expedient brand of justice. In fact, the Abbe family survivors and the Whitakers were much criticized for insisting that due process take its course. Elsewhere, neighbors of some defendants began threatening potential state witnesses; not until Henry Hawkins defied such threats and exposed the link between the Riley and Abbe slayings did others feel encouraged to come forth. By the time of the first trial in May, 1885, the affair was drawing national press coverage, with the *New York Times* writing of "an Assassination Society . . . one of the most atrocious organizations ever heard of. . . ."

Presiding in the Pine Level courtroom, Tampa's Judge Henry L. Mitchell heard Dr. Hunter, who had turned state's evidence, describe the bizarre workings of a "political" club with all the trappings of a secret society. New members were sworn to secrecy and could be punished by death for failure to perform certain "duties" delegated by the recognized leaders Bidwell, Alford, and Andrews. Severe whippings were administered for minor club infractions. Their "duties" included the murders of Riley and Abbe; further targets disclosed in testimony were Stephen Goings, Furman Whitaker, Robert Greer, and others. A blatant myth that arose long after the trial, namely, that the vigilantes acted out of sympathy for squatters whose homesteads faced seizure by agents of foreign "speculators," and that Abbe and Riley colluded somehow with the latter, was more than refuted by scores of settlers who testified that they heard the defendants make repeated and violent comments and threats toward Abbe, evidence of a bitter hostility they had been nursing years before the Disston purchase.

In three successive trials for the two murders, Willard, Anderson, Cato, and Dryman were convicted of first-degree murder and drew life sentences; Hunter was acquitted; Bidwell, Dr. Andrews, and Bacon were convicted of murder and of being accessories to first-degree murder and were sentenced to hang, but legal maneuvering delayed their execution.

A typical press reaction came from the Florida *Times-Union*, which hailed "a judicial victory; a vindication of the law; a source of congratulations to (local) citizens...."

Unfortunately, such accolades proved premature. After a year at the Pine Level jail, Dr. Andrews and Bacon managed to secure two shotguns and escaped. They fled the state and were never captured. Some political string-pulling won Bidwell a commutation to a life sentence. A sympathy petition won pardon for Tom Dryman in 1887, noting the "club's" intimidation of the 21-year-old illiterate, crippled farm hand. But this in turn would spawn a flurry of petitions and political manueverings by various factions during the next few years that would, by 1892, see the release of the last of the vigilantes, only eight years after the murders. Alford, later caught in Georgia, was given a rather perfunctory trial and acquitted.

But people would long remember the cavalier wantonness by which justice was eventually mocked, nor would they ever forget those terrible days when, as one settler truly lamented: "The devil was in the soil of Sara Sota."

22.
The Odd Couple:
Merchant and Gunslinger

Sober, even-tempered E.C. May seemed an unlikely companion for the erratic, gun-toting Fields.

They were an odd couple, surely, the good and temperate merchant and his violent bootlegger friend whom the former himself once dubbed "the worst white man I ever saw."

But strange bedfellows were as often the rule as the exception in the wild and lawless phosphate mining boom towns that stretched southeasterly from Florida's Suwanee River country, near the close of the 19th century.

Discovery of the valuable fossil rock in Marion County some years earlier had sparked the mushrooming of turbulent frontier camp towns from Live Oak to Brooksville, and, like all such "gold rush" boom towns, guns and whiskey played as strong a part in judicial processes as did the bench and gavel.

In fact, it was guns and whiskey that catalyzed the strange friendship between E.C. May, of Inverness, and John Fields in the "tough little town" of Hernando in north Citrus County. And, fatefully enough, guns and whiskey would end it in due time. But it was a singular experience for May and he would put it down in his memoirs before he died.

May later became a legislator and a county judge for 24 years, but in the spring of 1895, at the height of the boom, he had scraped together $74 in cash with which he bought a stock of goods for a general store he opened in Hernando.

Next to May's store was a building he had thought was vacant, but he observed much traffic going in and out of it. More pointedly, he also heard much screaming and shouting and, occasionally, shooting resounding from the place. Now and then, a man would stagger or fall out the door, sometimes seriously wounded. He soon learned that it was one of a number of "blind tigers" that trafficked in illicit liquor in the dry county of Citrus. Its operator, reputedly the county's top bootlegger, was a wild and "gruesome-looking" fellow named John Fields. An upright citizen and grand jury member who stopped by his place once to investigate was simply advised by Fields to "get out or I'll kill you." The juror hastily departed.

With or without a gun, Fields was no doubt a scary-looking customer. His left hand had been torn off at the wrist by a shotgun blast, and his right hand had only two fingers and a nub of thumb. His left eye and a portion of the left side of his head had been torn out by a rifle bullet, and on his body, legs, and arms were numerous bullet and knife wounds. The right eye could fix you with a "horribly baleful and penetrating" glance, May recalled. He was still an expert draw and a dead shot with his "good" hand and had dispatched from the earth so many men that he had lost count.

May's first encounter with Fields came when the latter walked into his store one morning and told May he had come "to have a settlement" with him. May knew this meant only one thing, since he had reported Fields to the grand jury earlier. May was standing with his right hand in the pocket of a light overcoat and, as Fields advanced, the storekeeper pointed his finger outward against the coat, as if he had a gun, and told Fields to stop. The latter did, but then accused May of reporting him to the grand jury. May quickly admitted it and even added other unflattering remarks about Fields's nuisance business activities. Surprisingly, Fields admitted the truth of the charges and then, assured by May that he would not be shot in the back, walked out of the store.

After this, Fields became a frequent customer of May's. Neither ever mentioned their initial encounter, and the two soon became friends. In fact, when Fields was drunk, which was frequently, he would offer to be May's bodyguard, while May would hastily but goodnaturedly decline the service. May soon learned that he was the only man whom Fields held in any kind of friendship. The bootlegger's wild behavior and fearsome reputation prompted most men to step very gingerly in or around his presence.

But an unusual surprise relating to the life of this notorious character still awaited May. One day, Fields invited May to his home on the Homosassa River for a fishing trip. May agreed to go, on condition that Fields took no liquor along. Driving through a soaking rain, they arrived that night, and May was surprised to find himself entering an imposing, large frame home which contained the "most magnificent" furniture he had ever seen. Fields explained that it came from his home in Georgia which he and his family had been forced to leave due to Fields's dissipation and violence. May was even more awed by Fields's wife, "a lovely and cultured lady," and their two beautiful and well-mannered children, a boy and a girl. Fields described his wife as the "angel woman," explaining how she had stood by him unfalteringly in his stormy life, nursing his near fatal wounds and encouraging him. The bootlegger lamented that he had ruined her life, forcing her to leave kin and friends due to his behavior and come to a frontier wilderness. He then explained that his infamous way of life began at age 18 when he shot and killed a schoolteacher who had punished him. Later on, he killed three men in a barroom brawl in Macon, Georgia. From then on, some driving demonic spirit impelled him to a series of countless violent acts, a spirit only the more inflamed by strong drink. At this disclosure, Fields suddenly made a strange request of May. He assured May of his friendship for him but warned him that if he were drunk sometime, he might fancy a grievance against May and attempt to shoot him. "He asked me to take no chances with him—to shoot first and shoot to kill." The gunman impressed this request on him with such deadly earnest that May promised him he would be on guard at those times.

Fields later moved his store over to the black section of town but, May learned, his conduct "continued bad to worse." He once shot in the shoulder a small black boy who worked for him when the boy hesitated at an errand. But at once Fields became contrite and rushed the boy to the doctor in Inverness. For a while, he kept the boy around his place in bandages to illustrate "the horrible example I've set."

Meanwhile, a Clarence O'Bannon had rented Fields's old store, using it for a "blind tiger." May described O'Bannon as a pleasant, easygoing man, but one day he came into May's store with a shotgun and told May to shut his store and go home. May refused, and asked O'Bannon for an explanation. The latter said Fields had sent a note warning him to get out of town by five o'clock that day. He didn't want May involved in the affair, but May refused to leave, and O'Bannon returned to his store.

Just before five P.M., Fields approached from across the street, and O'Bannon, sighting him, reached behind his door and withdrew a shotgun. The men stood in position facing each other for some time, but neither apparently dared to make the first move.

May called to them twice, offering to stand between them and let them discuss and settle the quarrel peaceably. But both men told May to stay out of it. Finally, as darkness approached, May walked out and stood between them and quietly asked them to lower their guns. This calm strategy worked. O'Bannon withdrew inside his store, and Fields went into May's store informing May that he had accomplished nothing but only delayed the settlement.

But next day, to May's puzzlement, he saw both men chatting peaceably together. It seems that a tale-bearing foe of both bootleggers had falsely informed each separately of insulting remarks each had allegedly made against the other. Upon learning of this, both men hunted the culprit out and summarily prompted his disappearance.

The year 1896 was a bad year for business. The Hernando phosphate mines had been depleted and people were moving away. Fields himself moved his business to Holder, where a few mines were still open. But the demonic force possessing the man was unrelenting, and the inevitable conflict soon came.

Fields got into an argument with another bootlegger, Will Gaines, in the latter's place, over who had the best whiskey. The dispute waxed hot; each picked up a shotgun to settle the matter, but were finally persuaded by cronies to travel to Fields's place, sample his spirits, and then settle the question. So the two men, accompanied by a black friend of Gaines, set out in a buckboard. But on the way the argument flared again, until finally Fields "decided that he would have to kill Gaines sometime and might as well do it then." Seated somewhat to the rear of Gaines, he raised his shotgun toward the man but, at that moment, the black employee grabbed Gaines's pistol from the man's holster and fired at Fields, missing him. Fields fired back and the blast tore the black man's arm off, shattering his heart and chest. Before the fatally wounded man fell, however, he managed to fire one more time; the bullet struck Fields in the stomach, ranging upward and coming out of his back.

A doctor was summoned from Inverness and, after dressing Fields's wound, packed the man in ice, with orders not to remove or disturb the pack, if he ever wanted to recover. Fields meekly obeyed and remained in bed for several days, but his agitated spirit grew restless over his invalid status. Later that day, in a sudden convulsive moment, Fields threw off the ice pack and struggled into his clothes. He then went down to his "blind tiger" and got roaring drunk. A few of his customer friends finally managed to return him to his bed.

Next day, the doctor came to see him, and then gave him the prognosis—a prognosis that, with little doubt, unconsciously, Fields wanted to hear. He told the stricken man that he would develop a fever and then, within five or six days, he would die. The doctor was right; Fields was dead within a week.

A brother and other relatives came from Georgia and took the body home for burial. Fields's wife and two children apparently left the area later and were not heard of again.

Few would mourn this possessed man who had kept so many of them on the edge of fear for so long a time. And it mattered little to Fields now who had the best whiskey in town, because the "blind tiger" in his own soul had finally consumed him.

23.
The Uncertain Heroics of Colonel Titus

The colonel's checkered filibuster career evoked images of an American version of Colonel Blimp.

Colonel Henry T. Titus, whose bearing was as imperious as that of his Roman emperor namesake, seemed an unlikely settler of the sandy, mosquito-ridden trading post that came to be Brevard's county seat and took his name, Titusville, in the 1860s.

His turbulent soldier-trader-filibuster career, recounted in later years with Bunyan-like gusto and florid verbosity, belied the aging rheumatic cripple who, from a wheelchair on his hotel veranda, thundered forth like the monarch of all he surveyed—at least whatever he surveyed within range of the loaded rifle he often cradled in his lap.

He was tall and handsome, of huge physique. Still, he embodied a curious blend of traits—a Colonel Blimp, a swaggering General Custer, and yet a touch of pure Falstaff—traits which could detract from the dashing soldier-of-fortune image he so ardently cultivated.

Titus was born in the Oklahoma Territory, but little is known of his early years. At age 35, he appeared in Jacksonville, Florida, buying up arms and supplies and recruiting filibusters for the Cuban revolutionary, Narciso Lopez. But this adventure met an untimely end with the capture and execution of Lopez, even as the colonel was fleeing pursuit by a U.S. Coast Guard cutter on the St. Johns River, hastily dumping his contraband just in time to win later acquittal on U.S. charges of neutrality violations.

Titus next opened a general store in Jacksonville and wangled a contract to sell supplies to the Florida Militia. But soon after marrying the daughter of a prominent local planter, Mary Hopkins, he went in 1836 to the Kansas Territory where, he was certain, his military prowess was needed to advance the pro-slavery cause. (Titus's rank of colonel had the vaguest of origins—he had never served in the military—but it seemed modestly suited to his destiny, and he made it a permanent title.)

Plunging into the strife of "bleeding Kansas," he led pro-slavers in raids on the abolitionist town of Lawrence. He then built a log cabin, designated "Fort Titus," at Lecompton and continued raids on free-staters. But the colonel's cavalier image suffered acutely at times, such as with one free-stater housewife, scuffling with Titus in her cabin, when she wrested his gun away and ordered him to flee her premises. Or the day free-staters surrounded Fort Titus and captured everyone but Titus, whom they finally discovered hiding beneath the cabin floor. But he was freed in a prisoner exchange when peace was finally restored to Kansas.

The restless colonel sought new adventures, but there were none—until the 1850s when he joined the Tennessee filibuster, William Walker, who had recently designated himself—somewhat shakily—as president of Nicaragua. Promised lands and booty, Titus became Walker's aide when the band of 58 "colonists" entered Nicaragua in February, 1857. Walker then ordered his new aide to take the band and seize a small river fort held by 30 Costa Rican volunteers. But the fort's captain bluffed Titus, feigning that he, the captain, had just sneaked in reinforcements. Making up with loud and ferocious threats and noises what they lacked in numbers, the captain and his men caused Titus to panic and beat a hasty retreat with his men. But no sooner had Walker censured the colonel and placed him on inactive duty, than the colonel landed in an English brig for heaping "vile and foul" insults upon the person of Queen Victoria and then in an American brig for cursing the U.S. counsel who, he claimed, delayed his release from the English. An exasperated Walker then gave Titus another chance, sending him to a battle scene at Rivas to get information of enemy strength. But, valuing discretion as the better part of exposure, the colonel picked up some erroneous information from a stray soldier some distance from the battle line. The misinformation proved costly to Walker, and the enraged El Presidente fired his dubious aid permanently.

Somehow, Titus made his way back to Jacksonville, where earlier he had sent his family, and then moved to Sand Point (Titusville) and opened a general store and trading post. During the Civil War, Titus prospered, both by selling food and supplies to the rebels and then assisting deserters to flee the state to escape execution.

At the war's end, Titus had a thriving general store, an insurance agency, and a mule transport team hauling passengers, mail, and farm produce to and from the St. Johns River. Determined to make the town a prosperous trade center and tourist resort, he constructed a large hotel on Washington Street, the Titus House. He adjoined to it an ornate saloon which soon became a popular watering hole for Indian River settlers. As tourists poured south in the post-war years, hotel guests came from as far away as Europe, including English and Italian nobility.

The colonel himself became a popular raconteur. Though soon confined to a wheelchair with rheumatism, he spent hours enthralling his guests with fierce (and somewhat embellished) tales of his past exploits. Yet even here he seemed to sense foes lurking somewhere about—real or imagined—for he often sat on his hotel veranda cradling a loaded rifle.

But Titus took an active civic pride in his town, laying out its broad streets, planting rows of trees, and promoting work on the Haulover Canal to link the Indian River with the Halifax River northward. By now the town had been named for him; this spurred him on to his crowning achievement—making his town of 150 souls the seat of Brevard County in 1880.

In his late years, the colonel's adventurous blood could still churn with indignation. He could especially wax hotly over barbs from outside critics. One day such a critic labelled Titusville "a dreary waste of white sand . . . the poorest place on earth." But the colonel's furious retort to this "imbecile and liar" apparently taxed his ailing frame so severely that, a few days later, on August 7, 1881, he died.

Today, Titusville is a clean, progressive, modestly sized town of nearly 40,000 inhabitants. Its strong sense of community might have pleased the old colonel who, after years of pursuing—sometimes reluctantly—uncertain glories in far-off lands, had finally laid claim to a single and lasting achievement.

24.
The Last of the Wreckers

Wooden ships had already turned to iron when colorful "Hog" Johnson salvaged his last vessel.

His tall frame and powerful physique seemed evenly matched to the ingenious seafaring skills and derring-do that enabled him to win almost every race to a shipwreck, thus earning him the nickname "Hog."

Indeed Bradish W. "Hog" Johnson, the last of Key West's master wreckers up to the close of that colorful era in the early 1900s, earned that moniker. With a zestful and fearless kind of audacity, he did "hog" the richest share of Key West shipwreck salvage off the perilous Florida reef for nearly a quarter-century. He easily would have made John Wayne, who celebrated the wreckers in his film *Reap the Wild Wind*, look like an awkward landlubber.

But with Johnson it was a case of the temperament finding the calling. He was born November 9, 1846, into an old and wealthy Long Island, New York, family. He attended the U.S. Naval Academy at Annapolis, but, finding the discipline of a naval career distasteful, resigned after three years and served for a while as a mate on an ocean steamer. Later, he and his brother, Theodore, bought a schooner and engaged in California coastal trade, with periodic trips to the Bering Sea to hunt seals and sea otters. Later they found more lavish profits running arms shipments to the Mexican revolutionary, Porfirio Díaz. When Díaz came to power in 1877, he rewarded Johnson with exclusive rights to salvage $5 million in gold from a sunken ship off Port Angel. But one day on shore, anti-Díaz rebels captured Johnson and his crew and were about to line them up for a firing squad when quick-thinking brother Theodore, remaining on shipboard in port, rigged up a fake 10-pound cannon, trained it shoreward and threatened to destroy the rebels' village. The captives were released and quickly sailed away, forgetting the treasure hunt.

After Theodore's death from tuberculosis in 1882, Johnson accepted a post under Admiral Perry to build a lighthouse pier in Key West. Johnson, captivated with the colorful little town and its tropical climate, became even more fascinated with its wrecking business. To his individual nature, the adventure, the peril, and the huge profits in wrecking made for an irresistible lure. For a while, after leaving the government job, he worked for master wrecker Captain Ben Baker, but soon after he took in three partners to form his own firm, the Key West Wrecking Company.

The innate audacity that impelled Johnson to take high risks, combined with his broad technical training and experience, was soon earning his company from $10,000 to $20,000 from each of the two or three ships a month going on the rocks. He was quick to move at any hour and into any seas. In mountainous swells he would tease his vessel within a hair's breadth of the jagged undersea coral teeth, and few would dare, as he did often, the roaring reef in a pitch black northeaster. Thus his fellow wreckers so dubbed him "hog," and his firm would dominate the business over the next 25 years.

His life ashore was in deceptive contrast to this hazardous calling. He had found time to marry Irene Bethel, the daughter of a leading family, and he built a large home on the island's west end, with an adjoining warehouse and shipways where he would construct the 35-ton schooner, *Irene*, named for Mrs. Johnson. An avid collector of books and music, he led much the life of a cultured gentleman. His home was filled with fine furniture and rare decorative items collected from the seven seas. Friends described him as "shrewd but fair, genial, often generous" and an "A-1 water dog," or master mariner.

But in fair-weather slack season, unlike other wreckers, he did not remain idle. Typically, he made a trip to New York with pineapples, then loaded coal there for Maine, then hauled ice back to New York, where he took on general cargo for Key West, topping that load with a deckful of kerosene in cans. His brand of instant ingenuity proved valuable, as once when the propeller of a recently acquired sea tugboat bent on a rock. Johnson simply placed a small charge of dynamite on it to loosen the screw, dove 12 feet underwater, removed the old screw and installed a new spare. This saved the huge expense of a long tow to Jacksonville and a long stay in dry dock.

Law-abiding in the general sense, Johnson had his own code concerning "unjust laws," such as neutrality laws. At this time, future Governor Napoleon Broward was active with his famous seatug, *Three Friends*, running arms shipments to Cuban insurgents fighting Spain in the 1890s. The tug had a problem getting fuel, having to make a long dead run back to Jacksonville for it. Then one day a Mexican gunboat loaded with coal crashed on the Key West shoals. Broward quickly bought her from the vessel's underwriters, who sold her where she lay. He then hired Johnson to raise and salvage her but told him to take his time doing it. Authorities on shore were puzzled that it took this master wrecker so long—all summer and fall—to off-load the coal onto barges. They learned, too late, that Broward was coasting up on dark nights and quietly refueling his tugs.

As the 20th century moved in, so did iron ships equipped with more modern navigational apparatus, and the century-old wrecking business began a quick exit into history. It seemed only fitting, therefore, that the last of the great wreckers should be prize master over the last of the great wrecks.

In 1906, the steamer *Alicia*, bound from Bilbao, Spain, for Havana with a million-dollar cargo, struck Ajax Reef in a heavy gale and quickly bilged. Her crew was rescued and taken to Havana, but Key West wreckers, the "Hog" leading as usual, were soon on the scene, eager to get at holds packed with silks, laces, pianos, furniture, wines, liquors, and other valuable items. But the rich prize was located 35 miles south of Coconut Grove and quickly drew the Bahamian Black Fleet, the island's native wrecker-divers. As they swarmed aboard for their share of the salvage, fighting quickly broke out. Quick to see the loss of a no-win contest, Johnson waded into the bloody melee and finally stopped the brawl with promises of equal shares for all. He then painted a red line down the center of the deck, one side for the Bahamians, the other for the Key Westers. Harmony reigned. The men became gregarious. It seems the *Alicia* carried a huge consignment of bottled ale; later, in salvage court, Johnson was hard put to explain the presence of so many bottles strewn beneath the vessel. Well, he suggested, they probably had washed through a hole in the ship's bottom. "Strange," the underwriter noted, "not a single bottle had a cork in it."

With wrecking virtually defunct, Johnson remained active at home in later years, but perhaps too strenuously so. One day in April, 1915, at age 68, after leaping into the water to heave on lines hauling a schooner up his shipways, he suddenly passed out in the water and never regained consciousness. But with the end of an adventurous and colorful era, he might have preferred it that way.

25.
The Bogus Treasure of Key Largo

Writer Ben Hecht's elaborate hoax to sell Key Largo real estate proved too imaginative for his own good.

During the great 1920s land boom, Florida often was described as a colorful cauldron of bizarre, madcap dreams and impossible schemes.

But one of the least known and most original of all these manic mementos came not from any grandiose promoter or developer but from a literary figure of the day—the inimitable Ben Hecht, novelist, short-story writer, and celebrated playwright-to-be. Yet unlike most of his creations this was a true Florida tale; had he later turned it into a stage or film script, it might easily have rivalled his hit play, *The Front Page*, or later film scripts like *Scarface* or *Gone with the Wind*.

Many of Hecht's admirers gingerly omit or gloss over this episode for, in its baldest terms, it was a conscious, deliberate scam. Hecht himself had no such qualms and would fondly recount it later in his autobiography.

Hecht arrived in Miami in 1925 with his fiancée, Rose Caylor, and writer colleague, J.P. "Mac" McEvoy. The couple were McEvoy's guests since Hecht himself was flat broke, a chronic condition with him given his lavish life-style. The boom at this time was at its fever pitch; crowds of promoters, con men and plain John Does scurried frantically about peddling building lots to everyone and each other. Millions of dollars—albeit mostly on paper—changed hands every day. The bedlamic scene fascinated and excited Hecht. It also churned his creative and often mischievous wit. And so, with a tongue-in-cheek bonhomie spirit of "When in Rome . . .," Hecht set forth to challenge the system "in one of its most hooligan hours." And, hopefully perhaps, also to restore his solvency.

Hecht first checked around and drew up a list of the top names "running the boom." He then had a local friend pick one name, contact him, and give Hecht a little "build-up" for an introduction. The writer already had some "build-up" with a seven-column-headline story in the Miami *Herald*, heralding the arrival of a "prince of litterateurs." Soon after, Hecht found himself in the Flagler Building office of Charles Ort, president of Key Largo Corporation, a

$90 million group of "pioneers." Greeted enthusiastically, Hecht found the short, reddish-faced man very shy and modest—except when the writer asked about Key Largo. "Modesty fled his tongue and I listened for half an hour to a Barnum outside the gate of Paradise." Ort floridly described how this largest of Florida Keys, some 40 miles south of Miami, would be "the future playground of America—and Europe," replete with luxury hotels, casinos, yachts, and mansions.

When Ort finished, Hecht said he had sought Ort out simply because "I, too, was fascinated by the great future of Key Largo and had thought of something that might help sell its $90 million worth of building lots." Ort replied that a directors' board meeting next day would be "honored" to hear Hecht's proposal.

That night, Hecht told McEvoy of his plan, including asking $2500 a week for 10 weeks minimum. Mac offered to assist Hecht, asking as a share only what they earned over the $2500. Hecht agreed.

The pair were greeted warmly the next day by a dozen directors, most of whom "wore white suits and looked like distinguished coffee planters." Hecht then began his talk by soberly remarking on a Key Largo "distinction on which no one had yet touched." Tracing the key's history back to the Spanish Main, treasure ships, and pirates, he asserted what was "known to all students of pirate history": that the sea robbers often buried great treasures of gold and jewelry along the Keys, and that Key Largo undoubtedly had more than a few of these buried and unclaimed caches.

As he made these "fantastic statements," Hecht paused apprehensively, half-expecting one of his listeners to "rise and denounce me for my bouncing lies." But no one stirred.

Hecht then explained his plan to organize a treasure hunt, starting from New York City. He would invite 50 leading society women and other celebrities, rent the ex-Kaiser's black yacht then lying idle off Long Island, sail them to the key, and, with the aid of an old pirate map, let them dig up a treasure, one properly buried beforehand, of course. "Its discovery would inflame the nation and bring thousands of other treasure hunters to Key Largo . . . lots would sell as if an oil strike had occurred."

Having finished, Hecht duly noted the happy nods of approval. Then one director asked: "How much will all this cost?" Before the writer could reply, McEvoy interrupted, declaring he was "the business side" of the operation and it would cost them $5,000 a week for 12 weeks minimum. The tycoons sighed with relief. "Sounds all right," one responded. Of course, Mac continued, this sum did not include per diem expenditures, yacht rental, food, entertainment, and rental of a spacious office and equipment, preferably in some top Miami Beach hotel. "Of course," a tycoon agreed. An hour later, Hecht walked out with a contract draft in pocket and a new admiration for friend Mac.

Within 24 hours, the pair were set up in a large, luxurious office in the Beach's Fleetwood Hotel, with Hecht moving into a commodious suite above the office. Hecht then dashed off "a rococo essay" for a fancy Key Largo brochure; it so impressed Ort that he promptly read it aloud to the company's 1,000 salesmen. But days passed, and McEvoy, now in New York, was unable to recruit even one society dowager. Hecht had meanwhile hired a zesty young local reporter, Charles Samuels, mainly to keep tabs on Ort and his tycoons, and soon learned that the nabobs were grumbling mightily about the delays. Hecht decided then on a quick switch to a more practical version of treasure hunting. He summoned Mac home, and then hired a local man who had personal ties to Cuba's President Machado; the man persuaded Machado to temporarily loan him some old Spanish doubloons. These in hand, Hecht then located two 18th-century Spanish vases, each 100 pounds and five feet high. He then sent Samuels to Key Largo to prospect a buried treasure site and find some "native hero" to discover it.

Samuels found no one except a weathered old Conch beachcomber called Cap'n Loftus, but he assured Hecht that Loftus passed the test, namely, could not read or write and did not know the name of the current U.S. president. Hecht and Samuels then went to the Key with the vases and doubloons and rolled the former to the "treasure site." Hecht gave Loftus a $100 bill and carefully coached him on his new role. They then broke the pottery and began digging.

From Miami, Hecht wired 200 city editors asking how large a story they would like on a half-million-dollar buried treasure discovered by a Key Largo native. A horde of reporters was soon on the scene and Cap'n Loftus surprised Hecht with the most effortless theatrics. The Cap'n displayed the handful of doubloons and vase shards, then direly warned that the rest of the treasure was hidden away and he would "kill anyone he caught snooping after it." The story appeared in papers nationwide and within two days a swarm of every sized craft converged on the island, bearing treasure hunters with tents, spades, and provisions. Ort, meanwhile, rushed 100 crack salesmen to the key. The hunters would face trespass charges, unless...unless they wanted to buy a lot at 10 percent down. Within a week, over a million dollars in lots were sold, and Ort and his tycoons gratefully presented Hecht with a new 12-week contract.

But Hecht was chafing at his idleness and boredom. Moreover, he was certain that the boom was beginning to totter; so certain that he carried all his money on his person—at this time $22,000—figuring the banks would fall first.

He sent $10,000 of this to his estranged wife in Chicago in exchange for a divorce and promptly married Rose. He then quit his job with Ort and tried to persuade the latter to get out while he could. It was 1926 and the boom was fast collapsing. All over downtown Hecht spotted "crowds screaming around the real estate offices, waving documents in the air and shouting for their money back." Ort's tycoon partners, fearing the worst, had by now liquidated their interests and decamped. But Ort assured Hecht it was only "a little fluctuation" and the boom would come back. Soon after, Ben and Rose boarded the train for New York.

About three months later, Hecht got a letter from Samuels with a postscript on Ort. It seemed the builder of "the world's playground center" had plunged heavily into a massive advertising campaign proclaiming "the return of the boom." The tycoon was last seen with his wife, sleeping in a parking lot and eating beans out of a can. Hecht gave a little shudder and unconsciously wiped his brow.

26.
The Great Railroad Paper Caper

The Swepson-Littlefield duo's artful chicanery spelled financial disaster for Florida's railroads.

Florida has been the scene of some artful and ingenious frauds in the course of its phenomenal growth in this century, but it was no doubt the 19th century that spawned one of the granddaddy swindles of them all—the Swepson-Littlefield railroad scandal (1868-70).

Moreover, this $4 million-plus paper caper probably delayed the economic recovery of an impoverished war-bled state by almost a generation. In the post-Civil War Reconstruction era, Florida's government was mainly under northern Republican control, with a motley mix of Democratic conservatives, scalawags, freedmen, and carpetbaggers, plus a horde of renegade fortune hunters swarming in to take advantage of the political turmoil and endemic corruption that characterized the period. It was, in short, a con man's paradise.

At this time, railroads were perhaps the major key to the state's economic recovery, but Florida's lines were in financial shambles, virtually inoperable. And when three major lines became swamped under default on state-endorsed bonds, the state's Internal Improvement Fund (IIF) trustees forced them up for sale. They were the Florida Atlantic & Gulf Central, Jacksonville to Lake City; the Pensacola & Georgia, Lake City to Quincy; and the Tallahassee, a branch line to the port of St. Marks on the Gulf. Two new arrivals to the state in this period were George Swepson, a smooth and amiable self-styled North Carolina capitalist, and Milton Littlefield, a tall figure of ingratiating charm, a former Union general from Maine. Both gentlemen had a keen interest in railroads. They both liked Florida, too, mainly because it was some distance from North Carolina, where both men had just absconded with a major chunk of $6 million in bonds from the Western Division railroad branch of that state. With all that spare change, they were looking for some new investments.

When the first Florida railroad, the FA & GC, went up for sale on March 4, 1868, Swepson entered into an arrangement with Colonel Edward Houstoun, president of one of the other defaulted lines, the P & G, to buy up for Swepson a controlling interest in the FA & GC. This deal having succeeded, Swepson then had Houstoun arrange to quietly buy up about 1 million of the P & G and

the Tallahassee railroad bonds—at less than 35 cents on the face value dollar—
prior to the sale by the IIF of both lines on March 20, 1869. The actual owner
of both lines, Frank Dibble & Associates, then colluded with Swepson to use
these bonds against the total sale price of the lines ($1,415,000). Through
Swepson's influence with several venal IIF trustees (possibly through bribery),
he arranged to be named a "confidential agent" for the IIF. Hereby he persuaded
them to accept the bonds' face value toward the purchase price. They were still
short of the sale price, so Swepson, as an IIF agent, simply had Dibble write him
(Swepson) a worthless check in the amount of the balance, $472,065, and this
was deposited into the IIF treasury. The ultimate effect of these complex paper
maneuvers was to give Swepson control of all three railroads at a cost of less
then $350,000 (the bonds) and a worthless check. The lines originally cost over
$4 million; also thrown in were the rolling stock and buildings and over one
million acres of land from earlier state grants.

But the grand scam awaited. Here Littlefield's lobbying skills, so successfully employed in the North Carolina legislature, entered. Free food, whiskey,
and entertainment, plus covert cash gifts ranging from $250 to $3,000, persuaded the lawmakers to authorize chartering of Swepson and Littlefield's new
Jacksonville, Pensacola & Mobile Railroad Company. Another bill, passed in
January, 1870, authorized the new JP & M line to issue $16,000 in bonds for
every mile of railroad proposed for construction, then to exchange these bonds
for $4 million in state bonds and, finally, permission to sell the state bonds on
the open market.

But protests were gathering, too. The Tallahassee *Floridian* called the bill
"a cunning fraud, boldly and adroitly perpetrated." Several citizens claiming
liens against the former lines filed a suit; the circuit judge hearing it called the
affair "a skillful collusion" and ordered appointment of a receiver for the entire
railroad. But two weeks later, a Florida Supreme Court judge (reputedly a friend
of Littlefield) set the order aside. Swepson acted further to still the discontent
by meeting with Jacksonville civic and business leaders, many of them railroad
stockholders. Glowingly outlining the railroad's economic future, he said he
also planned a bank for Jacksonville plus a line of steamships to New York.
"What have I done?" he queried innocently. "Why should [Floridians] be
unwilling that I should bring my money into the state and aid in developing their
own interests?" The reaction to this by most leaders, desperate to lure outside
investors into a moribund economy, was echoed in a Jacksonville *Union*
editorial: "Why sacrifice our most important material interests" in the interests
of "such a costly article as abstract justice?"

The hook was set; the $4 million in bonds was transferred to Swepson and

Littlefield, and the latter hurried to New York to put them in the hands of the securities firm of S.W. Hopkins and Company. But the publicity, published in the New York *World*, proclaiming a "taint" on the bonds, forced Hopkins agents and Littlefield to travel to Europe. A London snag developed when a North Carolina state agent, N.W. Woodfin, citing the earlier Swepson-Littlefield swindle in that state, threatened to attach any bond sale. Only after Littlefield agreed to give Woodfin a token "good faith" sum of $350,000 in bonds was the firm able to sell the remainder (at two-thirds their face value) to a Dutch investors syndicate. Of the total amount, after Swepson and Littlefield's generous division of the loot, only $308,938 remained for Florida railroad construction.

But the long-range effect was to keep Florida's railroads and her economy virtually moribund for years; not until the 1880s would a track be laid between Pensacola and Quincy.

When the full scope of the fraud revealed itself, the now outraged Jacksonville boosters joined with other stockholders, creditors, agents of the Dutch syndicate, and the State of North Carolina in a series of lawsuits to wrest control of the railroads from the malefactors. They would spend 10 years in the courts of five different states and the U.S. Supreme Court—all unsuccessfully. A Florida grand jury tried to indict Littlefield, but no witnesses were obtainable. Florida Governor Harrison Reed (purported to have some stock interest in the lines) refused the North Carolina governor's pleas to extradite Littlefield. Swepson got by with merely having to post a $200,000 bond in a North Carolina case against him that never came to hearing.

Perhaps the nearest thing to a punitive measure ever received by either culprit was a rebuke from a majority of the U.S. Supreme Court justices, who concluded that the pair had "shown themselves capable of the most shameless frauds, and we cannot but look with suspicion upon everything they do or say."

It is not known how painfully this rebuke pierced the hearts of these two astute pioneers of con. But it is probable that the enjoyment of the bountiful fruits of their devious labors must have eased any such pains considerably.

27.
He Cracked His Whip Over an Empire

Jake Summerlin carved a beefsteak barony out of his wild-roaming herds of Spanish-descended "vacos."

They called him "King of the Crackers" and he rather liked the title, even though his business and his slightly studied profile were somewhat less than regal in nature.

However, Jacob (Jake) Summerlin (1820-1893), Florida's first cattle baron, certainly enjoyed the monarchical trappings of power and wealth as he developed a beefsteak barony that sprawled across the vast wire-grass prairies from Fort Meade to Fort Myers in the last half of the 19th century.

"I'm nothing but a Cracker, don't you see?," he asserted once to a curious visitor. "I don't try to ape the quality." Nevertheless, the skeptical visitor had seen a host of poor Crackers during his Florida sojourn, and none of them splashed their fingers through piles of Spanish gold doubloons on a hard pine table, as Summerlin did. And this glittering metal was quality. In fact, for many decades, it was virtually the coin of the realm for Southwest Florida, when the major cattle kings poured thousands of tons of beef into Havana harbor in exchange for the royal Spanish gold.

Aside from his Cracker kingship, Jake Summerlin was one of the wealthiest men in Florida before he was 40, and was probably the granddaddy of all the renowned cow titans of that wild frontier era—the Hendrys, the Kings, the Hollingsworths, the Lykes brothers, and numerous others.

In speech, dress, and lifestyle, he certainly resembled the "po' folk" image that he sought to cultivate; however, the image concealed, but never sidetracked, the canny trader instinct that would build his empire. He influenced much of the course of Central and Southwest Florida history. He made sure, for example, that Orlando and Bartow were the respective county seats for Orange and Polk counties. But he did it all in his chosen style—low-key Cracker.

Jacob Summerlin was born in Alachua County in 1820 near the old town of Newnansville. His father raised a few cattle, and young Jake took easily to the cow business; he could ride a horse and crack a long cowhide whip at the age of seven. When he was 16, his father gave him a few calves, and the boy headed south to the wild, unsettled frontier of Southwest Florida to try his own hand as a stockman. He could not have picked a better time, location, or business.

In those years, the great ranges stretching across the pine and palmetto land for miles along either side of the Peace River Valley were wide open and free for everyone's use. But even more propitious, large numbers of wild cattle—descendants of the little Spanish *vacos* brought into Florida by the early Spanish conquistadors—roamed freely over that vast territory, available to anyone who would trouble to round them up. They were not like the fat cattle and improved breeds grazing in those areas today; today's cattle could not have survived in that pasture or environment. But these coarse-haired, gaunt, and bony little "scrubs" had adapted over more than two centuries, developing an unusual stamina and resistance to floods, heat, and insects. One carcass rarely dressed out to more than 300 pounds of beef—a tough and sinewy meat at that—but they were a hardy, nourishing food staple and free for the taking. Summerlin, like others later, took freely.

The Cracker King's good fortune was not confined to free pasture and cattle, but also included a flourishing nearby market with an insatiable beef appetite. It is somewhat ironic that the descendants of the men who gave the cattle freely to the state would one day be shelling out thousands of dollars in gold doubloons to buy back the progeny of those ancient *vacos*. But the Spanish government in Havana, Cuba, was glad to pay the $12 to $16 a head for every cow Jake could deliver to the little port of Punta Rassa, just south of Fort Myers.

It was here on this desolate, storm-swept, sandy little cape at Punta Rassa that Summerlin began to amass a fortune in gold and silver. He bought the wharf and several small buildings at the port and also 1,000 acres adjacent to it. The port would also be the site of the first underwater telegraphic cable to Key West and Havana, laid by the U.S. government in 1868.

Summerlin would later rent usage of the cowpens to other cattlemen and would even send his cowboys out to buy cows direct from stockmen in the area—at a fat profit margin. Overhead for cattlemen in those days was negligible. Few businesses required so little care, cost, or attention. The animals roamed freely and fed mainly on the tough wire-grass that blanketed those flatlands. Then, in late spring and early summer, the cowhands fanned out over the countryside to search for their cattle and bring them in for branding or marketing.

Wolves were the only inventory problem, and they were gradually eradicated by a $5 bounty on wolf scalps, plus the generous application of strychnine to a slaughtered carcass left on the range.

Summerlin was dubbed "King of the Crackers," not merely for the huge piles of Spanish gold and silver he had amassed, or his ascetic lifestyle, but also his mastery of the whip. Poor Floridians were called Crackers because of their singular diet of cracked corn, but cowmen were so labelled due to their proficiency with the long (sometimes 18 feet) cowhide whips they used for herding cattle. The crack of these whips sounded like rifle shots and were often mistaken for such by soldiers fighting Seminoles during that war. Summerlin was an expert in the art; reportedly he could decapitate a snake or gut a hen with one snap.

Banks were unheard of in that area then, and cattlemen like Summerlin kept their fortunes lying around their crude cabins, the coins poured into meal sacks, shirt sleeves, old woolen socks, cigar boxes, or tin meat cans, and tossed under a bed, in a corner, up on a rafter, or behind a door frame. On paydays, cowboys would leave their bags of doubloons carelessly—but safely—on the porches of local saloons.

Summerlin's empire thrived during the Civil War, supplying beef to the Confederacy and, when that currency became worthless, selling it to the Union forces at Fort Myers. Patriotic loyalties to either cause could not compete with gold doubloons, and Summerlin soon joined Tampa Captain James McKay in eluding the Union blockade and resuming shipments of cattle to Havana. But the shrewd Jake used some of his rebel script to pay for the 160-acre Blount homestead which he later surveyed, turning 120 acres of it over to Polk County, provided they made the homestead (later named Bartow) the county seat. Again, in a reported effort to thwart the scheme of General Sanford (for whom the town of Sanford is named) to locate Orange County's seat in his town, Summerlin contributed the funds to build the county's first courthouse in Orlando, and threw in a chunk of acreage as well.

But it was after the Civil War, when most of the state was—and remained for years—in the deepest war-wracked depression, that Summerlin's empire flourished, as did those of other cattle barons moving onto the scene. When the Cuban revolution of 1868 erupted and continued off and on up to the Spanish-American War in 1898, a torrential flood of gold doubloons poured into the saddlebags of cattlemen and shippers. Summerlin capitalized on his investments at Punta Rassa by charging cattlemen a fee to use his pens and shipping wharf. Bawling rivers of cattle moved in clouds of dust along the old military trails to the wharf pens, where Spanish officers rode their fine mounts off steamers to inspect the herds before the beasts were loaded aboard with winch chains around their horns.

A New York newspaperman who visited Punta Rassa wrote: "I could not realize that the little old man whom I found the next morning engaged in cutting up a slaughtered beef was the 'King of the Crackers,' whose name is known throughout Florida and Cuba. He hoes his own garden and waters his pet mule with perhaps an ostentatious humility. He dresses, lives, talks, trades as a poor man might, but he gives to the poor and defends the fatherless against the land sharks."

Summerlin informed his guest: "I'm nothing but a Cracker, don't you see? I don't try to ape the quality. I ain't wore a coat in 20 years. I ain't settin' for a fine gentlemen." He didn't mind if his boys dressed up and went off to college, but he himself would always remain "nothin'...but a sun-baked old Cracker."

Nevertheless, those "Cracker" cattle kings stood out like wealthy mandarins amid the mass poverty of Reconstruction Florida. While little fishing villages like Tampa had to survive on a crude barter system for cotton, hides, beeswax or sugar, the gold doubloon out-circulated American currency. Moreover, the cattle barons wielded such political power that their cows were protected as they roamed at will over railroads, city streets, or even someone's yard. It was not until the turn of the century that cattle were finally kept off the streets of Tampa, Sarasota, St. Petersburg, and Fort Myers. (In fact, their power remained so entrenched that it took a concentrated attack on the cattle interests by Governor Fuller Warren in the 1940s to finally fence them in, after cow-car highway accidents reached intolerable levels.)

Unlike some cattlemen who drank and gambled away their windfall fortunes, Summerlin, who shunned both vices, shrewdly invested in citrus groves, homes, and acreage. He also engaged in philanthropic endeavors, such as aiding General Francis Hendry in cutting a water link from the Caloosahatchie River to Lake Okeechobee. He was the driving force, and funder, for the development of Polk and Orange counties. And, in spite of his affected disdain for education, he founded the Summerlin Institute at Bartow in May, 1887; it would become a major educational center for the area well into the 20th century.

When he died in Orlando, on November 1, 1893, Florida's first cattle baron was hailed as a major pioneer developer of Central and Southwest Florida during a heyday era that the state would never see again. But the title that Jake coveted above all was the one given him in those early days when he cracked his whip over the wild-roaming Spanish *vacos* that would make his fortune, namely, "King of the Crackers."

28.
Those Intrepid Key West Wreckers

Early Key West wreckers engaged in a perilous occupation, but the salvage rewards were often bountiful.

It was often marked by a shrill blast from a conch-shell horn and the piercing cry of "Wreck ashore!" but it heralded one of the most turbulent and colorful chapters of Florida history—the era of the Key West "wreckers."

It was an exciting, hazardous, and sometimes fatal business, pitting fragile man against the most powerful and capricious elements of nature, but by the mid-19th century it made Key West the richest city in Florida and its citizenry the richest per capita in the nation.

Out of the misfortunes, fortunes were made, lives were crippled or lost, and sturdy ships met the supreme test against their natural adversary—the sea. And yet the entire wrecking industry was almost ordained by a bizarre phenomenon of nature, namely: one of the trickiest and most deadly combinations of natural elements ever packed together in one geographic spot—the Florida Straits.

Over the centuries, the Florida Straits became the most dreaded sea lane ever negotiated by marine navigators, a literal "ship's graveyard" perhaps unparalleled since ancient Greeks met their doom in the Straits of Scylla and Charybdis. But it was caused by a subtle triad of elements that confounded even the most skilled of mariners.

Swinging in a huge 200-mile arc just offshore, from Key Biscayne and along the Florida Keys to the Dry Tortugas, is the great Florida Reef, a massive line of coral rock set like jagged teeth beneath the water. Outward from the reef is that huge powerful blue river, the Gulf Stream, pushing northeasterly through the Straits on up toward the North Atlantic. Its unpredictable currents played the most fatal tricks with crude charts and speed measure devices, as ships "on course" inexplicably found themselves—too late—miles off course. Above water, a third portentous element was the Straits' freakish weather patterns. The steady Northeast Trade Winds, prevailing year-round in the Keys, mixed into other Caribbean weather patterns—notably tropic depressions—often with chaotic and volatile results, causing everything from squalls and gales to furious hurricanes. Thus the wrecking industry had early origins.

When Ponce De Leon first spotted through the clear waters the writhing, twisted shapes of the Reef's coral formations, he thought they resembled agonized martyrs impaled on stakes, and so he called the rocks "Los Martires." But ships, not martyrs, were fated to be impaled on these rocks. For over three centuries, countless Spanish galleons laden with gold, jewelry, and silver plate were skewered on "Los Martires." Treasure hunters today still retrieve valuable remnants of their bounty. Sounding leads gave little warning to these early mariners; the great coral ledges rose up sheer from the bottom, like cliff walls, and by the time they were spotted, the frantic dropping of anchors was useless. Many of the deadliest reefs were named for the famous ships they destroyed, such as Fowey, Ledbury, Carysfort, and others.

The Calusa and Carib Indians were South Florida's first wreckers. As the wrecks piled up along the Keys, they quickly learned the value of the glittering metal shining under the waters and the useful ships' stores. But human survivors usually met a fate worse than the one they escaped; those the Indians did not kill, they enslaved. Later, the Spanish befriended the Indians and taught them to become skilled divers and boatmen, thereby salvaging at least portions of their wreck-strewn treasures.

The Conchs (Konks) came next, Scotch-Irish-English descendants of early colonists of the British Grand Bahamas. These turtlers and woodcutters gradually emigrated to the Keys—mainly Key West—when they discovered the lucrative potential of wrecking. Named for their long-staple diet of Queen Conch stews and chowders, the Conchs were God-fearing, honest, hard-working people, close-knit in family ties yet kind and generous of disposition, traits reflected in a voice of Southern lilt, softened by an English accent. They would produce the hardiest of wrecking captains. By 1828, they had produced such a flourishing wrecking business that the United States had to take jurisdiction over the industry, licensing wreckers, directing fees and settlements of salvage shares, and overseeing auction sales of both cargoes and vessels.

Yet for all its excitement and rich profits, wrecking was a hazardous business. Wreckers had to be masters of sailing, navigation, and diving. It took wit and daring to sail into gale winds and mountainous seas and secure their ships precariously to the foundering vessels. The slightest sudden shift in seas could maim a salvager or wash him overboard; divers met watery deaths in murky undersea cargo holds as ship timbers heaved or splintered, or were permanently blinded by toxic cargo dyes. A wrecker captain's first duty was to rescue all aboard the disabled ship, then salvage cargo. If the vessel were not hopelessly bilged he tried to refloat it or tow it to port. (Many of Key West's early settlers were shipwreck victims who vowed never to board a ship again.) The first captain to reach a wreck was designated Wrecking Master. He received the largest shares of salvage and hired whatever other boats and men he needed.

The cry of "Wreck ashore!" brought all work on the island to an instant halt as men hastily gathered food and water provisions and raced to their boats. Key West historian Jefferson Browne vividly recollected this scene: "A more thrilling sight cannot be conceived than that of 20 or 30 sailing craft starting for a wreck. As if upon a preconcerted signal, sails would be hoisted, and as soon as jib and mainsail were up, moorings would be slipped and vessels got underway, crowding on all the sail they could carry. The sight of these, dashing out of the harbor, with a stiff northeast wind, bunched together in groups of threes and fours, jibing with everything standing as they swung around the bend in the harbor off the foot of Duval Street, was a scene never to be forgotten."

In such a remote, isolated island town, it seemed a little incongruous to find ladies attired in the finest fashions, and homes furnished in the grandest manner; Key West would long lead the country with the richest per capita income. Whatever the risks, the spoils were huge and richly diverse—brocades, linens, silks, cottons, fine leather, carriages, shoes, mahogany, silver- and glassware, machinery, fine wines and rums, elegant furniture, hides, textiles, jewelry, and sometimes chests of gold and silver, or paper specie. It was not an uncommon sight to see bolts and bolts of fine cloth stretched out to dry over mangrove treetops along the shore.

The riches were even cumbersome at times. Captain John Lowe, for example, retrieved several grand pianos, and, at one time, his house was so crammed with salvage goods he had to live and sleep in his kitchen and cook in his woodshed.

Another Conch, Ben Baker, became "King of the Wreckers" for many years. A stern, gaunt man with hawk-like features, he came to resemble a hawk as he almost flew in his swift, 14-ton schooner, "The Rapid," usually first to reach the prize.

Some reaped fortunes and never left shore, like William Curry, Florida's first official millionaire, who built a thriving business dealing in ship equipment and supplies, then either building, or buying interests in, wrecking vessels. He amassed such wealth over 60 years that every purchase by him seemed casual, whether spending $80,000 to build the finest ship, or simply sauntering into Tiffany's in New York to buy a complete dinner service made of solid gold.

One of the most notorious wreckers was Captain Jacob Housman, who for years enraged Key Westers by cleverly dodging salvage courts, diverting cargoes, and conniving with ship captains to split their shipwreck spoils. He built a small empire on his 11-acre islet of Indian Key, a sort of wrecking company town, until a U.S. Court caught him fraudulently diverting cargo and revoked his license. He later lost everything in the infamous Indian massacre raid on that key and had to find work as an ordinary wrecking hand. In 1841, while trying to board a storm-tossed wreck, Housman slipped and was crushed to death between the two heaving vessels.

The wrecking industry reached its peak in the decade 1850-60 when 500 ships, valued at $16 million, piled up on the reefs, an average of one a week. But by this time, the U.S. government was spurred to replace the flimsy, ineffective lightships with towering lighthouses on solid rock, from Fowey Rocks off Miami to Loggerhead Key in the Dry Tortugas. (There were isolated instances of unscrupulous wreckers using false lights to steer vessels off course, but most were honest salvagers, eager to assist in apprehending such "wrecker pirates.")

As lighthouses went up and navigation methods improved in the late 19th century, the wrecking industry declined steadily. But enough hapless vessels strayed off course to keep the business alive. The last "King of the Wreckers" was Bradish W. "Hog" Johnson, an energetic and daring captain who simply out-smarted and out-navigated other vessels with his powerful 35-ton schooner, "Irene." "Hog" Johnson did in fact get a hoggish share of most wrecks at the century's close and became a wealthy man. Big steam vessels of iron were now replacing wooden ships, but Johnson, as if to ironically stamp the ultimate superiority of wooden craft, made his final salvage job a heroic one by rescuing and salvaging one of these "unsinkable" vessels, the "Alicia," during a roaring hurricane in 1906.

Nevertheless, better design and engineering of ships and modernized navigational procedures literally dissolved the wrecking business in the 20th century. The Wrecking Register at the U.S. Courthouse in Key West was officially closed in 1921, and the U.S. Coast Guard assumed full attendance over all disabled vessels.

Yet oldtimers of the Keys still relate harrowing stories of the legendary wreckers, and as they weave their tales, one can almost hear the plaintive shrill of the conch shell and the echoing cry of "Wreck ashore!" as the imagination relives one of the most colorful and exciting chapters in Florida history.

29.
Florida's Mystery Land Grab

He bought a mammoth chunk of Florida real estate, coast to coast, but something happened to it on Tampa Bay.

Was the first settler of the future city of Tampa a double victim in an international shell game and a military squeeze play?

And did this "official" swindle impede by 60 years the development of Tampa and the bay area, while leaving the victim's heirs tied up in litigation for some 80 years, ending in the U.S. Supreme Court in 1905?

The Fort Brooke-Hackley affair is a true tale that may never be completely told, but the silence that shrouds so much of its genesis impels as much interest as does the affair itself.

In February 1818, King Ferdinand VII of Spain, concerned about his tenuous grip on his Florida territory and almost resigned to its eventual loss to the United States, decided to give huge Florida land grants to three of his favorite courtiers. He was convinced that America would have to honor such grants in any eventual purchase treaty. One courtier, the Duke of Alagon, was given some 11 million acres (almost a third of Florida) stretching from the Tampa Bay region cross-state to the Atlantic. But in those shaky times of Napoleonic conflict, the Duke became pressed for hard cash and decided to sell his grant. Richard S. Hackley, a prominent New York attorney then serving as U.S. consul in Madrid, saw a buy with vast potential and, after informing U.S. embassy officials of his intent, bought it. (The sale price was never disclosed.) This was in May, 1819, by which time the United States and Spain were hashing out terms of a Florida purchase treaty. But neither the Duke nor Hackley was informed that one proviso in the treaty, which was ratified in 1821, nullified all land grants made in Florida after 1802.

In the years following, Hackley's expanding New York law business left him little time to inspect his valuable purchase, so he sent his son, Robert J., 21, to Tampa Bay to create a settlement. With his father's new schooner loaded with lumber, oxen, cows, chickens, and 16 men employed to assist him, Robert sailed into Tampa Bay in early November, 1823. After a survey, Hackley picked a fertile, live-oak-studded tract on the east bank of the Hillsborough River at the point it faced the bay.

The industrious young settler began at once to clear land, plant citrus and vegetables, and construct barns, sheds, a wharf, and a house. Hackley had the first bona fide settlement not only at Tampa but on the entire mainland west coast. It seemed a wilderness paradise—balmy weather, shrubs, flowers, giant oaks, plentiful deer, bear, and turkey, river and bay replete with fish and thick beds of oysters, clams, and stone crabs. By January, 1824, his task finished, Hackley decided to sail to Pensacola for a brief vacation, leaving a foreman named Rhodes in charge.

Meanwhile, in the same month Hackley arrived at Tampa Bay, the U.S. War Department ordered Colonel George M. Brooke, then at Pensacola, to establish an Army post on Tampa Bay to oversee Seminole Indian occupation of the four-million-acre Central Florida reservation granted to them by the 1823 Moultrie Creek Treaty. Brooke, apparently reluctant to leave this lively city to live in a howling wilderness, delayed his departure until proddings by Washington officials prompted him finally to set sail. He arrived at Tampa Bay with four infantry companies on January 20, 1824.

A roving scouting party may or may not have spotted Hackley's settlement, but why Brooke chose the site for his post and indeed appropriated the plantation for his own use seems less explicable. The shallow draft of the bay made it impossible to access by military vessel. His troops had to march six miles to

Young Hackley's home turned into an officers' quarters by Colonel George M. Brooke.

reach the site. And there were numerous other sites on the bay of far more physical and strategic advantage as well as navigational access. Possibly Brooke simply decided that here was a commodious, "ready-made" post, so why sweat the labors of fort-building? More significant was the fact that in his February 5 report to Washington, the colonel omitted any reference to the existence of the settlement, much less his appropriation of it. Not surprisingly, the cantonment was soon designated Fort Brooke.

A curious feature of this episode is the total absence of any historical record, such as the responses of foreman Rhodes and the workmen to the seizure, the disposal of Hackley's equipment and furnishings, or the reasons for Brooke's failure to inform Washington of the dispossession. (Not until 1834, in an affidavit filed with the Interior Department, did Brooke acknowledge that the settlement was "occupied by Hackley.") Nor is there a record of Hackley's response on his return, other than that the astonished young settler sailed at once for New York and, soon after, his incensed father had legal proceedings in motion. The son also returned to Florida to file land claims and, later, claims under the federal Right-of-Pre-emption Act of 1826.

While court proceedings and hearings before the Interior Department dragged slowly through the 1820s and into the 1830s, many civilian settlers were moving into the immediate vicinity of Fort Brooke, enough to acquire a U.S. Post Office (Tampa Bay, later simply Tampa). In 1829, 16 square miles around the fort were declared a military reservation, but this did not deter settlers from creating a community in what is now downtown Tampa. Nor did it deter the Hackleys from selling lots and tracts of land to the new arrivals, since they were so confident of the validity of their claims. One buyer, Judge Augustus Steele, began platting the "town of Tampa" and subdividing his land into lots which, by the mid-1830s, enjoyed a brisk sale. Judge Steele also pushed for the act creating a huge new county of Hillsborough (8,580 square miles). By now, even official state maps designated the entire bay area as "Hackley's," and in 1837 the elder Hackley organized the Florida Peninsula Land Company.

But in 1838, a federal court ruled Hackley's grant purchase invalid, referring to the treaty nullification clause. This voided all tract and lot sales and financially ruined Steele, who left Tampa in disgust and settled at Cedar Key. By 1840 there were only 96 civilians in the entire county.

Hackley, Sr., appealed but died soon after the ruling. Robert Hackley died in Tallahassee in 1845, but the Hackley heirs continued the litigation. Meanwhile, Tampa, although incorporated, remained a sleepy undeveloped fishing village until 1883, when Washington abandoned the fort and reservation and threw the area open to homesteaders. Settlers already "squatting" on the land filed claims, the largest of which was filed by Dr. Edmund S. Carew. But they conflicted with the Hackleys' claim, and so the homesteaders joined in a case against the Hackley heirs.

The case seesawed through the courts for years, favoring one party, then another, until it reached the U.S. Supreme Court which, in 1905, ruled in favor of the homesteaders. The court ruled mainly that Hackley could not claim Right of Pre-emption since that act was not in effect until 1826. Strangely enough, questions of the legality of the colonel's initial dispossession of Hackley's settlement were not posed in the court arguments even though, aside from the purchases's invalidity, it was the common right of citizens then to homestead in the U.S. territory and to enjoy protection against illegal property seizures. The record was certainly clear that no official attempts were ever made to compensate the Hackleys for their losses.

And thus, despite the final ruling, the murky historical record of the Fort Brooke-Hackley affair poses more questions than it ever answered and today remains what historian Karl Grismer called "a mystery" of history.

Heroes and Heroines

30.
Booker T. Sweeps Gainesville

Gainesville honored Booker T. Washington during his 1903
visit, but political connivance thwarted his larger roles.

For all the furor that preceded the night that Booker T. Washington came to town, one might have thought it was a black General Sherman marching on Gainesville that February 5, 1903.

The renowned black educator had simply been invited by Florida's state superintendent of education, William N. Sheats, to address a Gainesville convention of county school superintendents on black educational needs. But contention arose from the fact that this black man would be talking to white people, maybe even whites of both sexes, thus invoking the dire specter of social parity. And in the racial lexicon of the white South of the early 1900s, no phrase could so incite raw emotion as that of "social equality," rooted as it so often was in unconscious sexual fears.

Washington's visit also fanned embers of an earlier national furor back in 1901 when President Theodore Roosevelt, who often consulted the "Tuskegee wizard" on racial matters, invited him to dine with him and his family at the White House. Most of the Southern press castigated the invitation, with one journal hinting darkly of a "conspiracy" by both men to encourage "social equality between the races."

The idea of inviting Booker T. Washington to Gainesville originated with Gainesville Baptist pastor J.B. Holley, Alachua lawmaker J.N. Rivers, and local black educator Sam DeBose, who hoped to organize a black industrial school. Sheats, who admired Washington's ideas on black education, agreed to extend the invitation. Gainesville Mayor W.R. Thomas also endorsed it. But some local resentment was fueled by the misunderstanding that Washington would speak in the auditorium of the white high school. Alachua School Superintendent W.M. Holloway promptly announced that the educator would be prohibited from using the white auditorium as long as he, Holloway, was school chief. The statement, however, only thinly veiled Holloway's perception of a campaign issue in his prospective bid later that year to unseat Sheats from his post.

His words ignited a flurry of commentary, statewide and nationally. The Jacksonville *Times-Union* saw nothing to fear by the visit since Washington knew he "must keep his place" while there. But other state newspapers shared the alarms of state railroad official Jefferson B. Browne, who viewed such mingling with white educators as "a threat to the preservation and purity of the white race." Elsewhere, the New York World "pitied" Southerners if the dignity of some "one-horse school officials . . . could be compromised . . . by a man of [Washington's] brains and character." And the St. Louis Globe-Democrat saw no harm in barring the address since Washington "would have talked over their heads" anyway.

In Gainesville itself, some leading citizens called an "indignation" meeting to censure Sheats, but Sheats, who happened to be in town that evening, walked in on the meeting. When the clamor died down, he calmly explained that Washington would likely be speaking in the courthouse, not the white school, that he would be speaking on black education, not "social equality," and that "whites could attend if they desired to." The high school's principal, J.W. Wideman, a friend of Sheats, then moved that the group endorse the visit; eventually, Holloway himself was persuaded to co-sign with Sheats, and the mayor sent a telegram to Washington urging him to come and promising "a kindly and friendly welcome." Washington, who earlier offered to withdraw from the invitation, now accepted, and, on February 5, took a train to Jacksonville, where he was met by a friend, black lawyer and businessman J.D. Wetmore.

Wetmore, still concerned for Washington's safety, decided to go to Gainesville with him. However, both men were pleased when at each train stop both whites and blacks came aboard to greet the educator. At a stop in Waldo, both men were bemused by the curious and ambivalent nature of prejudice when a "typical cracker" shook Washington's hand and called him the "greatest man" in America. Washington modestly deferred this title to Roosevelt. "Huh" Roosevelt?" the cracker snorted. "I used to think [he] was a great man until he ate dinner with you." Hearing this story later, Roosevelt reportedly "laughed uproariously."

The ex-slave, who had transformed a chicken coop in an Alabama pine woods into a famous Tuskegee Normal and Industrial Institute, viewed his Gainesville visit beyond simply a golden opportunity to publicize his economic and educational programs for blacks. He also hoped to refute charges from black critics that the educator was little more than an "Uncle Tom" who cowered before white racism; he would demonstrate his own methods for dealing with prejudice.

Washington's warm Gainesville welcome caused Wetmore to reflect that "all this noise" about the visit must have originated with "the political enemies of Mr. Sheats," especially when an overflow crowd of 2,000 men and women, white and black, jammed into the courthouse to hear the Tuskegeean give one of his most forceful and eloquent speeches, one marked often with applause. Wetmore was even more impressed when Washington digressed from his educational theme to roundly score white Southerners for their past racial misdeeds and warn that the races "are bound together in a way that we cannot tear ourselves asunder.... As one race is lifted up and made more intelligent, useful and honest...so are both races strengthened." Then, on a conciliatory note, he concluded: "I do not believe, I cannot believe, that the Negro will ever appeal to the Southern white man in vain."

The speech ended to sustained cheers and applause, with both men and women crowding onto the platform to congratulate the speaker. Wetmore later wrote that if Washington's black critics could have been there, they would never again accuse him of being "a good nigger." The press, North and South, generally hailed the speech and agreed in the tenor of one commentary that it was "wisely, prudently and nobly done." Washington himself quietly recorded it as a "distinct victory."

But for those who sponsored the visit, the victory had Pyrrhic overtones. The duplicitous Holloway, resurrecting the bogus "school auditorium" issue and falsely accusing Sheats of promoting "social equality" with the visit, defeated Sheats in November. School principal Wideman, a Sheats ally, was dismissed from his post and, thereafter, was unable to secure even a teaching position in the state. Under censure for allegedly offering his white church for the speech, Pastor Holley moved to Jacksonville. Black educator DeBose was soon forced to close his newly opened normal school for lack of funds.

A broader and more devastating offspin of Holloway's election was his successful advocacy of reducing state funding for black schools. This only compounded an inequity since, as Sheats once estimated, the poll and property taxes paid by black Floridians exceeded the amount spent on their education.

And so despite Washington's historic Florida triumph, it seemed, as one historian observed, to have the ironic effect of enabling white Southerners to defuse Northern criticism even as they quietly and covertly withdrew black educational opportunities. Perhaps their action stemmed from the fears expressed by Jefferson Browne that black young people themselves might get the notion they could aspire to "dine with the white president in the North and sit on the rostrum with the white educators of the South."

31.
The Tragedy of a Native Pocahontas

An Indian princess saves a soldier's life, but official recognition of the deed comes tragically too late.

Many authorities agree today that the romantic tale of Captain John Smith and Pocahontas was just that, an apocryphal tale deriving less from fact than febrile fancy.

Yet Florida could once boast its own Pocahontas, one who really did save a soldier from execution and who one day would be uniquely honored as the only woman in history for whom the U.S. Congress, in gratitude, minted a medal.

But the story of Milly (Malee) Francis, youngest of two daughters of the Seminole Indian Chief, Francis the Prophet, held a poignant epilogue for its heroine, one that would also mirror an ignominious chapter in the history of that day.

In the War of 1812, and later during General Andrew Jackson's punitive raids into Spanish-held Florida in 1818, the Creek and Seminole Indians often sided with the English, mainly due to the Yazoo land grant scandals earlier, during which Georgians had illegally seized much Indian territory. Specifically, the Indians often raided Georgia settlements, taking slaves or giving runaway slaves refuge. Chief Francis, whose village was on the Wakulla River south of Tallahassee and seven miles from the Spanish Fort St. Marks, was honored by the English for his efforts. In 1815, he was escorted to London, hailed as "the patriot Francis," and introduced to Prince Regent George IV. The Prince commissioned Francis a brigadier-general, also presenting him a splendid red and gold uniform, a diamond snuff-box, and a gold-mounted tomahawk. However, Francis had by now become wearied by the incessant warring and, upon returning home, vowed that he would, if possible, "live at peace with the white man." He had sufficient stock and property, a wife and two young daughters, and now desired to live out his days contentedly. The family, except the wife, all spoke English passably well. The youngest daughter, Milly, 15, was a beautiful girl of graceful form and movement and possessed of a keen intelligence. She had many admiring suitors among both Indians and white English officers.

When General Jackson moved into west Florida on his second punitive raid in March, 1818, he erected a camp, Fort Gadsden, not too distant from Tallahassee. While the troops rested there one day, a young private, Duncan McKrimmon, of a Georgia militia unit, decided to go fishing. On his return, he lost his way in the wilderness and was captured by two Seminole warriors who took him back to Francis's village. Here they stripped off his clothing, tied him to a tree, and began whooping and dancing around him with their rifles raised, preparatory to executing him.

Milly and her sister, playing on the riverbank, heard the war-cries, indicating a prisoner taken, and went with other villagers to the scene. She saw that the prisoner was a very young man who "seemed very much frightened and looked wildly around to see if anybody would help him." She took pity on him at once and went to her father to ask his intervention, telling him the youth was too young and "had no head" for war (meaning not old enough to go to war on his own account). But the chief explained that the prisoner, by custom, belonged to his captors; he, Francis, could not interfere, but he advised Milly to speak to the two Indians. She went and did so, enraging one of them who said he had two sisters lost in the war and would, therefore, kill the soldier. But Milly continued pleading, explaining that killing the youth would not bring his sisters back. She continued her pleas until, at length, the Indian relented, but he set certain conditions. McKrimmon must have his head shorn, Indian-style, adopt Indian dress, and live among them. When Milly explained these terms to the soldier, he, in joyful relief, thrust his head forward and cried: "Yes, yes, cut it all off if you choose." The youth then spent several days in the village but later was taken to Fort St. Marks by his two captors where a sympathetic Spanish commander ransomed the private for 7-1/2 gallons of rum. Later he was released.

The next month, April, shortly before General Jackson's attack upon and capture of Fort St. Marks, Chief Francis and another chief had been lured aboard a U.S. vessel disguised as an English ship and arrested. Hearing of it, Jackson ordered them hung at once, "as a warning to other Indians." Here the general acted in total violation of then war conventions, but his violent prejudice against Indians—described by some historians as almost psychotic—superseded law.

McKrimmon, whose unit disbanded several weeks later, returned to his home in Milledgeville, Georgia, where he regaled to everyone the heroic act of the Seminole "Pocahontas." When he learned that, after Chief Francis's death, his village had fallen on hard times, his town took up a collection and McKrimmon personally took the gift to the village, for he was also determined to ask Milly to marry him. While expressing grateful thanks for the gift, which she shared with her destitute villagers, Milly declined McKrimmon's marriage offer, telling him she had acted "from feelings of humanity alone" and would have done the same for any white man similarly circumstanced.

But conditions worsened for her village, and, on August 27, 1818, Milly, her family, and 188 other Seminoles, near starvation, surrendered to the commandant at Fort Gadsden. The officer did all he could to relieve their needs. While there, Milly, whose benevolent act had become widely known, was treated with much deference by officers and men who referred to her as "the princess."

But later, when she and other Seminoles were relocated to government reservations in the Oklahoma territory, along with many other tribes, they would fare even worse. Whole families and even tribes were nearly decimated by starvation at the hands of corrupt Indian agents and government contractors—a scandal that by 1842 would reach national proportions. In that year, President John Tyler had picked an officer then serving in Florida in the Seminole War to go west as a special investigator into the alleged frauds. For political reasons, Tyler hoped to downplay or defuse a volatile situation for his administration. But in this he picked the wrong man—Major Ethan Allen Hitchcock, grandson of the revolutionary war hero and, years later, as major-general, top military advisor to President Lincoln in the Civil War. Conscientious, dedicated, and relentless, Hitchcock scoured the territory, taking testimony from Indians and whites, gathering documents, and filling a voluminous report with countless cases of fraud, bribery, perjury, forgery, land swindles, and theft on the part of agents and contractors—"a cruel robbery," he found that had swept entire families away by starvation, leaving many others in near-starving destitution. Influential cronies of the administration were also named in the report. Tyler attempted to suppress the report from scrutiny by Congress, but the cry of outrage from that body was too loud and persistent, and the report finally saw public light. Under severe pressure, Hitchcock firmly held his ground on the truth of the report; many arrests, shake-ups, and reforms soon followed.

While in Oklahoma, Hitchcock had heard the story of Milly Francis and searched her out. She was now near 40, still "an attractive woman," but living in poverty on the banks of the Arkansas River, hard put to support herself and three small children. Her husband, a Seminole, had died earlier, along with five other children. Confirming the truth of her story, which she related matter-of-factly, without rancor, Hitchcock became incensed, especially at the "cruel and inhumane" conduct of Jackson in Florida. On his return to Washington, he strongly urged Congress to provide a pension for her, "in consideration of her extraordinary and humane act." Congress was favorable, and a bill was proposed granting Milly an annual pension of $96 for life, further providing that a gold medal be struck "with appropriate devices thereon, as additional testimonial of the gratitude of the United States." But, dilatory as usual, Congress did not pass the bill until 1844. It then took the administration four more years to finally send the award.

But Milly no longer needed it; she received it on her deathbed where she lay ravaged by poverty and tuberculosis. She died that same year, 1848.

The story of the authentic "Pocahontas" of Florida, and the belated justice accorded her, would long after remain a legend and example among the Seminole Indians. But, unfortunately, in the years ahead, it would be the white man who proved more sorely in need of such as example.

32.
Martyrdom Cracks an Evil System

A young Dakota wayfarer falls victim to a notorious penal system, but public outcry brings the system's abolition.

It weighed a hefty 7-1/2 pounds and from its handle stretched a two-ply leather strap five feet long and four inches wide. It was called a "Black Aunty"; often it was first smeared with oil and dragged over sand to enhance its searing effects.

For over half a century, from post-Civil War days to post-World War I, the "Black Aunty" had evolved into a sordid symbol of Florida's notorious convict-lease system, a penal practice that encrusted the state's civil image like a scabrous relic from the Dark Ages. The horror stories of brutal beatings and abuse, disease and death seeped into the public consciousness over the years, until outrage finally forced the state to end the system in 1919.

But the new law applied only to *state* prisoners; the leasing of county prisoners to turpentine, lumber, phosphate, railroad, and other private interests continued unabated. The law was merely a palliative; a system so entrenched and lucrative would not be easily wrested from the encysted grasp of public venality and private avarice. It would take the unwilling martyrdom of a North Dakota farm boy and the harsh glare of a national spotlight to abolish the system completely.

Twenty-two-year-old Martin Tabert had worked hard since childhood on his parents' 560-acre farm in Munich, North Dakota, and now, in the fall of 1921, he decided it was his turn, like his brothers and sisters before him, to go out and "see the world." He had saved some money. He would travel about, working part time, and then head south for the winter. All went well until he reached north Florida. Jobs were scarce, and he ran out of funds. He decided to leave Florida by train—without benefit of a ticket—but was arrested in Leon County for vagrancy. Brought before Judge B.F. Willis in Tallahassee on December 15, 1921, he was fined $25 or 90 days. The penniless youth was then turned over to Leon Sheriff J.R. Jones, who, under county policy, leased Tabert to the Putnam Lumber Company 60 miles away at Clara in Dixie County. But first Tabert wired home; his parents sent a letter and a $75 bank draft. But the sheriff returned the letter, stamping it "Unclaimed . . . Party gone." Assuming Martin had found another means of release, the Taberts waited to hear from him.

Then, weeks later, the Taberts received a letter from a Putnam Lumber official saying their son had died in their camp on February 1 of malaria fever. They had arranged for his burial. The aggrieved family was perplexed, and they hired local attorney Norris Nelson to make inquiries. The lumber company informed Nelson that Martin developed malaria and complications because he would not take his medicine regularly. The sheriff replied that he returned their letter because the draft was in Martin's name, preventing him (the sheriff) from getting the funds. The fuller explanation compelled the Taberts to accept Putnam's story of their son's death.

But, in July, 1922, a letter sent via the Munich postmaster reached the Taberts. The writer, Glen Thompson, wanted them to know "the particulars" of their son's death to which Thompson had been an eyewitness. The Taberts wrote at once to Thompson who gave them the names and addresses of many other eyewitnesses in other states. A flurry of correspondence followed. Gradually, the story of a monstrous deception unfolded as one after another of the former Florida inmates attested to "a horrible death" Martin suffered at the hands of a camp whipping boss, Walter Higginbotham, and the "many tortures" other black and white inmates had suffered.

Stunned and incredulous over this information, the outraged parents took the matter to State's Attorney G. Grimson, who personally went to Florida to investigate. A relentless Grimson soon substantiated the allegations. He also reported Sheriff Jones to be "little more than a slave catcher" who earned $20 a head picking up "unfortunate men" on trivial law violations and sending them to Putnam. His findings went to the Dakota legislature which, in turn, demanded that the Florida legislature make a thorough investigation. Florida Governor Cary Hardee wrote North Dakota's Governor R.A. Nestus, defending Florida's "humane" penal system but promising "vigorous prosecution" if criminal acts were involved. By spring of 1923, a joint Florida House-Senate committee began hearings with numerous witnesses—former camp inmates, former guards, Putnam employees, and others. On April 10, a Madison County grand jury also began a probe.

In testimony, an evasive Higginbotham repeatedly insisted that he gave Martin only a light whipping of "ten licks" for shirking his duties. But too many other witnesses presented a more compellingly graphic account of Martin's camp stay. Former inmates testified that a "strong and sturdy" Martin was soon reduced to a haggard 125 pounds, and that Higginbotham refused the youth's request to exchange his undersized shoes. Martin's feet were badly swollen from the swamp water the men were forced to work in. He developed groin swellings, one of which the visiting camp doctor lanced, and suffered chronic headaches and fever chills. The fever-ridden youth received no attention except for the blankets "some of the boys" threw over him. At the end of January, Martin was given a severe beating with a Black Aunty before a group of 85 inmates. They alleged that the whipping boss often flogged men "just for the sport of it." Former guard A.P. Shivers testified that a healthy Martin soon suffered running sores and feet so swollen he could "barely drag around" and only with difficulty walked the two miles to the swamp to work. The night of the beating, Shivers related, the already-ill Tabert had had 30 licks with the strap when he groaned and screamed for mercy. At this point, Higginbotham placed the heel of his boot on Martin's neck to hold him in place and gave him some 70 more strokes. Thereafter, Shivers said, the fever-ridden and delirious youth was unable to move from his cot and died two days later.

On April 23, Higginbotham was indicted by the grand jury for first-degree murder. The Taberts also filed a $50,000 civil suit against Putnam.

Lawmakers also heard former Leon jailor Jerry Poppell describe how Sheriff Jones made sizable profits in a deal "to railroad" men to Putnam, and how court appearances often took place late at night without formal due process. The camp physician, Dr. T. Caper Jones, suddenly changed his story and alleged that Martin had actually died of syphilis but that he, the doctor, wished to spare the Tabert family embarrassment. The committee eventually recommended removal from office of Leon Judge Willis and the sheriff and asked the medical board to purge this "seemingly unworthy member [Dr. Jones]" from the profession. Nor did the committee have to look far for other brutality cases: State Senator T.J. Knabb owned turpentine camps. A supervisor, J.B. Thomas, said that Knabb ran "a human slaughter pen" at which at least nine inmates died from brutal beatings. Although a camp captain was later indicted for cruelty, nothing came of efforts to remove Knabb from office.

Throughout the period, these revelations were aired almost daily in the press, which was joined by church, civic, business, and social clubs demanding abolition of "a barbarous system." On-the-scene stories by the New York *World* were picked up around the country, igniting a barrage of editorials and galvanizing a sense of national outrage. Thus, it was no surprise when, in May, committee bills abolishing both the lease system and corporal punishment passed and were signed by the governor.

The Taberts won a $20,000 settlement from Putnam, but this must have remained a painfully ambiguous consolation for their son's unwilling martyrdom, since retribution otherwise would prove elusive. Higginbotham was convicted of second-degree murder and sentenced to 20 years in prison that July. Out on bond and pulling strings legal and otherwise, Higginbotham won a case review before the Florida Supreme Court which, on a technicality, reversed his conviction and granted him a new trial in Dixie County. Records were then transferred to the Dixie Court Clerk in January, 1925. But a second trial was never held and Higginbotham remained free. It seemed to "disappear" as cryptically as Martin Tabert's burial site, which no one could ever exactly locate.

33.
The Deliverance of Jonathan Dickinson

A Quaker shipwreck victim in 17th-century Florida, along with his party, is delivered from a harrowing ordeal.

Shipwrecks off the Florida coast were fairly common in early centuries, but one of the most memorable ever recorded occurred in 1696 north of Palm Beach when the barkentine Reformation, out from Port Royal, Jamaica, bound for Philadelphia, was washed aground off Jupiter Island in a heavy storm.

Its occupants of 24 men, women, and children not only survived the shipwreck but also experienced a near miraculous deliverance from savage Indians, beatings, starvation, raw exposure, and constant threats of death in a harrowing journey up 230 miles of wild and desolate Florida coast to the freedom and safety of St. Augustine.

The ship, chartered by a young Quaker merchant, Jonathan Dickinson, his wife, Mary, and six-month-old son, also carried Robert Barrow, an elderly Quaker missionary, Benjamin Allen, a Quaker kinsman, its captain, Joseph Kirle, a crew of eight, and Dickinson's ten black servants—four men, a child, and five women.

The barkentine had become separated from its convoy of 12 vessels when the storm smashed it onto the long shallows off Jupiter on September 23, 1696. Fortunately, ebb tide gave the survivors virtually dry land over which to reach a nearby island and carry whatever trunks, chests, and provisions they could salvage. Dickinson and the crew began at once to set up a tent with ship spars and sails. They had no sooner finished this when two Indians, with knives drawn and of "wild, furious countenance," came running toward them. They seized two crewmen, hauled them up to where Dickinson stood and jabbered excitedly. Dickinson stayed the hand of a crewman who would have shot the pair and, instead, offered them some tobacco and pipes which they greedily snatched and then ran away.

But the Quaker knew they had only gone to round up their people; the survivors shuddered at the possible terrible fate awaiting them. Dickinson knew that while the Florida tribes were friendly with and even in awe of the Spanish, they considered the English, whom they called "Nickaleer," to be mortal enemies. The group thereupon proposed to pass themselves off as Spaniards and were greatly aided in this plan by a young French crewman, Solomon Cresson, who looked Spanish and spoke the language fluently. Within hours, as expected, a large horde of Indians and their chief (cacique) swooped down upon them, shouting: "Nickaleer, Nickaleer." The savages refused to believe their protests of Spanish nationality and encircled each person with large Spanish knives drawn, holding them in positions of execution. The Quakers had been fervently praying during this time and then, according to Dickinson, "it pleased the Lord to work wonderfully for our preservation," as the savages, inexplicably, seemed struck mute for nearly a quarter-hour and then loosed their holds of the victims. But then they began stripping the survivors of almost all their clothing, after which they all proceeded to loot the ship.

The group, through Cresson, began talking to the chief who, they perceived, had taken a protective role toward them, turning away those who attempted to molest them. But the cacique refused to let them proceed north toward St. a Lucca (St. Lucie) and, instead, next morning marched the near-naked, barefoot survivors a few miles south to his village. The chief then questioned them again. "Nickaleer?" he snapped. They chorused back, "No, Espainia," but were almost given away by missionary Barrow who, ever truthful, replied, "Yes." Dickinson, his wife, and his child stayed in the chief's tent and were fed boiled fish and the acrid palm berries, which they could not stomach. At night they listened to the "hideous" ceremonial shrieks and yells and the heated Indian "debates" over whether to kill the captives. Many younger braves were convinced they were "Nickaleer" and Dickinson was "startled" to hear one of them utter in clear phrase, "English son of a bitch." The group spent most of their time in prayer and Bible reading which, strangely, seemed to silence the savages as they sat listening with curious, pleased attentiveness.

Finally, the chief, providing men for escort, permitted the group to head northward in their salvaged ship's longboat. With the barest food supply, dressed in ragged patches of canvas sail, exposed to night cold, mosquitoes, and sand flies, the haggard ban struggled slowly up the intercoastal islets—the captain, his leg still disabled from a voyage mishap, led most of the group by shoreline; the family, plus Barrow and Allen, who were both wracked with fever and ague, went by boat.

Upon reaching St. Lucie, the earlier terror scene was reenacted as the deadly Aix tribes swarmed down upon them, shouting: "Nickaleer," and rending and tearing their few rags from them. The small band was pushed, kicked, and beaten along, stark naked, to the village, one savage only barely prevented from cutting the wife's throat as another stuffed sea-sand into the infant's mouth, all raging, "thirsting to shed our blood, and a mighty strife was amongst them; some would kill us, others would prevent it." Again, their cacique intervened and all lives were spared. The women were given some raw deer skins to wear, the men merely straw-like breech belts. Their exhaustion and exposure prevented them from eating the scaly boiled fish given them and they passed a wretched night in the vermin-infested, garbage-strewn grass huts, fearfully listening to the eerie howling of the savages as they danced and drank casseena, a liquor made from leaves of a shrub. Next day, however, the chief gave Mrs. Dickinson some roasted clams and even an Indian mother to suckle her child "since its mother's milk was almost gone" from hunger.

That night they were furnished a guide to the Jece village (Vero Beach). On the way, they passed the wreck of the Nantwitch, a convoy vessel which, they learned, was beached the same night as the Reformation. Totally exhausted, they arrived at Jece on October 2, and met the five men and one woman survivors of the Nantwitch. Their lives had been spared thus far even though they had admitted they were Nickaleer. The new arrivals were given huts and fed fish, and the elderly cacique promised them he would escort them to St. Augustine as soon as he returned from a trip from Hoe-Bay to recover some of the ship's booty. Soon after, a rainstorm and flood almost inundated the islet, washing their huts away and stranding them on an oyster-shell mound for five days, with little water and no food; the palm berries, which Dickinson first said tasted like "rotten cheese steeped in tobacco," were now forced down. They were also able to beg several Indian women to suckle the baby, its mother now worn almost dry. When the old cacique returned, he angrily displayed some of their ship's articles as "Nickaleer." The survivors insisted they had taken them from the English, but the chief was still suspicious and put off plans to take them to St. Augustine. They would spend a hard month at Jece.

Then, on October 18, the cacique and six Indians consented to take Solomon Cresson to St. Augustine for aid. But at their departure, rough days set in. The Indians would feed them only rarely a fish or two, and the starving captives sought out "any manner of thing...the gills and guts of fish, picked off a dung-hill...the scraps the Indians threw away and the water they boiled their fish in." Other Indians taunted them with how they would kill the other ship's company of "Nickaleer" and how the new captives, too, might suffer similarly. But "our hope never failed, trusting in the Lord to work for our deliverance." After much forced fasting, they were given a bag of berries which they devoured, and then some fish. Finally, on November 2, help arrived—11 Spanish soldiers sent by the Governor of St. Augustine.

The Spanish took charge at once in the village, ordering the Indians to lash two canoes together for the group and to return one of the stolen longboats. When the Indians soon learned that their captives were in fact "Nickaleer" they yelled and raged, but would do nothing to them for fear of the Spaniards. But the worst trip lay ahead, since the Spanish had no extra provisions, and the Indians would provide none. A freezing cold was also moving in, and they wore the scantiest of rags. Six of them would perish.

Through storm, rain, rough seas, around the treacherous point now called Cape Kennedy, overland through boggy marsh and barren sand, with but a few palm berries and an occasional fish for sustenance, the stricken, barefooted survivors inched onward. "Some of our people were for selling our rags to the Indians (met along the way) for fish," but the freeze worsened, "every day grew colder than the other and we feared that if we were much longer exposed to it, we should not live it out," Dickinson wrote. One Negro woman's small boy was first to die of the cold and hunger. Benjamin Allen fell out next and, while Dickinson searched for help to carry him, died from fever and exposure. Three other blacks, two men and a girl, became separated—as did many in the group—and froze to death. Yet, miraculously, the baby still survived, "black with cold from head to foot, and its flesh as cold as stone," but Dickinson and his wife "dared not stop...for if we did, we should perceive our limbs to fail."

When they spotted the first Spanish sentinel posthouse just below St. Augustine it so restored them that they almost ran to the outpost. Here they found most of the remainder of the party of both ships, then collapsed before a log fire and feasted on Indian cornbread and hot casseena. They were about to send out a search party for the elderly, ailing Barrow when he suddenly stumbled onto the site, unable to speak he was so overcome by joy. But the venerable missionary was to die in Charles Town (Charleston, South Carolina) a few weeks later from the journey's ravages. However, the few miles to their goal seemed impossible since neither guide nor boat was available. "We were in extraordinary pain, so that we could not rest; and our feet were extremely bruised, the skin was off and the sand caked with the blood that we could hardly set our feet to the ground after we had been some time in the house," Dickinson recalled.

But providence smiled once more. A governor's delegation soon appeared with rescue boats, and, on November 15, the governor personally welcomed and cared for them, supplying them with clothes, blankets, and provisions, two weeks of rest in his home, and boats to take them to Charles Town, where they caught a ship to Philadelphia.

Except for the six, the entire remaining party survived and lived well in years after. At Philadelphia, Dickinson built a prosperous merchant trade, transporting much commerce by ships under Captain Kirle. The infant, Jonathan, Jr., grew to healthy manhood, and the wife gave birth to two more boys and two girls.

And the descendants of the inexpendable Solomon Cresson helped preserve to this day the record of Dickinson's journal about this remarkable ordeal and the faith, endurance, and courage that wrought a miraculous deliverance along Florida's savage wilderness coast nearly three centuries ago.

34.
Colonel Newnan Sidesteps
a Massacre

A bold Army colonel leads a small unit into hostile Indian country, and his outnumbered force narrowly escapes massacre.

If Colonel Daniel Newnan had only half tried back in 1812, he might have achieved the celebrated memorial of Major Francis L. Dade who, with all but three of his men, was massacred near Bushnell by the Seminole chief Micanopy in 1835.

But Colonel Newnan went more than halfway and miraculously escaped in an almost forgotten battle against the Seminole chief King Payne near what is now Gainesville. Only an obscure sign on an unnumbered country road east of Newnan's Lake marks this episode today. But Newnan's bold foray against the Indians was the first American venture of its kind; it punctuated a critical juncture in not merely Florida but also U.S. history.

The episode came on the eve of the War of 1812. The young U.S. republic, facing official hostilities from Great Britain and unofficial enmity from Spain, had at its back a formidable group of Indian nations, stretching from Florida to Canada, that covertly aided the European belligerents. Central Florida's Seminoles, who had been raiding white settlers with a free hand for years, responded eagerly to the call of the great northern warrior, Tecumseh, for a grand alliance of all American Indians to stop America's westward encroachment.

During this time, Congress had met in secret sessions to discuss means of seizing Florida from Spain on the pretext that the English might use it as a base of operations. And though this bit of intrigue was abandoned, a group of some 200 East Florida planters calling themselves "The Patriots" drew up a provisional plan for a U.S. Territory of East Florida. They actually seized the fort at Fernandina from the Spanish, but failed in an attack on St. Augustine and, thereafter, turned their attentions to the rampaging Indians.

To implement this aim, Colonel Newnan and a detachment of 250 Georgia volunteers arrived on the St. Johns River on August 15, 1812, to begin an inland march against the Seminoles.

But, as if under some ominous portent, the expedition seemed plagued from the start. Newnan and half his men were laid up for several weeks with fever. Finally, when they were ready to go in September, Lieutenant Colonel Thomas A. Smith, who had just been attacked by the Spanish troops near St. Augustine, called Newnan to return to aid his stricken forces. Several days later, the men who had only a week or less to serve on their enlistments decided to drop out of the march. Newnan called for volunteers to extend their enlistments by three more weeks; only 84 men accepted. Along with some of Smith's troops who joined him, Newnan set out on September 24 with 117 officers and men, 12 horses, and four days of provisions.

The men marched through forest and broad open country without incident until the morning of the fourth day, a few miles from what is now Newnan's Lake. An advance patrol surprised a party of some 75 Indians proceeding toward them on the same path. The Indians fell back at once and set up a hasty defense, while Newnan had his men advance, under cover of trees, to within 130 yards of them. When the enemy opened fire, the colonel ordered a charge; the Indians retreated, swiftly pursued by the soldiers, who slew several of them before the redskins reached the shelter of a large swamp.

Here Newnan set up an attack position; a battle raged for two and a half hours, with the soldiers repelling several attempts by Indians to flank them or attack on their rear. Finally, one of the privates scored a plus. He caught in his sights a stalwart figure surveying the scene from his fine-looking mount. He fired, and the figure fell. Three warriors frantically retrieved the body and carried it away. It was their chief, the famous warrior King Payne, still alive but suffering from wounds that later proved fatal. The Indians ceased firing soon after, and a long, uneasy silence fell over the battle scene.

During this lull, the Indians sent for reinforcements, and, a half hour before sunset, a force more than twice Newnan's strength advanced toward his line with wild and frantic gestures and "the most horrid yells imaginable." At 200 yards the Indians began firing. Newnan waited until the foe moved in much closer and then ordered a brisk and well-directed fire which sent the Indians running back to their original ground. Several more attacks were similarly repelled, and then, at nightfall, silence fell again.

Newnan's now exhausted men worked through the night; by dawn they had constructed a sturdy breastwork of logs and earth with firing portholes. The previous night, Newnan sent an officer to the St. Johns camp for reinforcements, but "six more men took the liberty to accompany him, taking with them our best horses," he recalled.

The Indians remained quiet until the third evening and then began firing from a greater distance. This sporadic harassment continued for six days but without accomplishing any deaths.

By the eighth day, Newnan faced not only starvation but rebellion, as he wrote: "Expecting relief every hour, I was unwilling to leave our breastworks while we had a horse to eat, but I understood from some of my officers that a certain captain was determined to leave us with his company, and that many of the men, giving up all hope of relief, talked of deserting in the night rather than perish or fall a sacrifice to the merciless [enemy], whom they were taught to believe would surround us in great numbers in a few days. In this trying situation, when our few remaining horses were shot down by the Indians, and the number of our sick daily increasing, I reluctantly assented to leave our works that night, and directed the litters to be prepared to carry the wounded. About nine o'clock we commenced our distressing march."

However, after only eight miles, the exhausted troop fell out from hunger and fatigue. Newnan now sent another messenger to seek aid and then set up another defense post on the spot, fearing an Indian ambush if the men tried to march in their weakened condition.

At this time, some of the men were again stirred to leave the breastworks, and Newnan discovered that the same captain before mentioned was responsible for this dissension. "This gentleman [the captain], if innocent, will have an opportunity of proving himself so before a court martial," Newnan wrote later in his official report. Nevertheless, the colonel, burning with fever and scarcely able to walk himself, agreed to march on.

But his forebodings proved correct. The contingent had barely marched five miles when they ran straight into an ambush from both sides of the trail. Four of the advance soldiers were killed, and Newnan ordered an immediate charge. Within 15 minutes, the Indians began fleeing, even dropping their guns in their haste and leaving a half dozen of their own dead behind.

The exhausted, hungry troops camped on this scene for the night. Next morning they marched five more miles and again threw up a breastwork in a strategic spot between two ponds. During this period, they subsisted solely on gophers, palmetto cabbage, and alligator, while tending their sick and wounded as best they could. They were grimly aware of their position. They knew that if the main Indian force caught up to them, the enfeebled, ragged outfit would be slaughtered; time was against them.

But the sergeant-major that Newnan had dispatched previously to seek aid had wasted none of that time. Finally, after almost two weeks of warfare, hunger, illness, and death, and constantly under the threat of massacre, the soldiers whooped with relief as their messenger rode into camp with food, provisions, and 14 fresh horses. Even better, considering their physical condition, the men learned that they would be taking a short-cut back to camp. They had only to alternately march and ride a relatively few more miles to a point on the lower St. Johns River. Here Colonel Smith had sent a gunboat to pick them up, and they sailed most of the way home.

Newnan and his men were honored and decorated for the bold raid, the first of its kind ever conducted. And they had left more than 60 dead foe behind, including the great King Payne, plus numerous wounded.

The first settlers of Alachua County named their county seat Newnansville in memory of the colonel, around 1820. The town thrived as the most populous in Central and South Florida until the Civil War. But when the railroad came through in 1854, it bypassed Newnansville, and Gainesville, which lay on the rail line, became the new county seat. Gradually, the original town disappeared; only a few farmhouses remain on the site today.

But the little marker on the Rochelle-Windsor road near Newnan's Lake still attests to the day when history could record "Newnan's Miraculous Escape," instead of "Newnan's Massacre."

35.
Florida's First Reform Mayor

Jefferson's grandson, Francis Eppes, tries his hand at scouring vice, corruption, and violence in old Tallahassee.

Among the requisites for "useful citizenship," the grandfather counseled the 15-year-old, "honesty, disinterestedness and good nature are indispensable . . . [and] at all times, practice yourself in good humor."

In later years, however, Francis Eppes, the grandson of Thomas Jefferson, may have balked over the advice on "good humor," for there was not much that was amusing about conditions in antebellum Tallahassee during its territorial days. The capital was a wild frontier town. Its dingy slabwood buildings and muddy streets were the scene of recurrent brawls, shootings, drinking episodes, gambling, and assorted other vices and disorder.

And there was a proclivity to casual mayhem that was not confined to ruffian elements. The landed gentry indulged a more respectable mode of mayhem—the lethal sport of dueling. An issue might as easily be resolved with lead ball or Bowie knife as with study or debate. It was into such a milieu that Francis Eppes was thrust as the first "reform mayor" in Florida.

When he arrived in frontier Florida in 1827, the transplanted Virginian left behind any vestige of the political heritage of his famous grandfather. Eppes shunned the political arena in favor of moral and cultural pursuits. Indeed, when Jefferson's daughter, Maria, died two years after Francis's birth in 1801, and his son-in-law, John Wayles Eppes, a Virginia congressman, was so often away from home, the ex-president undertook to guide his grandson's education, first at the University of North Carolina and then during summers at his Monticello home. The boy became well read in Greek, Latin, Spanish, French, and Italian and in the classics. At age 20, Eppes married a distant cousin, Mary Elizabeth Cleland Randolph, and Jefferson provided the couple with a nearby estate, Poplar Forest.

But the gullied farmland proved inadequate to the needs of a growing family. In 1827, Eppes joined other Virginians and Carolinians making the trek to the new Florida territory. He first homesteaded about 12 miles from Tallahassee, but when his wife died after the birth of their sixth child, Eppes purchased and moved to a 1,900-acre plantation on nearby Lake Lafayette. He also built a home in Tallahassee and married Susan Margaret Ware, daughter of Georgia's governor. Eppes served for a while as a district peace justice in Leon County, but he avoided the capital's turbulent streets and political scene. He devoted much of his time to establishing the area's first Episcopal church, St. Johns, and would later serve as its Florida diocese secretary. In 1836, he became a trustee of a project to establish a "seminary of learning" in Florida. This effort bore fruit 20 years later with the establishment of the "Seminary West of the Suwannee," out of which evolved Florida State University.

But by 1840, vice, violence, and disorder far outpaced all efforts to raise the territory's moral and cultural tone. Furthermore, the flush prosperity engendered among the planters by the freewheeling Union Bank induced a kind of social euphoria that found release in a whirl of parties, balls, tournaments, and lavish expenditures. Neither pulpit nor academia could compete, for example, with the sybaritic lifestyles found at the nearby Marion racetrack.

Indulgence of the deadly Code Duello also became chronic. Eppes had been deeply affected by the death of a close friend who was challenged over a very trivial difference. The tragic consequences of the famous duel between two rival political leaders, Leigh Read and Augustus Alston, prompted the St. Joseph *Times* to remark on the "disturbed state of society in Leon County," its editor wondering why "the gentlemen . . . cannot differ in politics [without] violence and proscription."

When a yellow fever epidemic wiped out 450 Tallahassee residents in 1841, visiting New Englander John Tappan thought it was providence. "A year ago," he wrote, "you could not walk the streets [here] without being armed to the teeth. Now it's different. God has seen fit to take away . . . most all of the Gamblers and Blacklegs."'

Eppes himself gradually came to see that he could no longer stand back from public affairs, and that same year, when some reform-minded citizens urged him to become the capital's mayor, he accepted.

In early 1842 he also became foreman of a county grand jury that issued a stinging criticism of the Marion Race Course, declaring it to be "a public nuisance, a hotbed of vice, intemperance, gambling and profanity." Within a year the track was shut down. The reform campaign was spurred on by two more calamities occurring in 1843—the collapse of Union Bank and a fire that destroyed most of Tallahassee's shacklike downtown business section.

Eppes and his council zealously set about to enact a variety of strict and unprecedented city ordinances. Stiff fines and jail sentences were prescribed against disorderly conduct, drunkenness, gambling, profane or obscene language, "scandalous" drawings, pamphlets, or signs, the firing of guns or pistols, brawling, and various other civil disturbances. Eppes then organized a compulsory "night watch" consisting of four or more men who patrolled the city in two shifts.

By the close of Mayor Eppes's second term, the restoration of "virtue and good order" in the capital seemed so marked that a grateful citizenry honored the mayor for his "untiring and successful services" and awarded him an engraved solid silver pitcher.

Eppes would serve as mayor again in 1856 and 1857; in 1856 he had declined the presidency of the newly established "Seminary West of the Suwannee" but became a trustee nonetheless. Eppes's reform movement seemed to have taken durable effect in the capital; the riotous vice and lawlessness of earlier years had become, by the 1850s, only an occasional occurrence.

Eppes's reformist zeal did not diminish, even when federal forces under General John G. Foster occupied Tallahassee in 1866 after the Civil War; the occupiers asked Eppes to serve once more as mayor, and he consented. The role seemed merely titular—but not to the ex-reformer, according to an incident recalled by his daughter-in-law, Susan Bradford Eppes. Walking to church one Sunday morning, Eppes chanced to glance through a basement window and spied General Foster and a local general merchant playing poker. Eppes headed downstairs and, getting no response from knocking, forced the door open. The game abruptly ended. Word of the incident circulated, and the Eppes family grew apprehensive, even more so when the general and his wife called on the Eppeses the next day. Somewhat alarmed but with customary poise, Mrs. Eppes greeted her guests. Her alarm quickly changed to relief as she listened to the general praise her husband for his courage, sense of justice, and fair-minded execution of the laws.

But the war had reduced Eppes to insolvency. In 1864, he had sold his Lafayette acreage for Confederate money—worthless currency—and by 1869 was forced to sell his Tallahassee home to pay debts. He moved to Orange County, near Orlando, to begin a new life as a citrus grower. Here he organized another Episcopal church, and, when he died in 1881, Orlandoans recalled him as a "spiritual, intellectual and cultural force" in the community. Thus, while Eppes attained none of the political stature of his illustrious grandfather-mentor, the latter's early counsel on "useful citizenship" seemed more than fulfilled by Florida's first reform mayor.

36.
Sarasota's
Redoubtable
Dowager Queen

*Mrs. Potter Palmer forsook the salons
of the social register set to awaken and
revitalize a torpid backwoods town.*

When the drowsy little fishing village of Sarasota (900 souls) heard that the
queen was coming, they perked up, wet down their cowlicks, shined their shoes,
primped and preened, and with a certain awkward deference turned out to meet
her.

The year was 1910, and the queen was Mrs. Potter Palmer, Chicago's
bejeweled and regal Grande Dame and social arbiter, late also of Newport,
London, and Paris, friend of presidents, kings, and assorted royalty, now about
to lend a little courtly sheen to the Florida backwoods.

After all, nothing much good had happened around the little town in the
past several years. The hardware store burned down last year, as did the 16-room
Bay View Hotel and the livery stable the year before, all following on the
financial Panic of 1907, which had snuffed the high hopes for big Northern
investments in local citrus groves. Things were tight, with nothing much to do
except fish or shuffle sand. But now—the queen was coming. And everyone
knew that queens did good things for folks—things like providing jobs, largesse,
and benevolence in general.

Only weeks before, Mrs. Palmer was sitting in her chilly shoreside castle
on Lake Michigan, reading the *Chicago Tribune*, when she spied an advertisement telling of crystal waters, balmy clime, and land galore (for sale, cheap) in
sunny Florida. She called the advertiser, Chicago realtor J.H. Lord, they talked,
and soon Lord was notifying his partner in Sarasota, A.B. Edwards, to spread a
royal welcome for Guess Who? Also, P.S., "She will buy heavily if interested."
With no lodgings in town deemed suitable for the widow of a man who built the
famous Palmer House, an anxious Edwards persuaded local Dr. Jack Halton to
temporarily vacate his brand-new sanitorium overlooking Sarasota Bay so it

could be "fixed up" for Mrs. Palmer. The doctor consented readily, and on February 10, 1910, the 61-year-old dowager, with her father, H. H. Honore, staff and servants in tow, arrived in her private railroad car. It would be a milestone in Sarasota's history, for with her customary shrewdness, aplomb, and daring, the good lady would soon be turning the little town around.

In 1855, when Bertha Honore Palmer was six years old, she moved from Louisville, Kentucky, to Chicago with her father, H. H. Honore, mother Eliza, sister Ida, and four brothers. Honore was a prosperous businessman who saw a booming future for the burgeoning city of 80,000. The fruits of the plains were already pouring into the bustling metropolis—grain, cattle, hogs, produce, lumber, and railroads—and Honore would successfully invest heavily in real estate. So would a younger friend who had preceded him to the city, one with whom he would be closely associated, Potter Palmer. Palmer began with a dry goods store (later sold to and made famous by young entrepreneur Marshall Field), purchased large downtown tracts, built business houses on them, and became a millionaire before he was 40. Often in the Honore home, he was taken with Bertha, then barely a teenager, and vowed to himself he would marry her when she came of age. Sent off to private schools in Washington, D.C., Bertha returned—well-educated, accomplished, beautiful, and 21. Palmer began his suit, and soon Bertha began to see him as someone besides her father's friend. They were married July 28, 1870—the bride 21, the groom 44. There were a few clucks of disapproval, but the marriage proved to be intimate, durable, and happy. They had two sons, Honore and Potter, Jr. Her wedding gift—the $3.5 million Palmer House, a luxurious hostelry.

The Palmer House—and nearly every other building in Chicago—was wiped out in the great fire of 1871. But Palmer, Honore, and others were determined to rebuild, and they did. Loans were floated to the stricken city, buildings went up (including many on Palmer's State Street tracts), business recovered and boomed. Once more, Palmer built a larger and even more lavish Palmer House, one that became a famous mecca for political figures, hog and cattle kings, royalty, and celebrities of every stripe. The first prominent guests were President and Mrs. U.S. Grant, whose eldest son, Frederick Dent, was married to Bertha's sister Ida.

The vital and vibrant Bertha quickly rose to prominence on the social scene, the reigning hostess in a whirl of parties, receptions, charity balls, and philanthropic and worthy causes. She was also caught up in that era's foment of social reforms. She strongly backed Jane Addams's experimental Hull House and became a spokeswoman for the rights of working girls. In England and Europe, her efforts to build the imposing Women's Building for the famous World

Columbian Exposition in Chicago in 1893 won her the regard and cooperation of kings, prime ministers, duchesses, and princesses, many of whom, like the Prince of Wales (Edward VII), later became close friends. Yet she never shared the fawning awe over royalty so common in her social milieu. (She once sharply described a noted princess as "this bibulous representative of a degenerate monarch.") In her Gothic castle home on Lake Shore Drive she often entertained social reformers, temperance women, and labor leaders along with her gilded social guests.

But after her husband's death in 1902, Bertha found herself wearying of the taxing and artificial obligations of her social role. Still of radiant vitality and verve, she grew restless. Her solid Midwestern values and strenuous nature sent her searching for simpler, more basic modes of living and working. This she was to find in the wildlands of Sarasota.

"Here is heaven at last!" she exclaimed to her father as they pondered the shimmering beauty of Sarasota Bay. "It reminds me of the Bay of Naples." She absorbed every word as Edwards, a native, explained the topography and history of the area while they buggied over bumpy dirt roads. Cruising down Little Sarasota Bay, she was captivated with the tropical growth and huge Indian mounds around a small house at Osprey. Edwards told her he had the house and 13 acres listed for $13,000. Too high, she said. Edwards agreed. But later she went directly to the owner, Lawrence Jones, of Kentucky's Paul Jones whiskey family. Unable to bargain him down, she paid the $13,000. Later, with the purchase of additional acreage, this home, The Oaks, would become a show-place residence.

Edwards was not miffed over his commission loss on this sale. He and Lord profited generously from Mrs. Palmer's later acquisitions, although they found her to be a shrewd and astute bargainer, imbued with the strong tutoring of her late husband. She would buy 80,000 acres around Sarasota; at peak, including property in Tampa and Venice, her holdings would total 140,000 acres. Before purchasing 50,000 acres from her home south to Venice, where there was little transport access, she stipulated that Seaboard Air Line railroad would have to run a spur to her property. Nudged by pleas and pressure, wheels turned, and within 30 days SAL had a spur not only to Osprey but all the way to Venice.

Almost at once she put hundreds of area people to work—extending and remodeling her home, clearing woods and brush, laying out gardens and spacious landscapes, building seawalls and docks, and tending her large (1,300 acres) citrus grove. Her sons came down to be executives in her newly formed Sarasota-Venice Company. Her uncle, Benjamin Honore, came and built a colonnaded mansion, The Acacias, on top of an Indian mound overlooking the bay.

Publicity, such as picture layouts of Sarasota in the *Chicago Tribune*, was soon bringing in many Northern visitors, among them the John Ringlings. And the little town itself was coming alive as new hotels and lodges went up to accommodate the visitors. A small electric plant powered the first two street lights on Main Street. A water works and sewage system were installed. Seawalls went up, the Yacht Club was revived, a new bank opened. With workers being hired in batches of 300 at a time, supply soon fell short of demand and Mrs. Palmer began importing others—blacks, Italians, mixed races and nationalities. This would spark among some homesteaders a resentment that later led to friction and open clashes. But she also paid the highest wages along the seaboard, and, for now, local business coffers jingled with a new prosperity.

Always quick to inform herself, Bertha began studying every scientific and agricultural paper available on land and crops as well as consulting state field experts. Her citrus groves were soon thriving, and she began shipping boxcar loads of grapefruit to fellow Chicagoans. She next drained and irrigated large areas of muck eastward toward Bee Ridge for vegetable crops; her celery would later become a major local industry. But she met failure on one big venture—The Bee Ridge model farm development where 7,000 acres were sliced into 10-to-40-acre tracts. Local buyers found that the land did not come up to their expectations. Souring public disappointment plus meager sales prompted her to drop the project and move on to another.

Mrs. Palmer purchased three large ranches including 3,000 head of cattle to begin a model cattle ranch, Meadow Sweet Pastures, in the beautiful Myakka River region. She also built a ranch camp retreat at Upper Myakka Lake, with a power system and portable guest cottages. It was in this outdoor setting that she began to experience a new sense of freedom and exhilaration and of intimacy with the land and the ordinary people who worked for her, an intimacy that had eluded her in the ornate salons and drawing rooms of Chicago. Her able ranch manager, Albert Blackburn, and the new ranch hands generally found her to be relaxed, easy, and informal, eager to hear and take note of their needs or grievances. But troubles would come, too.

She started off with one mistake that made rival area ranchers laugh derisively. Unaware that in Florida cattle could graze year-round, she built silos. They laughed again when she constructed cement vats to dip her cattle for ticks, the age-old scourge of Florida cattle. Everyone knew that ticks originated inside cows, so how could you bathe them away? Smiles faded when all her cattle emerged tick-free. They were less than amused when she imported 17 Brahma bulls to infuse the scrawny Florida cow with new heft, and openly angry when she fenced in her ranch. The open range, however obsolete, was Florida custom.

By the time she shipped the first trainload of prize beef cattle ever to go out of the state, to Texas, they were furious.

At first, local woodsmen and rednecks were encouraged to cut her fences and kill some of her cows, but soon they were shooting up her property and assaulting and intimidating her black workers. These incidents always occurred after she left on trips out of the state. Mrs. Palmer began sending terse warning notes, one to the owner of a store where the marauders gathered at night. She would not have Sarasota returning to "the lawless Ku Klux era," and, while not wanting "to put any man in the chain gang," she kept up a frontal assault on both ranchers and townspeople until finally the harassment ceased.

She devised another grand project—a plan to make Venice a resort colony to surpass Palm Beach—but backed off after getting cost estimates that, even to her, seemed "staggering." Instead, she devoted most of her time to civic projects in Sarasota and organized and financed a women's group to continue them. In 1916, the year her father died at age 93, she learned she had cancer. She fought a losing two-year battle with the disease but remained active up to the last weeks before her death on May 5, 1918.

All of Sarasota turned out to mourn the lady who had been so often described as "the most elegant American woman of her day." They noted acutely and long remembered that such elegance had not prevented her from coming to a wilderness village, infusing it with new life and hope, and charting the course that would make it the unique and thriving resort community it is today.

37.
The Ordeal of Juan Ortiz

A 16th-century Spanish youth, captured by Tampa Bay Indians,
endures cruel torment until an Indian girl helps him escape.

Sixteenth-century Spanish explorers who were captured by Florida Indians usually endured painful deaths or else were held in permanent slavery; this is the story of one who survived a harrowing ordeal and escaped to tell of it.

In 1527, when Panfilo de Narvaez first explored the inland area around Tampa Bay, he encountered the tribe of the Indian cacique (chief) Hirrihigua with whom he first fought, then formed an uneasy friendship. But before sailing away from the region, the cruel and volatile Narvaez, after a fierce argument with Hirrihigua, resolved the matter by having the Indian's mother torn to pieces by dogs and then cutting off the nose of the cacique.

The bitter chieftain vowed to avenge the atrocity; some time later, his opportunity came. A stray Spanish patrol ship searching for Narvaez sailed into the bay. Hirrihigua contrived a clever ruse to lure four of the soldiers to shore by claiming to have a written message left by Narvaez. Once ashore, the four Spaniards were seized and bound; outnumbered, the ship's contingent quickly weighed anchor and sailed away.

Shortly after, during a ritual feast day, Hirrihigua celebrated by having three of the soldiers stripped naked and forced to run back and forth in the village plaza while Indians shot arrows at them—only a few at a time so as to prolong the execution over many hours. But when it came time to bring out the fourth captive, 18-year-old Juan Ortiz, the cacique's wife and three daughters, noting the boy's tender age and the fact that he was not of Narvaez's group and therefore guiltless, pleaded with the chief to spare the youth such a cruel death and, instead, keep him as a slave. Reluctantly, the cacique consented.

But in the months ahead, Ortiz came almost to envy his dead companions. He was forced to work to exhaustion at hard manual tasks; the Indians struck and whipped him almost daily; and, on feast days, he was forced to run around the plaza from sunup to sundown, with the threat of arrows if he faltered. At such a day's end, more dead than alive, the youth was ministered to by the chief's wife and daughters, whose aid alone helped him to sustain life.

Still, every time Hirrihigua reached up to scratch the air where his nose once was, his fury against the Spanish burned anew. He decided, finally, to have Ortiz roasted alive. For this, a wooden grill-like structure was mounted over a bed of hot embers and Ortiz was tied to the framework. Overwhelmed by the shrieks of the wretched victim, the wife and daughters first pleaded with and then began scolding their lord for his cruelty. Once more, the cacique relented. The women removed the youth from the rack, but only after many days of treatment with the juices of herbs did Ortiz recover. His back remained a snarled mass of deforming scars.

Now wanting his captive at least out of sight, the chief assigned him 24-hour guard duty at the cemetery a mile from the village. A fiery death penalty awaited the captive if any foraging animal disturbed the corpses in their crude, above-ground coffins. Ortiz was greatly relieved to be out of the village. But one night the exhausted youth dozed off and was suddenly awakened by a noise. Investigating, he discovered that the body of a recently deceased child had been dragged from its box. Frantically, he ran down a forest trail to find the culprit. Soon he heard a faint gnawing sound and stopped. Unable to see in the thick darkness, he took one of the heavy darts furnished him and hurled it with all his strength in the direction of the sound. The gnawing noise stopped, and Ortiz waited in suspense for the dawn's light.

At daybreak, he was exultant when he spotted the child's remains alongside the lifeless body of a large panther, the dart almost embedded in its entrails. Returning the corpse to its chest, he dragged the beast back to the village. The Indians were amazed at Ortiz's feat; to them, killing a "lion" was one of the highest deeds of valor. The cacique's family and villagers now held Ortiz in such esteem that, for a while, the chief ceased to harass the youth and assigned to him less exhausting tasks.

But Hirrihigua's obsessive hatred was too strong. He decided he could not rest until Ortiz was dead and forever out of his sight. Informing his wife and daughters of his intentions to execute Ortiz in the same way as his companions, he told them not to dare intercede in the matter again. His anger carried such seething finality that the women accepted the decision without argument. Ortiz's fate seemed sealed.

But the chief's eldest daughter, whose compassion for the youth's plight had not wavered, was emboldened to carry out a plan of her own, albeit at some personal risk. A few days before the scheduled fateful day, she secretly informed Ortiz of her father's decision and told him of her plan for his escape. A certain Chief Mucozo, head of a village some 25 miles north of her own, loved her and desired to wed her. While the village slept that same night, Ortiz was to meet one of her trusted Indian friends and be guided to a bridge, from whence he would make his way alone on the trail to Mucozo's village. He was to tell the chief that he, Ortiz, came in her name and that she trusted the cacique to care for his needs. At this, the youth fell at the maiden's feet with tears of gratitude and swore to follow her plan faithfully. The plan succeeded without hitch, and, by dawn the next day, a jubilant Ortiz walked into Mucozo's village.

The 28-year-old chieftain, whose generous, kind, and honorable disposition contrasted sharply with Hirrihigua's, heard out the youth's story, observed his scar-ridden body, and, also mindful of his beloved's entreaties, vowed to give Ortiz care and asylum.

Learning of his slave's refuge, Hirrihigua made repeated demands for Ortiz's return, but Mucozo, disgusted by the treatment the youth had undergone, angrily reminded his antagonist of Florida tribal laws permitting asylum for abused or mistreated subjects. Even threat of the loss of Hirrihigua's daughter would not move the stalwart chieftain. And for more than eight years after, Ortiz and Mucozo developed the closest of friendships; the chief honored him as a brother and appointed him as tribal chamberlain.

Thus, after 10 years among the Floridians, Ortiz took a sad farewell of the village upon the arrival in Tampa Bay of Hernando de Soto in May, 1539. De Soto recruited Ortiz as an interpreter for his gold-seeking expedition up the Florida coast.

But that long bitter journey yielded not gold but hardship, Indian wars, fevers, and decimating casualties; doubtless there were many times when Ortiz thought longingly of the beautiful maiden who had effected his miraculous survival and escape and of the peaceful, idyllic years he led with his Indian brother, Mucozo. For after crossing the Great River (Mississippi), Ortiz—along with many of his company, including de Soto himself—died of fever in the winter of 1542.

38.
The Foiled Plot to Steal Florida

*A French-born revolutionary veteran scuttles government
intrigue in a plot to seize Florida from Spain.*

Covert operations by one nation against another are not a strictly modern
phenomenon. For centuries the Borgias, Metternichs, and Talleyrands honed
the practice into consummate statecraft.

But America's first venture into this dubious antonym of diplomacy—the
1812 plot to pry Florida away from the colonial clutches of Spain—ended up
like an early version of the Bay of Pigs. The operation had every chance of
success, but it became tangled in a duel of wills between the special agent in
charge of the plan and a stubborn French-born U.S. Army major. It was a case
of Gallic idealism versus frontier *realpolitik*. Surprisingly, the former prevailed.

Spain in 1812, struggling to throw off a Napoleonic dictatorship, held a
tenuous grip on its two Floridas, East and West, and had no desire to part with
this strategic safeguard for its colonial commerce in Latin America. Nonetheless, the United States was anxious to acquire this "natural Southeastern U.S.
border" where many Americans, by Spanish invitation, already had settled.
After President James Madison failed to acquire West Florida through a combination of intrigue and diplomacy in 1810, he turned his attention to East
Florida. In January, 1811, he won secret authorization from Congress to invade
and occupy either of the Floridas on two conditions—namely, if "patriot"
settlers in either Florida declared their independence from Spanish authority and
requested U.S. support; or, if a foreign power threatened to invade the territories.

In June, 1811, Madison sent George Mathews as a special secret agent to
St. Mary's, Georgia, North Florida's border on the St. Mary's River, to organize
a "patriot" revolution in East Florida.

Crusty, impulsive, and rough-hewn, the 72-year-old Mathews had been a
Revolutionary War officer, twice Georgia's governor, a U.S. congressman, and
a Georgia militia general (he retained the latter title). At St. Mary's, Mathews
shared a summer cottage with another Revolutionary War veteran, U.S. Army
Major Jacinte Laval, who, in the temporary absence of the regular commander,
Lieutenant Colonel Thomas Smith, was acting commander over 200 regular
troops at nearby Point Petre. Laval had left his native France full of ideals about

liberty and "inalienable rights," and he fought and was wounded in the American struggle. Later, he married and settled his family in South Carolina. But when England once more threatened war, he reenlisted and rose to the rank of major.

Despite their proximity to each other, Mathews and Laval rarely spoke. The general was preoccupied day and night with trying to recruit Florida settlers into the "Patriots of East Florida" who would first revolt against Spanish authority and then request U.S. support. Mathews' secret instructions, sent also to the absent Lieutenant Colonel Smith, authorized him to apply for U.S. Army or naval assistance as needed. (Neither Laval nor Commodore Hugh Campbell, who commanded five U.S. gunboats near the mouth of the St. Mary's River, received any such secret instructions.)

Through the thin partition of their rooms, Laval was often kept awake nights by the intense discussions Mathews held with the settlers, urging them to join the "patriots" and promising them large free land grants and choice offices in a new government. The major was disgusted by what he heard.

The settlers, mostly planters, were sympathetic to U.S. annexation but balked at risking their prosperity in a revolution that might fail. By March, 1812, Mathews had nine Floridians, to be led by John Houstoun McIntosh, and some 70 Georgia militiamen organized as "patriots." U.S. aid could now be "officially" sought. The huge Fort Castillo de San Marcos at St. Augustine was in much disrepair (its main gate especially) and poorly defended, with fewer than 100 men.

Mathews planned a surprise Monday morning attack, which he believed could not fail. Therefore, the general was furious when Laval refused Mathews' request for cartridges and some 140 regular troops for the assault.

"Do you dare defy the orders of the President of the United States?" stormed Mathews. Replied Laval: "I have unbounded respect for the President and his wishes, but I have no orders to obey an unauthorized command. My orders are to hold and defend East Florida, as you say, when offered by the local authorities. These orders don't bind me to use troops to cause a revolution in [Florida]." Mathews calmed himself. "Major Laval, you fought for our freedoms in the revolution. I did.... We are all men of '76. You've seen my commission, you have your orders."

"General Mathews," Laval answered, "I fought for your American freedom, but I didn't leave my native land so that avaricious men could grab land by debasing the ideals of '76," adding that he did not refer to the general but to his associates as avaricious. "I see the advantage of acquiring Florida, but by negotiation, not by intrigue and theft." Mathews then shouted: "I tell you that it is authorized by the President!" "It is not!" Laval exclaimed. "And you, sir, I order to leave my post. I am in command here. I do not want you to set foot here again."

Mathews stomped away in anger muttering later to his secretary, Ralph Isaacs, about "that . . . Frenchman." But the general, through messages conveyed by Isaacs, kept pressuring Laval until the weary major finally consented to let him have 40 men. But they would have to "volunteer as a regular detachment of the U.S. Army." Aware the he could not endanger the friendly power and neutrality status between the United States and Spain by having U.S. troops officially participate in such a covert project, Mathews informed Laval that the troops should volunteer as individuals in the "patriot" army. Laval exploded, declaring that he was being asked, in effect, to let his men "abandon their post" to fight against a friendly state. The order for 40 men was thereby canceled.

Mathews, now desperate, decided to foment a mutiny against Laval using several disgruntled officers whom he directed, through Isaacs, to draw up some official charges against the major, specifics of which ranged from borrowing money and not repaying it to committing adultery with a soldier's wife. Carefully omitted was the disputed issue of the use of troops.

Laval promptly arrested one of the more abusive officers and then set 50 of his most loyal men to prevent any of the soldiers from leaving the post to join with the "patriots." Meanwhile, Lieutenant Colonel Smith returned and placed Laval under technical house arrest until he, Smith, could learn more about the "charges" and the nature of the imbroglio generally.

By this time, however, Mathews and his patriots had invaded and occupied Fernandina on Amelia Island and then marched on to St. Augustine. But here they faced a repaired and reinforced fort—Governor Estrada having been forewarned by the Fernandina attack. The governor refused to even confer with the "patriots," and they languished in camp at old Fort Mose two miles away. Commodore Campbell had also refused to bring his gunboats into the St. Johns River, and, although Lieutenant Colonel Smith would later join the "patriots" with some of his Point Petre troops, only substantial aid and reinforcement from the United States could now make the operation succeed.

But as the War of 1812 (declared that June) loomed against England over maritime violations against U.S. ships, an uneasy Congress refused to support Madison in Florida. On April 4, Madison was forced to repudiate Mathews and revoke his "special agent" powers. The "patriots" movement gradually disintegrated thereafter and the disheartened general died at his home the following August.

Nothing ever came of the "charges" against Laval (presumably they were mostly fabricated). He had written earlier to the U.S. Secretary of War requesting a transfer, preferably as far away from Mathews as possible. He was given a command on the Canadian frontier and later became a full colonel. He died at his home in 1822. But he never believed for a moment that his "hero" of the Revolution, President Madison, would have approved the covert operation in Florida. Despite Mathews, the men of '76 just wouldn't do such things.

39.
Dr. Adamo, Reluctant Hero

From a teenage Ybor City cigar-roller, Dr. Adamo rose to fame
as a medical hero when Japan invaded the Philippines.

The blow to his head from the flat side of the rifle butt, swung by the Japanese guard, only stunned him briefly; he remained conscious.

He had forgotten the smoking rules. Lately his thinking had become "befuddled," and he simply did not care much about anything, even the rumors, always the rumors, about bombings, landings, troops coming. He was convinced anyway that he would not last that long. And so, as the hunger gnawed incessantly at his disease-wracked, 90-pound frame, he fantasized about food—a favorite pasta dish of spaghetti, veal, and chicken, or a thick steak.

But Lieutenant Colonel Dr. Frank S. Adamo, the physician hero of Bataan and Corregidor in the Philippines during World War II, written up by *Time, Life,* and other media for developing a life-saving treatment for gangrene, would survive and return to a hero's welcome in his native Tampa. This son of Sicilian immigrants had come a long way from a childhood view of the future that seemed to stretch no further than the tip of a cigar, or the number of them he could roll in a lifetime.

Frank Adamo was born on January 20, 1893, to Giuseppe and Maria Adamo in the colorful immigrant community of Ybor City in East Tampa. Hundreds of Cubans, Afro-Cubans, Spaniards, and Italians had left other lands and come to Tampa, transforming the sleepy village into a thriving cigar-making industrial city. Like many other immigrant children, Adamo dropped out of school early and began to roll cigars. The Havana stogies seemed to be the measure of young Frank's future until one day the 17-year-old chanced to read the biography of a noted Canadian doctor. This so fired Adamo's ambition that in April, 1911, he set off with two friends for Chicago.

Working days in a cigar factory and studying nights, the diligent youth earned his high school diploma within two years. He also learned English. Still working, he studied first at Chicago's Rush Medical Institute and finished his senior year at Loyola School of Medicine. An intern by 1919, he met and married a nurse, Euphemia, a native of Scotland. The couple soon moved to Tampa, where Adamo opened practice in the heart of Ybor's "Little Italy" on Seventh Avenue.

Among the numerous mutual aid societies formed by the Latin community, its system of collective medicine, begun in 1888, was the most popular and progressive. Clubs such as El Centro Asturiano and El Centro Espanol, contracting with doctors, provided cigar workers and their families with complete medical care, plus other benefits, for $1.50 a month or less. The system prospered. In 1906, when Tampa's city hospital was merely a run-down facility in an old abandoned building, El Centro Espanol had built a modern, three-story brick hospital on Bayshore Boulevard (today a school). But the Hillsborough County Medical Society fumed about "socialistic" and "radical" medicine and threatened to expel or "blacklist" any doctor who contracted to serve the Latin societies. "I didn't think it was right," Adamo recalled. "We [doctors] couldn't even go to the hospitals [Espanol and Asturiano] then." But the intense pressures and threats forced some doctors, including Adamo, to return solely to private practice. He returned to Chicago for a while to study medical specialties and in the late 1930s was appointed surgeon for the county hospital in Tampa.

But, as historian Gary Mormino notes, collective medicine under auspices of the societies flourished throughout the 1920s, 1930s, and 1940s.

Long an Army reservist, Adamo was called up as a lieutenant colonel in 1940 to practice a more acceptable form of collective medicine in the U.S. Army Medical Corps. Then in May, 1941, he was ordered to Camp McKinley near Manila in the Philippine Islands.

When the Japanese invaded the Philippines 24 hours after Pearl Harbor, the toll of U.S. and Filipino casualties on Bataan and then on Corregidor Island in Manila Bay kept doctors, including Adamo, toiling night and day. As in World War I, the fatality count from gas gangrene, caused by anaerobic bacilli, soared. Amputation was usually the sole remedy. But clearly this was no solution when, in the early Bataan days, Adamo had a chest gangrene case. With time critical, the physician decided on a bold experiment. He knew the gangrene bacillus could not live in the open air, and so, with extensive incisions, he split the infected muscles wide open, sprinkled them with sulfa drugs, and left the wound undressed, irrigating it every hour with peroxide. The wound healed, and the man recovered, as did nearly every case treated in that manner thereafter.

The story of this "miracle" breakthrough was splashed in the American press along with a famous photo of the shirtless doctor performing surgery in the field. *Time* and *Life* magazines hailed a "hero of Bataan," and, in a book, writer John Hersey praised the "slight, grayish doctor" for saving countless limbs and lives.

Adamo got the first glimpse of his captors when Corregidor fell on May 6, 1942. Their sight came as "a shock" to Adamo. Still, he continued with his exhausting caseload and even performed appendectomies on two Japanese patients at the request of a somewhat inept Japanese surgeon. The latter felt grateful enough to give Adamo a can of peaches. Moved later to the old Bilibid prison in Manila, where he shared a large room with some 55 other officers, Adamo had become so weakened by bacillus dysentery that he could no longer work.

The meager diet, made up mainly of rice dished up three times a day, afflicted the prisoners with numerous diseases—dysentery, pellagra, and especially beriberi, which gave Adamo severe optic neuritis. His poor eyesight was not helped when he accidentally sat on and broke his only pair of glasses. The Japanese replaced them with a deficient pair. By the second year of captivity, the doctor's weight had fallen from 160 to 90 pounds.

The boredom, illness, and unrelieved hunger were broken several times when Red Cross packages came through, especially one with badly needed vitamins, another with Spam and cheese. Adamo rationed out his portion of this latter "luxury" over four months. But as Adamo's condition weakened, he said his mind "began to get befuddled and I just didn't care much about anything." False rumors of U.S. troop landings proliferated, but Adamo was convinced that even if he survived he would be shipped off to Japan as had many other prisoners. Now and then they received a few cheap Filipino cigarettes. Smoking rules were rigid, and when Adamo strayed one day out of the smoking area, a Japanese guard struck his head with a rifle butt. "It shook me but didn't knock me out," Adamo recalled.

Finally, in the third year, one rumor came true. General MacArthur landed on Leyte and on February 3, 1945, retook Manila. The day of liberation "seemed unbelievable" to Adamo as American troops poured into the prison. Prisoners shouted or wept with joy, but Adamo said he only felt numb. He recalled a big sergeant half-carrying him to a table for "nothing fancy...but the most wonderful food I will ever eat."

At homecoming in Tampa that April, a "Dr. Adamo Day" parade was held in his honor. Recalling all the men who didn't return, the diffident doctor implored friends to keep "all this to-do" simple. Later, he did fulfill a recurrent prison fantasy; he shared with a friend their favorite dish of spaghetti, veal, and chicken. Hours later, he had the steak.

Adamo was awarded the U.S. Legion of Merit, and other honors followed. Tampa's First Avenue (State Road 60) was renamed Adamo Drive, and later a plaque on the Franklin Street Mall cited him.

Thus from uncertain cigarmaking days to medical crossfires to the long ordeal as a prisoner of war, Frank Adamo had been a survivor. He would also survive to the venerable age of 95. He died in Tampa on June 24, 1988.

War and Peace

40.
Politics Past: From Warts to Images

From its earthy, colorful past, Florida politics evolves into a bland, homogenous puff of dueling images.

Gov. Fuller Warren—An atypical politician.

Another political season is upon us, and while it may not be the time of the cuckoo, some might almost wish it were as they contemplate the sheeny, but bland, almost antiseptic aura that has come to define modern campaigning.

Was it always so? Have we swapped principles for pablum; warts, flesh, and blood for images? Are we more civilized today or merely more homogenized?

Such questions arise on reviewing the colorful vitality that was Florida's political past. It had passion, comedy, tragedy, idealism, and demagoguery. But it was never dull. It simply projected a raw human conflict that knew nothing of the "state of the art." Examples abound with spangled diversity.

Consider, for example, the curious amalgam of cosmopolite and homespun Cracker that was Governor Fuller Warren (1948-52). Here was a populist Porkchopper who assailed the Porkchop Gang, a silver-tongued Elizabethan orator, at ease in backwoods or drawing rooms, who imbued state politics with joy and zest even as he seriously tackled the titans of "special interest"—and often won. He was atypical; he could laugh at himself. He once wrote a whimsical book on how to win in politics wherein he advised candidates to "speak loudly" and "gesticulate wildly"; strike poses, such as "fists clenched, arms outstretched, head thrown back, and eyes toward heaven," a position that carries "the subtle suggestion of receiving inspiration from above." Again: "Use many adjectives. Never use a lone adjective where 10 can be crowded in" since your goal is "sound, not sense." "Don't just call an opponent 'a mean man.' Fulminate in stentorian tones that 'he is a snarling, snapping, hissing monstrosity.'"

155

Warren's levity might have been useful a century earlier when the infamous Code Duello was invoked to settle issues. Two Tallahasseans—Augustus Alston, a Whig leader and prominent planter, and Leigh Read, Democrat leader and a rising political star—were immersed in heated controversy over banking reforms; Read was for them, Alston opposed. When Alston, an expert duelist, challenged Read, and the latter accepted, his supporters considered Read a doomed man. But Read had shrewdly picked rare hair-trigger rifles for weapons. The hasty, hot-tempered Alston turned and fired too soon, off center. Read carefully fired one fatal bullet. Later, Alston's brother, Willis, fatally shot Read in the back as the latter strolled down a street. This, in turn, led to Willis's violent death later in Texas.

In turbulent Reconstruction days in the late 1860s, Republican Governor Harrison Reed had a shaky tenure. At one time, his own lieutenant governor, William Gleason, tried to seize the governorship by occupying Reed's office in the latter's absence. A loyal aide ousted Gleason at gunpoint. But Gleason supporters harassed Reed, fired shots at his home, and once hired a notorious gunman, Luke Lott, to assassinate Reed. Learning of the plot, planter and future governor William Bloxham persuaded Lott, by one means or other, to drop his plan. Reed also survived repeated attempts to impeach him. When his term ended, he had successfully held a fragile government together, guiding it into less stormy waters.

The 1890s were anything but gay in Jacksonville politics. Conservative forces had recently won an election by registering residents of local cemeteries, a move that tripled the town's voting population overnight. By next election, Duval County Sheriff Napoleon B. Broward moved to halt this practice by placing lawmen-inspectors at every polling place. Broward, a Progressive, acted in defiance of conservative Governor Henry L. Mitchell, who earlier had forbidden this monitoring. Using an obscure legal technicality, Mitchell removed Broward from office. But the sheriff ousted his replacement in the next election and went on to become a governor himself.

For sheer demagoguery, Governor Sidney Catts (1916-20) had no peer in Florida's past. He helped to feed, and then inflame, the virulent anti-Catholic bigotry of the time. Catts often carried two guns in either pocket at speech stops, hinting darkly of "Romanish" plots to kill him. He was perhaps the only governor ever to carry a gun to his own inauguration.

The practice of heckling flourished in earlier days. Once Governor John W. Martin (1924-28) faced a zealous Catts supporter (Catts was running a second time) who would repeatedly interrupt Martin's speech with: "Hurray for Catts!" While ignoring the heckler, Martin paused and remarked to the crowd on how people gave their support to Catts in 1916 on Catts's promise "to run the Pope out of business." But did Catts keep his promise? "No. While he was governor ... one Pope died and he [Catts] let them appoint another without raising a finger to stop it." It silenced his detractor.

Speaking in Miami one night, another candidate heard a heckler trying to identify the candidate with a group known as "Little Tammany." At every pause by the speaker, the heckler shouted: "You're a stooge for Little Tammany." Finally the candidate turned toward the voice and retorted: "You thought Little Tammany was all right when they got your nephew out of prison." Of course, there was no nephew, and the candidate could not even see the heckler. But the crowd did not know this—or care. The heckler was laughed out of the park.

Often a single issue or a single error could make or break a candidate. Governor Doyle Carlton (1928-32), running against state road board chairman Fons Hathaway, hit pay dirt with the discovery of a repair bill for rear-end work on a road department Ford truck, a bill totaling more than the cost of the truck when it was brand new. With a platform decrying waste in government, Carlton rode the rear end of that Ford truck into the governor's mansion.

In 1931, political pundits were asking: What is a nice Jewish boy from Brooklyn, New York (via Daytona Beach), David Sholtz, doing in a Florida gubernatorial race against seven formidable native-son candidates? "They'll cut him up like fish bait," the seers agreed. But Sholtz, in low-key style, had an infectious self-confidence and conveyed personal warmth and sincerity. While the big boys attacked each other, Sholtz stuck to the hard Depression-year issues; people sensed a fresh face among the old-line machine politicos, and the pundits were baffled when he finished in second place in the first primary. In top place, former governor John W. Martin took another look at this dark horse and became desperate. Martin even wrote to Germany to get depositions attesting to the Jewish origin of Sholtz's immigrant parents. This offended even the Bible Belt Crackers that he, Martin, sought to inflame. Sholtz won the race handily and was finally elected by the biggest majority in history up to that time.

But the Big Smear could also be effective at times. Powerful interests in Florida were out to unseat U.S. Senator Claude Pepper in the 1950 race. They picked candidate George Smathers, the smooth-as-oil "Golden Hatchetman." Speaking to rural Cracker crowds, Smathers would, for example, lower his voice and solemnly intone: "Are you aware that Claude Pepper is known all over Washington as a shameless extrovert? Not only that, but this man is reliably reported to practice nepotism with his sister-in-law, and he has a sister who was once a thespian in wicked New York. Worst of all, it is an established fact that Mr. Pepper, before his marriage, practiced celibacy." In fairness, this episode must remain apocryphal since both a Pepper spokesman and Smathers deny its occurrence. Smathers informed the author that the story was the whimsical concoction of a certain press club. Such tactics, enforced with a rather sordid "red-baiting" campaign, put Smathers over and in by 60,000 votes.

Admittedly, the "warts, flesh, and blood" campaigning of yesteryear harbored excesses that we might gladly, and rightly, forego today. Nevertheless, the fluid banality of the modern scene—diversionary forays into "mom and apple pie" issues to the exclusion of hard, critical issues, the obsessive cultivation of images instead of ideas—often tend to induce a stifling vacuum and an indifferent electorate. In such a time, it is easy to understand the nostalgic yearning to swap the era of "hype" for a few tree stumps and a fiery debate or two.

41.
Almost the State's First Town

*Pensacola, not St. Augustine, almost became America's oldest
city when explorer Tristan de Luna tried to colonize it.*

Well before Roanoke and Jamestown were founded, and even before St.
Augustine was fully settled, Pensacola Bay was an object of European interest
in America.

Few are aware that this "fine jewel" of a natural, deep water harbor was
once a coveted fulcrum in the perilous New World, the prize in a fight pitting
France and Spain in a race for Gulf Coast hegemony. A different outcome easily
might have meant the state would come to be called Le Fleur instead of La
Florida.

By the late 17th century, the once powerful kingdom of Spain was in
decline. The costs of maintaining a lavish empire had depleted the great wealth
garnered from New Spain (Mexico, Peru and the West Indies). Moreover,
Dutch, French, and English pirates had long infested the Spanish Main, harassing and even capturing ships in Spain's gold and silver fleets. Spain had even
lost Caribbean strongholds like Jamaica, the Lesser Antilles, and parts of the
Dominican Republic. Compounding Spain's woes were numerous wars, a
still-primitive and stagnated economy and the rule of an imbecilic king, Charles
II. More than ever, Spain's 17th-century existence depended on her expansion
in America. Any threat to New Spain was thus a threat to the entire kingdom.
And by the 1680s, such a threat began to loom with menace.

For years Spain had viewed the vast unsettled and unexplored inlands of
the Mississippi Valley and the Gulf Coast as a comfortable buffer zone against
foreign encroachment in New Spain's northeastern periphery. She further had
an interest in the region because Spaniards were the first to discover, and settle,
a spot on this uncharted northern coast, a place called Panzacola by the Indians.
The Miruelos and Pineda Indians were probably the first to discover the
beautiful harbor in 1519, followed by Panfilo de Narvaez in 1528. Hernando de
Soto's fleet commander, Cristobal Maldonado, spent the winter of 1539-40
there and tried, unsuccessfully, to convince the king to make it a major supply
port. In 1558, Tristan de Luna settled a colony of 1,500 at Pensacola, exclaiming
to King Philip II, "It is the best port in the Indies!" But after two years of

hardships, capped by a hurricane that all but destroyed the colony, it was abandoned. Spain forgot about Pensacola and Florida for the next 124 years.

In 1682 French explorer Robert Cavelier de La Salle pushed south from the Great Lakes, journeyed down the Mississippi River, and discovered its mouth. He then claimed the entire river valley for Louis XIV, naming it Louisiana. La Salle also announced that he would settle and fortify a major port on the river's mouth. Louis XIV had long had designs on New Spain. Here now would be a dagger poised directly at the Spanish empire, which stretched from Florida to Mexico City.

Wary and on guard, Spain watched—but nothing more was heard of La Salle or his plans for several years. In fact, La Salle had returned to France where, in greatest secrecy, the king had outfitted him with four ships and 300 colonists. In July, 1684, La Salle's party sailed for the Caribbean. Spain would not learn of this except by chance in 1686. A French youth captured on a pirate ship near Vera Cruz explained how he had deserted an expedition under a man named "Monsieur de Salas" who was bound for a place called "Micipipi." Her direst fears confirmed, Spain acted fast to "pluck out the thorn that had been thrust into the heart of America." For almost four years, with no less than 11

Pensacola and harbor at the time of the French-Spanish War in the 1760s.

expeditions, she unsuccessfully scoured the Gulf Coast in search of the French. She finally learned of the colony's location and fate in 1690 from a handful of its survivors. La Salle had sailed far past his Mississippi destination and landed instead at Matagorda Bay in Texas. For two years, the colonists fruitlessly searched for the Mississippi by land; their last ship had been wrecked. Slowly they were decimated by hunger and disease. A mutinous soldier assassinated La Salle, and hostile Indians killed most of the remaining colonists.

By now, Spain was on full alert; there would be other La Salles. Besides, during her search for the French, Spain had rediscovered "the magnificent" harbor of Panzacola which New Spain viceroy Conde de Galve and naval captain Andres de Pez urged the king to occupy and fortify at once. The famous Mexican mathematician, Siguenza y Gongora, who personally charted and mapped the bay, called it "the finest jewel possessed by his Majesty." It was spacious, landlocked, eight to 10 fathoms deep, and surrounded with abundant pine and oak timber for shipbuilding; nearby were bounteous supplies of fresh water, fish, and game. Most importantly, it was of critical strategic value to the defense of the entire Gulf Coast. Gongora warned, prophetically, that King Louis would quickly occupy this "excellent harbor" if Spain did not. The Spanish king quickly decreed its occupation in 1694, but, for lack of funds, the project lay in limbo for several years until, once more, the indolent court was galvanized into action on learning of another French expedition being prepared for the Gulf. This time, the famous Spanish naval officer Andres d'Arriola was quickly dispatched to Pensacola with three ships and 357 men in late 1698. Hastily assembled and scantily equipped with provisions, the fleet had barely set up fortification before an encounter with the French.

On the morning of January 26, 1699, the firing of five cannons announced the arrival of three large French war frigates and two ketches near the harbor's entrance. In response, d'Arriola fired three cannon shots and quickly prepared his men for attack. But nothing happened. The next morning a French launch came ashore to request entrance to the harbor to secure wood and water. In the manners of the day, lavish compliments were exchanged between hosts and visitors while d'Arriola politely informed them that, under his king's orders, no foreign vessels could be permitted entrance to the harbor. The French commander Marquis de Chasteaumorant next sent d'Arriola a formal note citing the friendly relations then existing between the two countries and the great "personal esteem" he held for the Spaniard. He wanted only a little wood and water and he would be on his way. Fully aware of the ruse, d'Arriola lamented in reply how "it grieves me exceedingly" to have to refuse the request. Later, d'Arriola ordered the French away at cannon point. The French set up a garrison on Mobile

Bay, then entered the Mississippi River and built a fort at Biloxi. Had the North Florida bay been captured at that particular time, there would have been no stopping the French from penetrating the heart of Florida and also threatening Mexico and the Caribbean. Despite brief wars and skirmishes, Spain would control Pensacola Bay for more than another two centuries.

Even today, the indelible marks of Spanish culture pervade the city of Pensacola—in her ancient Spanish "creole" families and relaxed lifestyle, her architecture, and her street names—while the bay itself still reminds Pensacolans of their place in American history.

42.
When Tobacco was King

Florida's economy almost sank after financial panic and falling cotton prices, but the golden tobacco leaf came to its rescue.

Tobacco, hailed by early English courtiers as "that bewitching vegetable," once played a distinctive role in Florida's development by rescuing and stabilizing the state's entire economy.

For a golden era spanning nearly two decades, the "bewitching" leaf became an economic mainstay for both rich and poor alike. And across the rolling hills and hummocks of North Florida—which then *was* Florida—tobacco, not cotton, was king. Buyers from as far away as Europe poured into the state to purchase tons of the curiously spotted, silky, mahogany-colored leaf, and it became the world's most prized cigar wrapper. Farmers could not grow it fast enough as they planted it into every inch of soil they owned—even the front yard.

The tobacco boom came at no more propitious time, following on successive economic calamities: the national financial panic in 1837-38, the collapse of Florida's Union Bank, and a lingering depression in the cotton market. And it would end only with the advent of the Civil War.

Tobacco had always been native to Florida, but it took a curiously long and circuitous route into its economy. Europeans had never seen such a plant until Christopher Columbus learned of how the West Indian natives "drank smoke." Marveling, the explorer later wrote of how the Indians "perfume themselves with certain herbs." Later, the English privateer John Hawkins, visiting the French Huguenots on the St. Johns River in 1564, observed of the Indians there: "The Floridians when they travail have a kind of herb dried, who with cane and an earthen cup on the end, with fyre and dried herbs put together, do suck through the cane the smoke thereof, which smoke satisfieth hunger, and therewith do live four or five days without food or drink."

Hawkins took a packet of the "curious herb" back to England. Later, a fascinated Sir Walter Raleigh got hooked on the weed, and he introduced smoking as an acceptable vice. In fact, he learned to plant and cure the leaf and soon had most of the Elizabethan Court puffing away.

The Spanish in Cuba were the first to plant tobacco as a cash crop, but its

163

commercial cultivation in Florida came much later, largely at the instigation of the first territorial governor, William P. Duval.

While cotton was king elsewhere in the South, it didn't always cotton to the stubborn clay soil of North Florida. True, some planters thrived, but too many others were plagued by crop failures. A stable and dependable cash crop was urgently needed. Governor Duval believed that Florida's non-calcareous (limestone) soil was ideally suited to some tobacco leaf varieties, and in 1828 he introduced some Cuban seeds and encouraged farmers to plant it. They did, and initial production proved profitable. Tobacco was soon hailed as the coming crop, and, in deference to the governor, the first leaves were named "Little Duval." Planting expanded across the state, and the high and rolling little North Florida town of Quincy, in Gadsden County, became the center of the tobacco culture.

But the coming boom almost became a bust. After several years of "Little Duval" crops, the ultra-sensitive plant began acquiring unusual characteristics. Strange varieties began to appear, such as a very dark narrow leaf that one planter termed in flavor "third-rate Havana." Another crop produced a larger, brighter-colored leaf whose taste was labeled "insipid and flavorless." A third variety produced a silkier, broader leaf, mahogany in color and curiously but attractively spotted. But over the years, buyers became put off by these chameleon-like mutations, and this final spotty leaf was called just another "useless hybrid." By 1840, the state's tobacco market was becoming as shaky as one of its leaves in a strong wind. The "useless hybrid" was about to save it.

Some growers believed that the speckled leaf had a singular value and quality of its own, but they weren't quite sure what it was. And so, in 1842, acting more on hunch than hard knowledge, grower Arthur J. Forman, of the firm of Forman and Muse, shipped a whole cargo of the leaf to cigar makers in Bremen, Germany. For weeks they waited anxiously. Then came the reply. Yes, Bremen was delighted with the shipment. Yes, the leaf is an ideal cigar wrapper. Yes, we want more. Forman then sent a similar shipment to New York. It sold out at premium prices. The boom was on.

By the time the next year's crop rolled around, both European and Northern buyers were flocking into Quincy and the surrounding area to buy all the spotted leaf they could. Farmers were relocating their outhouses just to plant every square inch of soil they owned. And they couldn't grow it fast enough. The soil was ideal: no fertilizers, chemical or animal, were needed. A visiting reporter wrote: "Everybody here is going into the tobacco culture, which requires no machinery, and the poorest can engage it." True enough. An outlay of only $13 for the Havana seed could bring a return of up to $700. There were no Jeeter

Lesters on this Tobacco Road.

The aftereffects of the earlier financial panic, the Union Bank failure, and the depressed cotton market only gave sharper impetus to the boom. Not unexpectedly, bumper crops poured forth in the following years, and farmers were forced to cut back production by a third—500 pounds of good leaf to an acre—to work it off. Production had jumped from 75,000 pounds in 1839 to 998,000 pounds in 1849. But the boom continued right up through the 1850s; never was the general prosperity so equitably infused throughout the state, sweeping up the poorest dirt farmer along with the high-scale planter. Over a span of two decades, the "iniquitous weed" literally sustained the state's economy.

So prized was the leaf that wrapper growers elsewhere in the country even tried to imitate the spotted leaf by a chemical process. They got the spots right—but they also got holes in the leaf. They quickly let nature have it back.

By 1860, when production peaked at 1.2 million pounds, the long, lush, rich years seemed to some observers too good to be true. By the following year they were right. One of the first casualties of the Civil War's devastation was the spotted leaf. In the general ruin, the seed practically disappeared. There was barely enough stock for consumption, and, through the 1870s, growers struggled desperately to bring back the golden prewar days. But the crops were lean at best, and as spotty as the famous leaf.

The fatal blow to "spotty" came from cigar makers early in the 1880s, who began gauging a gradual shift in smoking customs. The capricious winds of consumer preference were definitely leaning to a much darker cigar wrapper. By the mid-1880s, hard market statistics convinced the makers. Spotty was out; it had to go. Its growth was discouraged everywhere, and the darker plants of Cuba and Sumatra were now in. Wrapper growers gradually switched cultivation as the darker leaves began pouring into the market.

The swelling dark-leaf tide soon engulfed Florida growers, and the combined factors of soil, climate, and variations in seed characteristics drove them under. Later, in 1896, some Florida growers began experimenting with, and producing, a bright—or yellow—flue-colored leaf. Over time, this would evolve into the substantial crop staple that is successfully produced across North Florida today. But as a dominant industry, tobacco has long since given way to the orange and the tourist.

43.
Restored: A Golden Era's Symbol

Coral Gables's Biltmore Hotel, a symbol of glittering boomtime Florida, is undergoing a rebirth.

The 55-year-old Biltmore Hotel, once the "Dowager Queen of Coral Gables" and a glittering 1920s showplace for tycoons, celebrities, and socialites, has just been reborn.

After $3.5 million worth of delicate inside-out surgery, the restored hotel, one of America's foremost, has been transformed into the Metropolitan Museum and Art Center for all of Dade County.

And it's a fitting rebirth for the towering Grand Dame, because, more than any other Gold Coast resort, she symbolizes a legend and an era. The legend: George E. Merrick, the ingenious developer who spent millions to carve a City Beautiful out of hard coral bedrock on the southwest edge of Miami. The era: that colorful, giddy, splendorous insanity of the 1920s Florida land boom.

Merrick, a would-be poet-writer, seemed destined to do all of his writing "in wood and steel and stone." But his organizational genius surpassed that of Carl Fisher (Miami Beach), and his artistic flair in architecture easily rivaled Addison Mizner (Boca Raton), two other boomtime city builders.

In 1922, when Merrick took his father's bequest—3,000 acres of lots on grove and pineland—and went into the real estate business, he was already laying out his dream of the first planned city in Florida—Coral Gables. By 1925, he had sold over $150 million in Coral Gables property and had extended his tract to Biscayne Bay, 19,000 acres in all. The city was laid out with broad tree-lined boulevards, huge swimming pools, Venetian waterways, plazas, fountains, golf courses, bridges, and massive archway gates; the excavated coral rock itself provided excellent building material. The project had been blueprinted to the finest detail before even a palmetto was grubbed, and Merrick demanded strict adherence to aesthetic quality of design. To preserve architectural harmony, no home or business could be built in Coral Gables without first meeting approval of an architectural board; the building style was Mediterranean, a blend of Spanish and Italian.

In one year, Merrick spent $3 million on promotion, with nationwide offices and salesmen. Prospects were bused from as far away as San Francisco, and his daily land auctions were fanfared with brass bands and song. Merrick was also able to attract men of national repute, such as writer Rex Beach, who earned $25,000 writing a popular book on the delights of Coral Gables. The renowned William Jennings Bryan earned $100,000 a year to speak 40 minutes a day from a platform in the large Venetian Pool. Orchestra leader Jan Garber even publicized a new song, "When the Moon Shines on Coral Gables." Lot sales hit a million dollars a week by the time Merrick contracted with American Builders Corporation to build $75 million in new homes.

The multi-million-dollar madness of the boom itself had made America Florida-conscious in the early 1920s. Nearly 1.5 million people a year poured into the state, heading mainly for Miami. Housing was nonexistent, so they slept in cars, on porches and park benches, and in boats or tents. By 1925, Miami swarmed with 5,917 real estate brokers. Woodland eight miles away was selling for $25,000 an acre, and downtown business property had soared to $50,000 a front-foot. The notorious "binder boys" swapped lots, for a 10 percent "binder," as often as eight times a day, each time at a higher price. In the manic get-rich-quick rush, people willingly paid up to a hundred times a property's real value, often not even bothering to inspect it. Fast fortunes were being made—at least on paper.

As a grand centerpiece for his new city, Merrick sought to build "two of the most stupendous edifices of their kind," a hotel and a country club. He informed builder John Bowman that he was "in a hurry for both," and so, within eight months, at a cost of $10 million, Bowman completed the 26-story Biltmore and its elegant clubhouse. The posh structure, with its illuminated Giralda tower, a replica of the Giralda in old Seville, drew praise even from Spain's King Alphonso. Complementing it were two 18-hole golf courses, tennis courts, a polo field, and a picturesque canal to transport hotel guests to Tahiti Beach on the bay. To its grand opening gala on January 15, 1926, two special trains from New York brought in financiers and celebrities, along with famous performers and artists such as Chaliapin, Galli-Curci, Paderewski, and Paul Whiteman. Olympic champion Pete Desjardins gave daily diving exhibitions in the Venetian Pool, while Red Grange and the Chicago Bears played football on the grounds.

This euphoric boom fever continued high for eight more months, but few, if any, could discern its fragile paper structure. The boom's collapse, ironically, was punctuated with an addendum of fury from Mother Nature. In September, 1926, a hurricane devastated the Gold Coast and Miami, along with much of its gimcrack new construction. Builders went bankrupt, paper fortunes collapsed, and banks failed throughout Florida. Merrick, like most developers, was wiped out. His assets had all been tied to profits from future projects that now had no future. Virtually penniless, Merrick operated a fish camp in the Florida Keys in the years before his death in 1942. Lacking credit, he once found himself unable even to buy a tire for his aging Cadillac, the only possession he salvaged from the boom, along with his devoted wife, the former Eunice Peacock of Coconut Grove.

During the Great Depression, the Biltmore struggled along under several owners and then, in World War II, it was taken over as an Army Air Force Hospital. After the war, from 1947 to 1968, it was used as a Veterans Administration Hospital and then remained vacant until the City of Coral Gables acquired it and raised $3.5 million to turn it into a thriving cultural center.

Hilario Candela, of the architectural firm that handled the restoration, says the project is the best example of the current trend to "restore and adapt the best buildings from our past for new uses today." And, perhaps, it might also be considered a fitting memorial to the poet-dreamer George Merrick and to a madcap resplendent era of history that Florida may never know again.

44.
David Yulee's Tragic Dream

The state's first U.S. Senator tried to build the first intercoastal railroad link, but his politics killed his dream.

David Levy Yulee was one of the brightest political stars illuminating Florida's antebellum era, and he had a dream that promised to transform the state's economy.

Momentous in its implications, the dream was nevertheless simple and practical. He proposed construction of a railroad linking the Atlantic Ocean and Gulf of Mexico across the northern half of the state. The rail line would be used to transfer freight from the flourishing European shipping trade to destinations throughout the South, and to transport U.S. goods on their way to Europe.

It was a dream that had instant appeal to shippers and merchants, from London and New York to New Orleans and other Gulf ports. The rail line not only would bring a substantial reduction in freight costs but also, more important, would bypass the roundabout and hazardous sea lanes of the Bahama Channel and Florida Reef, where shipwrecks were taking a staggering toll during the 1840s and 1850s.

Yulee's vision had the potential of giving the state a half-century's running start on two later rail titans, Henry Flagler and Henry Plant, who did transform the state. But Yulee's dream was fatally flawed by the star-crossed elements of both his own and Florida's destiny. He did indeed build his railroad, but only in time to flee for his life on the last train out of his Atlantic port at Fernandina, under a hail of gunfire.

David Levy Yulee's birthplace, the British West Indian island of St. Thomas, seemed in 1810 an unlikely precursor to the dynamic political career awaiting him in Florida. His father, Moses Levy, of Portuguese-Jewish ancestry, earned his fortune in lumbering and Spanish supply contracting in St. Thomas and Havana. (Moses substituted Levy for the family name of Yulee, but in 1845 David officially took the name of David Levy Yulee.)

169

The father sent David, at age 9, to Norfolk, Virginia, for schooling and the oldest son, Elias, to Harvard. Meanwhile, Moses began buying land in Florida just prior to its cession by Spain to the United States in 1821. He also immersed himself in ancient theological studies which, inexplicably, led him to withdraw school support for his two sons. Elias remained in the North while David returned to one of his father's plantations near St. Augustine.

David avidly continued his studies while also becoming popular in St. Augustine social circles. He soon decided to read for the law under U.S. Judge Robert R. Reid in that city, and in 1832 he was admitted to the Florida Bar. But his keen interest in politics led him to forego law practice and successfully seek the post of clerk to the Territorial Legislature. The distinctiveness of his work there led him to membership in the convention in St. Joseph in 1838 to write Florida's first constitution. By this time, Yulee was becoming an attractive and formidable figure in Tallahassee political circles; in 1841, he was elected territorial delegate to the U.S. Congress.

Young, handsome, intellectually brilliant, and skillful at debating, Yulee was unafraid to challenge congressional veterans. At the same time, Yulee, along with Governor Richard Keith Call, energetically promoted statehood for Florida, eloquently persuading divided Floridians of its advantages, including national voting strength and, at home, generous land grants by which to finance vital internal improvements. Of the latter, Yulee already was envisioning his Gulf-Atlantic railroad.

When statehood finally was granted in 1845, Yulee's diligent efforts were rewarded with his election, along with James D. Wescott, Jr., to one of the state's first two U.S. Senate seats. Except for an interlude of four years, he would serve as senator until secession in 1861.

Enhancing this political high mark in the same year, the 35-year-old senator married Nancy Wickliffe, daughter of Kentucky's ex-governor, Charles Wickliffe. A woman of unusual beauty and goodness, Nancy was commonly known as The Wickliffe Madonna; even Yulee's political foes deferred to her.

During the next years, Yulee slowly formulated his railroad plans. He and his associates already had decided on the respective termini—Fernandina, on Amelia Island east of Jacksonville, as the Atlantic port, and Cedar Key on the Gulf.

Although the Florida Railroad Company was incorporated in 1853, not until 1855 did Yulee and state lawmakers work out financing plans through the newly formed Internal Improvement Fund (IIF). After right-of-way was laid and crossties put in, the IIF would give the railroad land grants and then issue 7% coupon bonds at the rate of $10,000 per mile to pay for rails and equipment, plus additional bonds for bridges and trestles as needed. A sinking fund drawn from railroad profits would cover interest payments and the bonds' ultimate redemption, but financial liability rested legally with the IIF trustees (a stipulation that would return to haunt the state in later years).

Given its need, the railroad's future looked boundlessly bright. But snags soon developed. The New York firm hired to build the line, Finegan & Co., it soon was learned, had scant operating capital, and the sluggish sales of land, bonds, or stock could not stave off the firm's pending bankruptcy.

But the most serious obstacle was the divisiveness smoldering between North and South over slavery and other issues and hence the wariness of Northerners to invest below the Mason-Dixon line. A desperate Yulee finally maneuvered Finegan into surrendering the contract, and, in 1858, the senator renegotiated it with the eminent Northern lawyer, E.N. Dickerson, and his wealthy associates. But the price was painfully high—giving up dominant control of the railroad to the Dickerson group.

Nevertheless, by June, 1860, Yulee had announced that rail traffic was ready to roll. He already had acquired a cross-state telegraph line, plus a fast-mail ship route from Cedar Key to Havana. Fernandina bustled with growth as shops, wharves, and warehouses were completed. Yulee was soon enthusing over "a new emporium of commerce in the South—Fernandina." He could not then know that other people had other plans for Fernandina.

In the stormy sectional clashes growing out of the Missouri Compromise of 1850, Yulee could not perceive the flaw in his rationale concerning states' rights, a concept he ardently defended in Congress. For if states' rights superseded those of the federal union, then it legitimately followed that the state, or any region of states, could simply withdraw from that union and form its own government, at any time and in a peaceful context. Yulee expressed such solipsistic thinking in late 1860 when he wrote: "We should arrange together now, and at once for living in peace or parting in peace," as if such a momentous and disruptive fracture of a 70-year-old nation could be accomplished so lightly and arbitrarily.

And so when Florida's secession finally came in early 1861, he could, with his Senate colleague, Stephen Mallory, eagerly embrace it and resign his Senate seat. He could with equal ease ignore the lone and courageous voice of his former statehood compatriot, ex-Governor Call, who somberly warned the secessionists: "You have just opened the gates of hell."

It is possible that the ex-senator reflected upon these words on March 3, 1862, when he fled before invading federal forces on the last train out of Fernandina. As the train sped over the mainland trestle under a hail of rifle fire,

Yulee remained unharmed, but the man seated beside him was fatally wounded. Yulee's main wartime concern was to preserve the railroad for postwar operation, but a destitute Confederacy was later forced to confiscate and relocate the rails, despite Yulee's protests and court actions.

Yulee's railroad dream might very well have accelerated Florida's development by decades. But, like his dream of peaceful separation from the Union, its contradictory flaw would crush both.

45.
Florida's Haunted Gibraltar

*Our Caribbean "Gibraltar," massive Fort Jefferson, guarded
little more than the ghosts of its haunted past.*

Out in the Gulf of Mexico, some 68 miles due west of Key West, lie seven small
coral keys that mark the scene of some of the most notorious, colorful, tragic,
and ill-fated chapters in the history of the Americas—the Dry Tortugas.

Oldtimers will swear these keys bear a curse—and the events of more than
four and a half centuries might lend dark evidence to this notion. From here the
most vicious cutthroat pirates fanned out over the Spanish Main to plunder and
scuttle treasure-laden Spanish galleons and slaughter their occupants. Legend
to this day claims that millions in gold still lie buried on one or another key.
(One lighthouse keeper actually found some scattered pieces of eight worth
several thousand dollars.) Salvage wreckers waited anxiously here for victims
of the treacherous, storm-plagued shoals and reefs. Even in modern times, the
keys have hosted criminal fugitives, gun and rum runners, narcotic and alien
smugglers, and other miscreants. From here the mighty battleship Maine sailed
to its explosive doom in Havana Harbor in 1898, sparking the Spanish-American
War.

But the Tortugas are most famous for the giant citadel Fort Jefferson, its
ruins now a national monument situated on Garden Key. One of the most
massive fortresses ever built in this hemisphere, it was heralded in 1846 as the
"Gibraltar of the Gulf." However, its mammoth canonry never fired a shot. It
was a federal prison for years (some insist an American "Devil's Island"), with
its most notable occupant being Dr. Samuel A. Mudd, the unfortunate physician
who set the leg of Lincoln's assassin, John Wilkes Booth.

Ponce de Leon—history's first devotee of the youth cult—never found his
rejuvenating fountain, but he did discover these keys in 1513. He promptly
named them: "dry," because they had no water supply; "tortugas," for the huge
Loggerhead turtles that bred there and provided him and his men with fresh
meat.

The keys were strategically situated at the far west entrance to the Florida
Straits, the main passage route eastward for 17th and 18th century Spanish ships
bearing fabulous treasures of gold, silver, and jewels from Mexico and lands

south to Peru. From this convenient redoubt, freebooters terrorized ships of every kind. The sight of the fluttering skull and crossbones banner evoked terror on every quarterdeck, for soon the motley cutthroats would be swarming over the side, slaughtering crews in bloody abandon, looting holds and cabins, laughing and sword-prodding many a proud, deruffled Spanish don to the plank's edge. Back on the keys, they would portion the booty—bars of silver and gold, pieces of eight, pearls, beads, bales of wood and silk, precious stones, salted beef, maize, tobacco, sugar, casks of rum, weapons, and, often, female passengers. Many a maid might have preferred the plank or cutlass to entertaining these brigands at their drunken shoreside revels.

For over 200 years, their dread names became legends—Sawkins, Dampier, Sir Henry Morgan, Bartholomew Sharp, Ed "Blackbeard" Teach, Ambrose Cowley, L'Ollonois, Jose Gaspar, Brasiliere, Captain William Kidd, Black Caesar, and many others. Remains of their brickwork bastions can be seen on the keys today. As late as the period 1812-1823, over 3,000 piracies were reported in or near these waters. Finally, the U.S. Congress outfitted 22 vessels and 1,100 men to form the West Indian Squadron, headed by Commodore David Porter, who was a hero of the War of 1812 and veteran fighter of the pirates of Tripoli. Porter mercilessly scoured every coast from Jamaica to the Tortugas, burning ships and beach shacks, ransacking caves and coves to recover enormous booty, hanging captains and crews. This campaign effectively ended the long and bloody era of the pirate.

Cannonballs line a walkway on the fort's grounds. Not one of them was ever fired.
(FLORIDA TREND)

In 1846, still fearing Spanish or British encroachment in the Gulf and Caribbean, President James Polk ordered construction of one of the most gigantic forts ever conceived, to be located on Garden Key, to protect the vital ship commerce of the entire southern United States. Fleets of ships were soon voyaging 1,500 miles from New England to dump tons of ironwork, granite, cement, lime, mortar, lumber, bolts, and some 40 million bricks onto the barren 16-acre island. Over the next 15 years, some skilled, but mostly slave, labor would suffer broiling sun, savage mosquitoes, sea and sand storms, scurvy, dysentery, typhoid, and death to raise the monstrous citadel out of the sea. One contemporary observed: "The building conditions at Fort Jefferson were a hundred-fold worse than must have existed during the erection of Egypt's pyramids."

Constructed in hexagonal shape, the fort's walls rose a sheer 60 feet high from its coral bedrock. The six sides were each 450 feet long and five feet thick at the top. Its gunports were castellated enclosures, three tiers of them, designed to mount 243 huge cannons, 18 to 20 feet long and many tons in weight, 80 guns to a side.

Within the hexagon were officers' quarters in ornately finished brickwork, three stories high and 400 feet long, plus barracks to house six companies (maybe 800 men) and a large parade ground.

Adding a medieval touch, a moat was built around the fort 70 feet wide and 10 to 15 deep. It was bordered by an outer seawall to contain tidal action. (During its prison years, this moat was filled with shark and barracuda to discourage straying inmates.) Over the moat was a drawbridge and heavy gates leading to the hewn-granite sally port, the fort's only entrance.

Fort Jefferson took 30 years to build and was never completely finished. Its elephantine guns, which could have taken on whole armadas, never fired a shot. In fact, by the 1860s, the fort was rendered obsolete for defense purposes. The invention of the new rifled cannon could make quick rubble of the thickest walls. Thus, one of the mightiest edifices ever built may have been one of the greatest and most expensive "white elephants," or boondoggles, ever conceived. It was also soon to become a grim and isolated corner of hell.

By Civil War time, Fort Jefferson was designated a federal prison; the first prisoners arrived in September, 1861. In most years, the fort's population was about 1,500—nearly 1,000 prisoners, the remainder officers, families, and enlisted men. Its most famous prisoner, Dr. Samuel A. Mudd, arrived at the prison fortress July 24, 1865. Dr. Mudd had set the leg of Booth hours after Lincoln's assassination without any knowledge of the cause of Booth's mishap. He was the first to report to authorities when he learned of Booth's terrible crime.

But the highly emotional atmosphere of the period, and the hasty military trials of the real conspirators, caused Dr. Mudd to be implicated merely by proximity to the culprit; he was given a life term.

While serving as a hospital nurse and steward, he attempted an early escape on a supply ship but was caught. He had hoped to seek release by securing a writ of habeas corpus, which he might legally have done. After that he was kept in leg irons under heavy guard in a small damp dungeon where he described his treatment as "brutal and degrading."

Then, in August, a yellow fever epidemic struck the fort; terror spread as inmates were fatally seized one after the other. When the garrison surgeon, Major Joseph S. Smith, succumbed himself, Dr. Mudd's services were accepted, and he worked night and day to stem the rising death toll. "The whole island became one immense hospital," wrote an officer's wife later. "We seemed in some horrible nightmare." At one time, only 10 troops could be mustered, and just a few inmates were well enough to serve burial detail, removing the bodies to nearby Bird Key. One such detail of three men escaped to Cuba by stealing a small boat. (There were 25 reported escapes from Fort Jefferson. Over the years, most prisoners considered Tortugas "a death sentence"; one shipload of convicts attempted, but failed, mutiny on learning their destination.)

The death toll had reached the hundreds by the time Dr. Mudd was able to bring the disease under control. Officials and inmates alike praised his efforts, while petitioning authorities for his release. But the doctor did not win freedom until pardoned by President Andrew Johnson in March, 1869. He returned to his Maryland home "frail, weak, and sick," only to learn that still his "name was Mudd" (whence came the expression). He died in 1885, aged 49.

The fort was abandoned as a prison in the 1870s, becoming first a small navy station in the 1890s and then near-deserted for years save for a small U.S. Coast Guard patrol post. The U.S. battleship Maine was "coaled" here before sailing in 1898 to Havana Harbor, where a mysterious explosion sunk her. The incident was a catalyst for the Spanish-American War.

Battered over the decades by terrible hurricanes and tidal waves, the grim walls and brooding bastions of the ruins still overshadow the emerald waters, although within one finds a montage of ripped-off roofs, shattered walls, and awry tangles of beams, ironwork, brick heaps, and wreckage. Modern pirates have, over the years, stripped the fort and removed anything not fastened securely. Anonymous graffiti, incongruously, adorns every wall and surface with symbols, signs, remarks, warnings, sketches, threats, and so on.

Beneath the Tortugas' waters still lies one of the greatest marine gardens of the world where more than 600 varieties of sea life swarm in the crystal clear deeps.

Above, one still waits each spring to spy a long dark line rising out of the sea—solid birds—as the Noddy and Sooty Terns came back by the thousands to nest on the five-acre sand spit of Bush Key, just as they have each year since first seen by the naturalist visitors Audubon, in 1832, and Agassiz, in 1858. Under federal auspices, the Keys now shelter one of the world's largest tern rookeries.

Thus, the Tortugas have always remained a home to fish, fowl, and nature, but, over centuries, the "curse" on the isles seems to have, violently and tragically, rejected man as some alien despoiler.

46.
Of Red Hopes and White Politics

Early Florida Indians learned the white man's political ways when the latter rigged their election to get a safe candidate.

Chief Micanopy

Elections this year, as in the past, should be fairly much a set piece—a wide variety that varies little, shrill loudspeakers and strident claims, a tubeful of "images" rather than "issues," and an array of appeals ranging from bland "middle-of-the-road" pap to slightly cometicized demagoguery; all complete with straw boaters and balloons.

Therefore, one might recall with nostalgia a unique but simple election held in the state 150 years ago; it was, in fact, the first official federal-state election ever held in Florida. It was not for any president or lesser aspirant. It was for no less a post than the Supreme Chief of the Seminole Indian Nation. But it was a very important election held that July, 1826, an outdoor affair set in the primitive wilderness beauty near Silver Springs. It would draw hundreds from around the state, including a lot of U.S. blue coats who strolled up from Tampa's Fort Brooke to attend as "guests" (but really to see that no scalps were unnecessarily creased, and that one-man, one-vote prevailed).

The election was called by Colonel Gad Humphreys, U.S. Indian Agent for Florida, who hoped that the unified central leadership would make it easier to deal with all the Seminoles, not only in regard to their reserved land rights (over four million acres) and government compensation granted to them by the Moultrie Creek Treaty of 1823, but to stop the sporadic raids and clashes with white settlers, a prime cause of the first bloody Seminole War years earlier.

Three large Florida tribes would present two major candidates at this convention: the Tallassees (Tallahassees) and the Miccosukee, sponsoring Tukose Emathla (called John Hicks by white men), and the Alachuan Seminoles, headed by the formidable Micanopy, grandson of the famous warrior, King Payne. A "third-party" candidate, the bold Miccosukee chief Charlie Neamathla, had been ruled out of contention by Territorial Governor William

178

P. Duval: "Dangerous," Duval claimed. (Neamathla once warned General E.P. Gaines in an 1816 skirmish he would annihilate the officer if he crossed the Flint River to attack him. Gaines stayed put.)

Feelings grew more intense as election day drew near. Micanopy, who had never really relished the idea of being incorporated with the other two tribes, felt even less confident about his prospects of winning, since his own men were outnumbered. Humphreys, sensing the danger, appealed to Colonel George Brooke, at the fort so named, for a U.S. "presence"; Brooke responded with two full companies, led by a Captain F.L. Dade, and a young Lieutenant, George A. McCall.

McCall, who would later become a distinguished Civil War Union General, offers in his letters to father and brother a rare portrait of the early state, especially its lush wilderness beauty and its inhabitants, white or red. He gives therein some eyewitness accounts of this election, plus a glimpse of its idyllic natural setting.

Upon arrival from the five-day journey, 10 days before election day, Humphreys invited McCall for a canoe trip to nearby Silver Springs, then in its wild state. "How my heart swelled with astonishment as we neared the center of this grand basin of limpid water . . . so pellucid that the line of demarcation between the water and atmosphere was invisible . . . [as if] the canoe and its contents were suspended in midair," McCall wrote. Humphreys then cut a mother-of-pearl sleeve button and let it sink to the sand 40 feet below where "we distinguished clearly the four [sewing] holes in the button," while the tiniest fish feeding at bottom were seen as if at the surface. The men spent several hours almost entranced by this "magic theater of nature," surrounded by exotic trees, birdsong and wildflowers.

While in camp, McCall chatted with the two candidates and proffered his estimate of them. First is (John Hicks) Tukose Emathla, meaning Ant-chief, "in allusion, I suppose, to his industry in promoting the welfare of his people." McCall rated the six-foot-two-inch 50-year-old as "one of nature's noblemen...finely formed; his figure combining strength with gracefulness...perfect ease in all his attitude and gestures. The expression of his fine open countenance is habitually mild; but as he grows earnest in conversation, you see arise within him that flow of fervid feeling warming into determined energy which characterizes the man."

Of Micanopy, known also as "Governor": "I know him personally quite well. He is of medium height, stout, with a large, stolid face, heavy eyes and a general bearing and expression denoting lethargy. Though slow of speech, I have always found him communicative and good-tempered. He is rather too indolent to rule harshly." But the chief's official manager, Jumper, McCall tersely labeled as a man of "great cunning and effrontery."

It is not known what words passed between Micanopy and the senior captain, Francis L. Dade, but doubtless they met, as protocol demanded. However, neither could know that their destinies were fatally entwined, and that, nine years hence, the chief would surprise Major Dade on a wooded trail one cold December morning and kill him and over a hundred of his men, with only three survivors. This "Dade Massacre," less than 50 miles south of the election site, would be a major catalyst for the Second Seminole War.

Election day finally rolled around, and members of each band duly marked their ballots. To no one's surprise, the returns showed Emathla the winner by a decided majority. "No disturbance had occurred anywhere," McCall writes, "Micanopy, governed by the advice of the Agent [Humphreys] and the presence of the troops, having wisely yielded to circumstances he could not control."

Runners by now had fanned out in all directions to carry the election results to every tribal town and notify them of the grand inauguration day to be held 20 days hence. A party of Miccosukees took charge of this ceremony and began at once the erection of an amphitheater. McCall observes: "I was surprised to see how much mechanical skill they displayed, and before the appointed time arrived they had completed a structure of no mean character. A circular arbor, 50 feet wide and 200 feet in diameter on the outer circle, was well covered in with green boughs; under this were erected seats formed of post-oak, rising one above another, in true amphitheatrical style, and capable of seating near 2,000 warriors."

The crowds had already poured in—some 3,000—by the time McCall and the other officers were conducted by a Miccosukee chief to their reserved seats. "Every seat was already filled, and the most perfect order and silence prevailed," he noted, as the ceremonies began at 7 p.m. A rattlesnake dance, honoring the chief-elect, was conducted by 100 men led by a chief, a chanting dance "enacted with great dignity and grace." Other dances followed, and then a herald, bearing a small American Flag, stood in front of the officers, faced the arena, and called loudly three times, at slow intervals: "Tukose Emathla!" The chief came forward and bowed slightly, at which time the herald attached a small seven-inch-long war club to the leader's scalp-lock and proclaimed him the Supreme Chief, followed by prolonged shouts of assent from the packed assemblage.

The Tallahassean stood calmly until the applause subsided, then raised his head and looked steadily around upon his audience. "He commenced his address in a low tone, and with a slight tremor in his voice," McCall relates. "But as he proceeded and warmed with his subject, his voice swelled to its full, manly volume, and his words flowed in an unbroken stream, which manifested the fixedness of his purpose and the settled conviction of his mind as to what was the policy he should adopt and fearlessly carry out, in order to establish harmony and promote the welfare of the nation."

Noting that he had been elected "without any solicitation on his part," he would enforce the laws without favor to any . . . of the respective tribes which in the whole were, in the abstract, the same." He then enjoined all to hold "a kindly feeling" toward one another and concluded with a "kind of prayer or injunction to all to respect the law and live in peace." He then dismissed them.

McCall says he "felt as if I had been listening to an enlightened and, indeed, to a great man. All that he said evinced so much good sense, and was conveyed in so eloquent and forcible a manner, that I could not but accord him that place in my estimation."

But even as McCall wrote these words, die-hard sentiment was fomenting in Washington to force a scrapping of treaties and removal of the Indians completely from Florida. White settlers, too, who had already been violating Indian reserves and poaching the cattle and other goods of various tribes, were alarmed that runaway slaves so readily found refuge and freedom with the Seminoles and often became their fiercest warriors.

Sensing this keenly, the new chief took a delegation to the capitol that same year to petition President John Quincy Adams to let the tribes stay on their lands. "Here our navel strings were cut and the blood from them sunk into the earth, and made the country dear to us," Emathla pleaded.

But the pressures were too great, especially when reinforced by men like Andrew Jackson and Indian commissioner James Gadsen—near phobic in their fear and hatred of the Indian—who successfully agitated for the Indian Removal Act of 1830, violating at once the 20-year Moultrie Creek agreement.

But the Congress would pay dearly for this act. In fact, the Second Seminole War, in proportion to the relative handful of enemy engaged, was one of the longest (6-1/2 years), costliest, and bloodiest wars in American history. When at last the ragged remnant of Seminoles who escaped westward removal found permanent refuge in the Everglades, the "victory" of the white man seemed Pyrrhic indeed.

And thus the significance of Florida's first official federal-state election which, had it been honored by men as enlightened and fair-minded as Humphreys, McCall, and Emathla, might have changed a long chapter of Florida's history—for the better.

47.
The Indians' Last Warpath

Banana trees and white perfidy ignite the fury of Chief Billy
Bowlegs and propel him down the last fiery warpath.

The Seminole chief was wined and dined in the best hotels of Washington and New York; he found the cuisine sumptuous, and the claret and French brandy much smoother than the tart Indian brew, caseena.

Chief Bolechs, commonly known as Billy Bowlegs, did not at all mind these attentions, but he knew they were designed to induce him and his people to move from Florida to Arkansas. And he had no desire to leave his native state.

When the Second Seminole War officially ended in 1842, and most of the Seminoles had been removed westward, Bowlegs and several hundred Indians had fled to the Everglades and Big Cypress Swamp. Under the peace terms, federal authorities agreed to let them remain there unmolested. Reservation boundaries were even set, and, for some 10 years, the Indians lived there peacefully, hunting, fishing raising cattle and farming, far removed from the nearest white settler who normally shunned that soggy wildland anyway.

But with increasing regularity in the postwar years, Floridians clamored to have these Seminoles removed west. This made Billy angry. When he heard Florida Governor Thomas Brown refer to his people as "a few roving savages," he fumed in retort that if Brown tried to attack his people, "Me whip governor of Florida and his long knives damn quick."

Floridians were not altogether happy with the war's end in 1842. The lush windfall of millions of federal dollars spent annually in the state would be sorely missed. And they didn't like the idea of any Indians remaining behind, even if it was far away in the South Florida swamps. And even though the Seminoles had admirably kept to the terms of the peace accords, most Floridians agreed with the Florida *Peninsular* that it was time for the U.S. government to "rid Florida of this non-amalgamating and dangerous population."

But there was a more compelling motive behind this anti-Seminole chorus, a chorus largely orchestrated by North Florida planters, politicians, and land speculators. Both during and after the war, periodic surveying explorations in the Everglades had produced glowing and effusive reports of the availability of millions of acres of dark, rich, amazingly fertile muckland, awaiting only

drainage and reclamation. With no real knowledge then of the delicate intercon-
nected ecosystem of that vast river of grass, self-styled authorities confidently
assured state leaders that "two or three small canals" would do the job at a cost
of no more than $500,000. Glittering visions of huge, immensely lucrative sugar
and rice plantations, requiring perhaps only a handful of slaves, prompted the
state, in 1847, to send Buckingham Smith to the Glades to make a complete
study of the practicality of its drainage. Smith returned to enthuse that it not only
was practical but, within 10 years, it would also draw enough population to
create an entire new state composed of East and South Florida.

This latter commentary alluded to another prime motive behind the removal
outcry, namely, the serious discussion then about severing the "unnatural"
connection of West Florida to East and South Florida and creating two states—
more exactly, two "slave" states to give balance if not edge in Congress with
"free" states. Of course, the first priority would have to be Indian removal from
such a valuable region.

Memories of the long, costly, and bloody Indian war were too fresh in
Washington for the U.S. military to even think of resuming hostilities against a
relatively small, peaceful tribe inhabiting an impenetrable swamp. They did
establish a token presence at Fort Myers in 1850 and also told Floridians they
would do what they could to induce removal, but only if it could be done through
peaceful means.

Over the years, U.S. Indian agents had persuaded a number of Seminoles,
through small cash payments, to relocate. But Bowlegs and the main tribe
assured such agents that they liked it just fine on—they emphasized—their
"U.S. reservation." Even when agent Luther Blake took Billy and three other
Seminoles to talk with "great white fathers" in Washington, D.C., provided them
with a $600 spending spree in New York for clothes and fine wines, and won a
vaguely tentative agreement for removal, Billy returned to his Big Cypress home
and quietly forgot all about the agreement. Blake was fired.

Finally, a new administration and a new war secretary, Jefferson Davis, the
future Confederate head, approved a plan whereby a few U.S. troops and Florida
volunteers would cordon off the Seminoles by cutting off trade and supplies and
generally harassing the Indians with surveying incursions and other intrusions,
hoping to provoke the Indians out of their jungly sanctuary and thereupon
capture them. It proved to have more than its intended effect.

In December, 1855, a surveying party of 11 men under engineer Lieutenant
George L. Hartsuff came across an Indian village where Bowlegs had a prized
garden. In a senseless act of vandalism, the men began trampling down banana
stalks, smashing pumpkins, and uprooting potatoes. An enraged Billy con-

fronted the party, demanding an apology and compensation, but the group only laughed at him. As they later explained, they just wanted to see how "old Billy would cut up." Old Billy "cut up" all right. In a pre-dawn attack on the engineers' camp soon after, two men were killed and four others, including Hartsuff, wounded. The Third Seminole War was on.

It was actually less a war than a series of attacks and skirmishes. The Hartsuff incident had ignited the pent-up anger and desperation of the Indians, and small bands of them went out raiding in all directions, attacking and pillaging white settlements as far north as Manatee, Hillsborough, and Polk counties. Panicky settlers fled to nearby forts, and U.S. troops and Florida volunteers moved onto the scene. But the fast-moving small bands consistently eluded their hunters as they withdrew into the sawgrass, swamps, and forests. After nearly two years, only several dozen Indians, mostly women and children, were captured. By 1857, Washington conceded that the Seminoles had "baffled" all efforts to subjugate them, and a new president, James Buchanan, decided to take a different tack.

Fortunately, the government had earlier kept an overdue promise to the Arkansas Creeks and Seminoles to give these traditional foes not only separate reservations but cash payments totaling about $1 million to each tribe, a portion of which would be invested for them. This drastically changed the previously impoverished conditions and also provided a strong inducement for their migration.

Accordingly, Indian affairs supervisor Elias Rector arrived in Fort Myers in early 1858 with 40 Seminoles and six Creeks. The Indians made contact with Billy, gave him glowing reports of their new conditions, and persuaded him to come to Fort Myers for talks, under solemn assurances of safe conduct. Billy was promised immediate cash gifts totaling $7,500, with $1,000 to each warrior and $100 to each woman and child. A now war-weary Billy returned to his tribe to discuss the offer, and two weeks later he consented to migrate. On May 4, 1858, a total of 165 Seminoles sailed from Egmont Key in Tampa Bay and headed to Arkansas.

But not all the Indians left. The venerable old Sam Jones and between 150 and 300 others retreated farther into the wilderness recesses; there they remained permanently, the undefeated. Thus ended a 35-year struggle (1823-1858), at a cost of hundreds of lives and millions of dollars.

48.
Florida's
Presidential
Darkhorse

*University of Florida head,
Murphree, is touted as a
presidential candidate by none
other than William Jennings Bryan.*

Dr. A. A. Murphree
(FLORIDA TREND)

Many years before Jimmy Carter broke the 100-year-plus ban on a Southerner being nominated for the U.S. presidency, Florida once tried to herald its own "Woodrow Wilson."

The 1924 attempt failed, but, for a moment in history, a national klieg light was focused on a relatively unknown educator, Dr. A.A. Murphree, president of the University of Florida. His promoter was none other than the Great Commoner himself, William Jennings Bryan.

Bryan, who three times was a presidential candidate himself, was no novice at pushing candidates. His efforts to break a deadlocked convention in 1912 secured the nomination of another little-known educator, Woodrow Wilson. Bryan, who earlier had changed his residency to Miami, resigned as Secretary of State in Wilson's administration in June, 1915, over what he termed its "war preparedness" stance. But he was still a national figure. He rode the Florida circuit widely, speaking out on such issues as militarism, evolution, prohibition, and the Klan. His oratorical genius with an audience could still be reminiscent of the days when, as a young reformer, he once stirred a nation with his impassioned "Cross of Gold" speech at the 1896 Democratic convention.

Bryan was an especially popular speaker at the University of Florida, and it was here that his close friendship with Murphree developed. The two men were kindred spirits: Both were of genial and generous disposition, had strong religious faith, and were willing to take firm stands on moral issues.

Born in rural Alabama in 1870, Albert Alexander Murphree began teaching school at 18. He soon became a brilliant scholar and teacher and served in numerous academic posts before becoming president, at 32, of Florida State

185

College in Tallahassee, where he remained until 1905 when it was changed to Florida State College for Women. Then, in 1909, he was picked to head the struggling four-year-old University of Florida, and here his executive talents flowered. He expanded the faculty, raised academic standards, formed new colleges, spurred new fields of research, and, simultaneously, spearheaded pressures on the Legislature for more funding to meet educational needs.

Described by peers as "efficient, broadminded, progressive and energetic," Murphree saw enrollment grow from 186 in 1909 to more than 2,000 in the 1920s, with his university rated as one of the South's most distinctive.

But the educator was as surprised as anyone the day he learned that he had suddenly become a political figure.

Bryan ignited these political tinders in January, 1924, by announcing his candidacy as a delegate to the Democratic National Convention—for the sole purpose, he added, of presenting Murphree as a nominee for the presidency. The effect was sensational and sparked a flurry of debate and commentary, first statewide, then nationally. Most of the state's press took up the Murphree banner, likening him to another educator, Woodrow Wilson, and generally agreeing with one editorial comment that "Dr. Murphree is no politician and no seeker after office. He is a great teacher. But he would carry it [the presidency] with grace and wisdom."

By now, a skeptical but curious national press was flocking into the state, with Bryan repeatedly reminding them that Murphree's chances at a nomination "are a great deal better than mine were six months before the Chicago [1896] convention or President Wilson's were two years before 1912." It was time, he added, "to break the 60-year ban on a Southerner for president."

The modest "candidate," a little overwhelmed by the sudden spotlight and somewhat upset that Bryan had not consulted him beforehand, nevertheless dealt good-naturedly with the clamor of the press and the teasing of friends asking him for cabinet posts and offices. While he expressed gratitude for this "high compliment . . . from a great American," he emphasized that "Bryan alone is responsible for the [candidacy] suggestion." Such talk, he added, was "fiction. Nobody expects a Southern man to be nominated president, much less a Florida man."

But despite Murphree's disclaimers, Bryan intensified his campaigning. To one and all he extolled the educator's "high idealism . . . rare combination of intellect and heart...a splendid executive" who represented "a [prohibition] dry and progressive" Democrat as opposed to one (John W. Davis) "wet and reactionary."

By springtime a host of enthused political and civic leaders were on the bandwagon, while newspapers all over the country—and especially in the

South—were anxious to support the educator. Wires from editors urgently pleaded with Murphree to place his name on the Florida preferential primary ballot.

But the doctor was adamant. His ambition in life was education, not politics, and it would remain so. Yet, he personally praised Bryan's "faithfulness and friendship," congratulating him on winning his delegate seat and noting that "a little coterie of people would have given almost their lives to keep you out of the convention." He observed, too, the recognition given the state and its university "from every section of the United States."

But the progressive reform era symbolized by Bryan had long since passed; the "wets and reactionaries" were indeed in the convention saddle, and the old commoner was "humiliated" by the boos and heckling he received when he rose to speak on his Florida choice. This, followed later by the circus-like Scopes evolution trial in Tennessee, probably hastened Bryan's death on July 26, 1925. Murphree's untimely death, at 57, came two years later.

It would be another half-century before a Southerner would win a nomination—and election—for the highest office. But for a brief and exhilarating moment in history, Florida made its own bid to break the historical taboo and put a Southern "Woodrow Wilson" in the White House.

49.
The Legendary Island of Useppa

*Tales of buried treasure, captive beauties, pirates, and plunder
lend lurid mystery to this West Coast Florida island.*

There have been some famous retreats and playgrounds for the gilt-edged
moguls of wealth, power, and estate in America—Saratoga, Newport, Ormond
Beach, Palm Beach—but few know that one of the most popular hideaways for
the high polloi in this century has been an obscure little piece of land lying in
tropical, idyllic seclusion just off the southwest coast of Florida.

This is the tiny, beautiful, high-rising island of Useppa, situated five miles
south of Boca Grande, facing the mouth of Charlotte Harbor and accessible still
only by boat or small plane. One of a series of better-known islets (Gasparilla
Island, legendary home of the pirate Jose Gaspar, is a few miles north while
Captiva and Sanibel Islands lie southward), Useppa has quietly relished its
relative anonymity, as befits a host to the celebrated, the titled, and the tycoons
of the day.

Surrounded by the world's greatest tarpon fishing grounds, which first
spurred its resort development by the Florida land baron, Barron Collier, the
island also enjoys an aura of romantic legend. Here, it is said, the famous pirate
once gamboled with his favorite captive beauty, to whom he presented the
island, and for whom he named it. And more than a few treasure hunters have
probed beneath its verdant surface for some of the millions in gold that legend
assures them Gaspar buried there.

Its guest lists have been diverse since the turn of the century, not exclusively
the Vanderbilts, Rothschilds, and Rockefellers, or presidents like Roosevelt
(Teddy) and Hoover. Writers like Mary Roberts Rinehart (mysteries) or Zane
Grey (westerns), or the urbane pugilist Gene Tunney, or beauties like Hedy
Lamarr, Shirley Temple, and Gloria Swanson have frolicked on its silver sands.

Today, it is the home of the Useppa Island Club, where selective guests
(limit 75) enjoy a unique golf course and palm-shaded tennis courts in addition
to the uncrowded snow-sand beaches and world-renowned fishing. But its
history remains singular and colorful.

In the early 19th century, the story goes, Gasparilla seized a rich Spanish
merchantman as it sailed by his island hideaway. In anger at the resistance

shown by the bark, he ordered the survivors to walk the plank. Then suddenly he stopped the execution as he spied the next victim, a beautiful, proud, and disdainful young woman. He ordered her taken back to his island as a captive "bride" to join his many other wives, but soon became so enamored of her, and fearful for her person among so many angry and jealous women, that he set her up in queenly dominion on her own island just south of his base and named it for her—Joseffa. This was the official government name for it until years later it gradually took the name of Useppa; that is its legal name today. It is believed that the name grew out of the corrupted pronunciation of "Joseffa" by early Cracker settlers on the mainland.

The island remained tranquilly undisturbed until the 1890s when John M. Roach, a Chicago street car magnate, who passed the island by steamer on his way to winter in Fort Myers, became so impressed with its elevation and natural beauty that he bought it outright, intending to make it a winter home for his family. He built a cottage near where the present golf club stands and had a younger brother live there to make further developments.

Although many have searched the area islands for Gasparilla gold (unsuccessfully), young Roach relates the only incident that seemingly corroborates the treasure legend. One evening a schooner dropped anchor offshore; two rough-looking sailors asked Roach for permission to camp overnight and draw water from the island spring. Since this was a common request, he consented. But when he went to the spring for water next morning, he was surprised to find the campsite vacant, the schooner gone, and a large excavation dug out under the big tree. His real shock, however, was the clearly defined imprint of a box, the size of a common seachest, at the excavation's bottom. Grabbing a pistol, young Roach set out in a fast-sailing sharpie in pursuit but failed to locate the schooner after sailing 24 miles down to Punta Pass. This digging was never refilled, and, years later, when the golf course was being laid out in 1916, a greenskeeper discovered at its bottom a small octagonal Spanish coin about the size of a dime. This seemed to convince doubters that the outlined box was certainly a treasure chest.

In the meantime, the island passes had become so popular as a tarpon fishing ground that Roach was persuaded to build the 20-room Useppa Inn in 1902 to accommodate all visitors. Gradually, a discreet word-of-mouth advertising was making the island a winter haven for the country's elite-club set who coveted such newly-discovered hideaways. Winthrop Rockefeller, Erastus Foote, John Stewart, and Richmond Talbot would ply its waters for tarpon and other game fish, and Ben Crowinshield once took a record 25 tarpon in one day. One wag reports that even today, affluent transients at New York's famous Waldorf

Astoria can tell you more about Useppa than can any local resident of Fort Myers. The hard-fighting tarpon even spurred a noted visitor to contrive a now famous piece of tackle. Edward Vom Hofe, on snaring his noted record 210-pound tarpon, had such a struggle with his old-fashioned leather thumb-brake reel that he and his brother, Julius, invented the star-drag fishing reel which is the basis of all big-game fishing reels today.

In 1912, Barron Collier, the advertising titan and settler of Lee and Collier counties, bought the island and began extensive improvements. The high, rolling elevation (35 feet) prompted him to develop a highly original and beautiful golf course which remains a major attraction today.

Earlier, in 1907, the Charlotte Harbor and Northern Railway was built to Boca Grande on Gasparilla Island. Used for phosphate transport from inland mines, it soon made the great tarpon grounds more accessible. The exact route of this old railway was lost until the early 1960s, when it was uncovered running through the backyard of "Journey's End," the historic home now seasonally occupied by Dr. James Ingram, of Tampa.

Collier also instituted one of the most famous clubs in America—the Izaak Walton Club, named for the 17th century English author who wrote the fishing classic, "The Compleat Angler." The club's silver, gold, and diamond buttons, awarded for various record tarpon catches, soon became the most highly prized of awards.

But not all visitors sought only the great Silver King. President Theodore Roosevelt, typically, chased down the Giant Ray, or Devil Fish, which can weigh up to a ton. On one of his trips, some jokester sent a sensational story over the press wires that Teddy had become entangled in his harpoon line, jerked overboard, and drowned. On hearing this, William T. Dewart, of the *New York Sun*, a Useppa guest also, dashed quickly over to the president's boat near Captiva Island, only to find the executive enjoying a hearty breakfast of smoked mullet. "His big front teeth stood out like lighthouses as he laughed at the story," Dewart relates.

Herbert Hoover, on the other hand, enjoyed more the quiet and serenity of the island, "the chance to wash one's soul with pure air [and] rejoicing that you do not have to decide a darn thing until next week.

The tarpon is the major attraction of people from countries across the globe, but less strenuous fishing is also available. In fact, from the Useppa dock the amateur angler can readily fetch up any number of redfish, snappers, sheepshead, ladyfish, or jack crevalle. Mullet can be netted or gigged by the score. Farther out, sea bass, snook, bull reds, and black and red grouper are taken merely at the drop of a line. Useppa fishing truly seems Cornucopian alongside so many other spots long since "fished out."

Useppa Island was sold in 1968 to James Turner, of Turner's Plantation Dairies, in Tampa, for over a half-million dollars and has been developed since then into today's Useppa Island Club. Exactly one mile long from tip to tip and three-fourths of a mile at its widest, room has been found nevertheless to lay out a 2000-foot-long landing strip for single- and twin-engine planes, private or chartered. The old Collier hotel is now the clubhouse, and a modern swimming pool has been built, complementing the famous nine-hole golf course and tennis courts. It also has a marina for yacht club groups. By boat, the island can be reached easily from Boca Grande northward, or Bokeelia, on the mainland east.

The island does not quite boast today some of the celebrated names it once hosted. Today's visitor, while still from the upper ranks of affluency, is more often than not a bank or corporation president or government official, keeping strictly to his characteristic low-profile image.

But tales of lore and legend from the island's colorful bygone days are still bantered about over cocktail or coffee in the clubroom or on the terrace, and the individual of ways and means still seeks this tranquil, unspoiled natural beauty that lies so close to home—and yet so far away.

50.
Tilting for a County Seat

Haughty Colonel Sanford clashes with cattle tycoon Summerlin
in a bid to claim the seat of Orange County.

It was a duel of personalities as much as of public relations—the cattle king versus the haughty ex-diplomat—but the stakes were probably higher than either one could foresee at the time.

It was also a duel of two towns—Orlando and Sanford—to determine which was destined to be the hub of Central Florida's thriving metropolitan area today. Back then, 1875, history could have nudged it either way.

Neither of the protagonists—Jacob "Jake" Summerlin and General Henry S. Sanford—knew each other prior to their brief but decisive encounter to determine the permanent seat of Orange County. Yet each was a determined and formidable man.

Summerlin, whose wizened, slight figure and eccentric ways belied his reputation as "King of the Crackers," was a major Florida cattle king. Leaving his Lake City home in 1836, at age 16, he headed south with the gift of a few cattle from his father and over years built them into the largest herds in the state. He also bought up tracts of land at 25 cents an acre (almost half of Polk County and much land southward). His years-long beef market in Cuba netted him a fortune in gold doubloons. Although eccentric in dress and habits, he had a philanthropic bent and provided most of the funds to set up Bartow as the Polk County seat, where he also endowed a private school. His interest in Orange County prompted him to buy a home there after the Civil War. By this time, he was one of the wealthiest men in the state.

The tall, portly Sanford was almost a caricature opposite. Inheriting a fortune from his Connecticut manufacturer father, he began a career in the foreign service, serving in several U.S. legations in Europe until his appointment, in 1861, as Minister to Belgium. He married Parisian Gertrude du Puy, and had eight children by her. He returned to the U.S. in 1870 and purchased a large land tract on Lake Munroe on the St. Johns River. There he planted a large orange grove and platted out a model town which he named for himself. Peers described Sanford's manner as often pompous and overbearing; his habits in dress never varied—impeccable cutaway, high hat, and gold-knobbed cane.

Orange County at the time included Lake, Osceola, and Seminole counties with a population of less than 2500. In 1856, Orlando had wrested the county seat from Enterprise, but the former was still "a straggling" village of less than 200 souls with no foreseeable growth prospects. On the other hand, Sanford, 22 miles northward, was situated on the major transport artery of the day, the St. Johns River. It also had a thriving resort hotel, a wharf, a general store, a sawmill, and other new building planned—almost an ideal site for a future hub city.

Sanford saw only one essential complement to his "dream city"—the county seat. He was determined to move it, and more than a few area settlers shared his sentiments. But he soon learned of strong opposition coming from a single source—Jake Summerlin.

Determined to confront this "interloper" and also persuade the county commissioners of the advantages of his removal proposal, the general set out one day for Orlando. Arriving at the town's modest "Inn," he spotted a man reclined on the veranda apparently asleep—shirt open, garbed in drab clothes, with saddle bags under his head for a pillow. It was Summerlin himself, who slowly opened his eyes as the tall figure approached.

Condescendingly, the general inquired: "You seem, my good man, to be a native so perhaps you have met the self-styled cattle king Jacob Summerlin?"

"Wal', no, I have never met him," Summerlin replied, "but my wife knows him purty well; got acquainted with 'im a number of years ago, before we moved to Orlando, and I have heard considerably 'bout him and his doings."

Identifying himself, Sanford queried further: "Then tell me what reason has this ignorant cattleman when he defies me...in my efforts to move the county seat to the new town, where it properly belongs?"

"Wal' I reckon he thinks Orlando a purty good place, and people usta sorta tend court and do their trading here."

"I care nothing about what he thinks. He will find his stubborn opposition and insolent refusal to agree will gain nothing, for I say the county seat is going to be moved to Sanford."

At this, Summerlin rose, eyes flashing, and declared: "You may be General Sanford and a-goin' to move the courthouse, but I am Jacob Summerlin and I say there on Main Street, Orlando, stands the Orange County Courthouse and there it will stand when you and I, our children, and grandchildren are long since passed away." As if to punctuate the conversation's end, Summerlin lay back down again and closed his eyes. The general, nonplussed, turned finally and entered the lodging.

That evening, spotting Summerlin again at the dining table, Sanford joined him with a friendly greeting. Summoning his ablest diplomatic prowess, he proceeded to regale the cowman with a glowing description of the town's future and its progress thus far, plus its great commercial potential. Summerlin, just as polite in mien, nodded courteously at points in the general's spiel but said little himself. After dinner the two men shook hands and parted, Sanford with every confidence that his diplomatic skills had saved the day.

The next morning, rising to speak before the county commissioners, Sanford was at his most eloquent describing his town's bright future, its progressive plans developing, the benefits that would accrue to the entire county, and concluding with an offer to construct a beautiful new courthouse. The commissioners were duly impressed, especially with the courthouse offer. They then turned to hear Summerlin, who had been sitting quietly in a corner.

Speaking briefly, the cattle king described what he believed to be a great raw potential for Orlando's future, then reminded the solons that "the county seat has been located here by the free will of the majority of settlers," and so deeded for that purpose. He then concluded: "Now I will make my offer"—a sum of $10,000 immediately to construct a new courthouse. "And if the county is ever able to pay me, all right, and if not, that is also all right with me."

For nearly a quarter-hour, the commissioners buzzed intensely together in a huddle, then finally resumed their seats. The chairman then announced unanimous acceptance of Summerlin's offer. (They later repaid the $10,000 over a 10-year period.) Once more the general stood dumbfounded. Then, in an imperious huff, he walked out of the room. A few years later he would rejoin the diplomatic service, where he remained until his death in 1891.

The old cowman's faith in Orlando's future is certainly attested to by its bustling major metro status today. But the general would not live to see a—sort of—posthumous victory. In 1913, when Seminole County was formed, it chose as its county seat—Sanford.

51.
From Sawgrass to White House

The battle with Seminoles at Okeechobee was a doubtful victory, but it put Zachary Taylor on a road to the White House.

The battle of Okeechobee was the one and only major conventional battle ever fought in that long and costly guerrilla war called the Seminole Indian War (1835-1842).

It occurred on Christmas Day and lasted only three brief, gory hours, but the mix of mud and blood in the meanest swamp and sawgrass land would have a totally unexpected result—it would take a routinely competent career army officer (one not far from retirement), and catalyze a course for him leading straight to the White House.

The case of Colonel Zachary Taylor is perhaps merely illustration of the "bug" afflicting military leaders recurrently in American history, namely, political ambition. Or, to paraphrase an old military adage, "Old soldiers never die, they just make a bid for the presidency."

The Seminole War had been dragging on for two years, long past the time estimated by experts of the period, who had figured on a simple 30-day field trip to subdue "a small band of savages." The hundreds of Seminoles who fought westward expansion, claiming gross violation of their treaty rights, proved as tenacious in this refusal as they were elusive in their war tactics. Therefore, Taylor's victory at Okeechobee was effusively heralded in the nation's press as the war's "turning point," the "decisive victory" that would hasten its end. It was an exhilarating tonic to a weary war machine that had all but bogged down in the yellow fever-ridden forests, swamps, and tropical jungle that made up most of interior Florida in those years.

But it was not a turning point; in fact, one of America's costliest and bloodiest wars would drag on another five years. It was a war that saw a succession of various commanders—Clinch, Scott, Gaines, Jesup, Armistead— who found their classic military tactics, largely European-derived, mostly ineffective in a wilderness jungle against primitives who had not studied the West Point manuals on proper warfare. Within less than two years, Taylor himself would want out.

But the Battle of Okeechobee stamped Taylor's name indelibly in the country's mind as *the* hero of the Seminole War. He was suddenly being viewed as a true cut—however knotty—of Presidential timber. And yet, most historians agree that the battle itself was lauded much out of proportion to what it actually accomplished.

In any event, then-commander General Thomas Jesup could hardly have picked a more able officer for this "show of force." As one historian notes, Taylor "had already acquired a reputation as one of the best fighters and worst politicians in the armed services." He was vinegary, profane, informal, and even irreverent toward military protocol, and had thus earned the nickname "Old Rough and Ready."

When scouts informed the army that the Seminoles were moving toward a major rendezvous point just north of Lake Okeechobee, Colonel Taylor moved out of Fort Brooke at Tampa in November, 1837, with 800 regulars, 180 Missouri Indians, 70 Delaware Indians, a handful of Shawnees, and a few Florida volunteers.

On reaching the Kissimmee River, he established Fort Gardiner, where he dropped off his heavier baggage and artillery and then marched south, setting up another depot, Fort Basinger, some 20 miles northwest of the lake. On the evening of the first day of the march, Taylor surprised and captured 63 Indians, including Micanopy's sometime mentor, Chief Jumper. The next day, a small camp of 22 men, women, and children surrendered. Thereafter, they came across other deserted camps, the fires and half-cooked meals indicating hasty departures. After crossing Taylor's Creek near the present town of Okeechobee, scouts reported that Chief Alligator, joined by the ingenious Coacoochee, who had recently escaped from the federal fort at St. Augustine, was encamped with 400 warriors near the lake shore, ready to take their stand. At dawn, Christmas Day, Taylor would move his men out to attack. A young infantry lieutenant, Robert C. Buchanan, kept a diary record of the fray. At pre-dawn, he also began a Christmas letter home which he decided to finish only after the day's end. It began: "A merry Christmas to all of my friends at home, and may they have many happy returns of the season. Mine, I am inclined to think, will be more lively, but not so pleasant as theirs." He was right, of course.

Alligator had positioned his men in a large hammock that overlooked a swamp three-quarters of a mile wide and about three miles long, covered with sawgrass five feet high. The Indians had cut a wide swath in the sawgrass in order to have a clear shot at their foe. "The enemy was posted in the strongest position that I have ever seen in Florida," Buchanan wrote. He noted that the men were already exhausted from the march and became even more so as they turned their horses back and began inching through the knee-high mud and water. The Missouri volunteers took the first line of advance. The regulars took up the second line, with some on the flanks joining the Delawares and Shawnees. With the first volley of Indian fire, the Missourian line broke and retreated, "after which they could not be rallied again," Buchanan reported. Their commander was killed. The second line moved up quickly but under "so deadly a fire . . . that most of the officers and men were soon killed or wounded and they [the flanks] were forced to give way."

The battle had begun shortly after the noon hour, but by two o'clock, so many officers had been killed that Lieutenant Buchanan found himself commanding two extra companies. The Indians had entrenched themselves well, both in the tops of trees and behind them, the officer observed. Buchanan and another officer quickly decided then to regroup their men for a direct frontal charge.

During one of the several charges, Buchanan recorded a devastating trick pulled by the hostiles. Taylor's Delaware Indians so closely resembled the Seminoles in the thick of the fight that "as they [the Seminoles] came up within a few yards of our line, some of the men hailed them to know if they were Delawares. They [the Seminoles] answered, 'Yes, Delaware, Delaware!' but at the same time continued to take up their positions behind trees and stumps, from which they soon gave us a volley which caused more injury than all of the others during the fight."

But repeated infantry charges succeeded in pushing the Seminoles a mile back to the shore of the lake. Taylor then ordered a massive right flank turn. It was an overwhelming move. The Indians fired one more volley and then scattered in retreat. They were pursued, but with little success, up to nightfall.

It was a victory—but at a price. The Indians had suffered 11 killed and 14 wounded. The army: 26 killed (a large number officers), and 112 wounded. The men were so exhausted, Buchanan noted, that "it was with utmost difficulty that they could bring out the bodies of the dead [and wounded]." But before sleep that night, Buchanan closed his letter: "A sad Christmas this has been for us and our friends."

The six-week, 150-mile expedition had succeeded in overtaking and defeating the enemy for the first time. Taylor had also captured 180 of the enemy, plus 100 horses and 600 head of cattle. The victory was celebrated nationwide and Colonel Taylor became a hero virtually overnight. He was quickly raised to the brevet rank of brigadier general and, within months, would succeed Jesup as supreme commander in Florida.

But the war would thereafter remain a series of hit-and-run skirmishes. Beset by reductions in his troop strength, along with hostile attitudes from Tallahassee political leaders who sought massive federal funds to finance their rather unreliable militia forces, Taylor concluded that "the conflict could be ended only by allowing the hostiles to remain in Florida." Although this enraged state politicians, Washington agreed with him; specific boundaries were set out below the Peace River Valley. Taylor then asked for, and received, relief from his Florida command post in April, 1840. Florida politics would soon disrupt that peace; the "war" would continue until the various bands either turned themselves in to the army, were killed or captured, or retreated into the vast Everglades where their survivors remain today.

But Taylor's momentum in national politics and his "hero" status continued steadily upward, and within a few years he would clinch this status with a brilliant and resounding defeat of Mexican forces at Buena Vista in the Mexican-American War. His party—the Whigs—engineered an enthusiastic groundswell throughout the country for his nomination as Whig candidate for president in 1848. Although he reserved personal doubts earlier as to his desire, or even his ability, to serve in this highest office, the wooing gained in such spirit and intensity that the general succumbed to the garland. He was nominated and won a clear-cut victory over Louis Cass, a Democrat, that November.

His administration was often marred by party bickering and executive uncertainty, especially over the inflammatory Missouri Compromise that prompted widespread national divisions. These problems would fan the embers toward the conflagration of Civil War. Taylor would not live to see this event, however. He died in office of a fever in July, 1850.

But he must have wondered at the strange turns of history: How an old soldier in the twilight of his career would find his entire life—and history's course—suddenly changed, and all because of a bloody little battle with a band of Indians long ago in a Florida swamp.

52.
When Land Sold by the Gallon

Home and farm lots in the Everglades were promoted and peddled nationwide, but buyers often had to "row" to their plots.

Florida has seen many kinds of land booms in its history, from the early conquistadors, who killed for it, to the "binder boys" of the giddy 1920s, who swindled for it.

But for sheer tragedy, comedy, and outrage, few have exceeded the "swamp boom" of the early 1900s, when thousands of acres of "farmland" in the vast Everglades south of Okeechobee were peddled—mainly in the Midwest—by hucksters whose glib and colorful hyperbole was matched only by their amnesic attention to facts.

So much so that by the time this swamp fever had subsided, and the woeful stories of thousands of victimized buyers had sifted through a federal grand jury, a host of land companies were brought to trial in what one U.S. Congressman called "one of the meanest swindles ever devised."

The trial surely did attest to a bit of grand scale knavery, though leavened at moments with comic relief. Miss Mina Allen, an Illinois schoolteacher, testified that on a trip to inspect her farm, the Everglades "looked like a wheat field in June—until you got close." She said they motored as far as they could, then set out on foot "in water everywhere." By the time it got knee-deep, and her farm was still over a mile distant, she turned back. Asked her feelings on seeing her land underwater, she replied, "I was entirely at sea," demurely unaware of the pun—but the jury roared.

An Iowa purchaser swore: "I have bought land by the acre, I have bought land by the foot; but, by God, I have never bought land by the gallon."

Press wits had a field day advising hapless victims of plows that could be run by launches and how to raise fish instead of produce.

But to the thousands who lost their hard-earned savings, there was nothing funny about their submarine farms. Many officials and salesmen were convicted—some going to prison—and those who appealed found little sympathy from the U.S. Supreme Court, which decided: "Advertisers, even though they give purchasers value received, are guilty of fraud, if by exaggerated advertisement propaganda they had led clients to expect more."

The ironic tragedy of the "swamp boom" is that it began as a grand-scale progressive public project, designed to drain and open the rich mucklands to Florida homesteaders, and it was initiated by one of Florida's greatest governors, Napoleon B. Broward. In 1850, the federal government gave the state 20.5 million acres of "swamp and overflowed lands," but railroads and corporate interests had, by 1900, gobbled up over 15 million of these acres. Broward was determined to "save for the people" the largest state tract left—3,076,904 acres south of Lake Okeechobee. After a stormy election as governor in 1904, Broward won a violent and bitter contest with these corporate interests to begin his "dream" project, the colossal task of draining and reclaiming the Glades. He began at once by cutting three canals from Lake Okeechobee to the southeast Florida coast, but the mammoth effort proved so costly that, by the end of his term, Broward decided to let a successful Midwestern developer, R.J. Bolles, come into the project. The trustees of the state's Internal Improvement Fund sold 500,000 acres of the Everglades to Bolles for development at $2 an acre, half of which proceeds the state would use solely for drainage purposes.

After Broward left office, Bolles began organizing land companies; most of his purchase was soon divided into farm tracts of from 10 to 640 acres, with a bonus lot thrown in at a planned townsite called Progresso, near Fort Lauderdale.

The companies hired "supersalesmen" to fan out over rural Midwestern communities to promote "The Promised Land," a "Poor Man's Paradise," farmland "more fertile than the Nile Valley," where 10 acres of the fabulous muck would generously maintain a whole family. By 1911, fully 50 real estate agencies in Chicago—called "swampboomers" by the *New York World*—were selling Everglades land.

But soon enough the boom would backfire. When purchasers began visiting their farmsites, their shock slowly turned into a crescendo of outrage when they discovered the land not only undrained but almost inaccessible by boat through the thick sawgrass prairies. In their loquacious spiel, the supersalesmen had seen fit to gloss over this geographic detail. Meanwhile, the state once more had exhausted its reclamation funds, due in large part to the slow dribble of due payments from the land companies, but due also to the unforeseen intricacies of so vast an undertaking.

Missouri Congressman William P. Borland, many of whose constituents were among the victims, estimated that "about 25,000 people" had been defrauded in "one of the meanest swindles ever devised." He noted that many of these small investors would, financially and otherwise, be unable to redress their claims through the courts. Joined by other lawmakers, Borland set out to initiate a grand jury probe; by November, 1913, the first indictments of land company officials and salesmen were handed down.

To a degree, it had to be said that some responsibility for the tragedy rested with the buyers themselves. As chronicler Winthrop Packard put it: "A man who buys land for settlement which he has never seen is a fool, but that does not alter the misery of it." That some of the buyers were indeed somewhat untutored in more ways than one was never more poignantly, if humorously, illustrated than when defense attorneys at the trial asked one farm buyer if there was nitrogen as well as H_2O in the rain water in Florida. The witness allowed that he had never seen any H_2O in the water, that he was doubtful about the presence of letters and figures of any kind there, but he was positive about the nitrogen.

In the end, dozens of both land company officials and salesmen were convicted, and more than a few served up to five years in prison. But Bolles himself eluded trial on 22 counts when, after boarding a train in Palm Beach, he was discovered dead in his berth the next morning, possibly from cardiac arrest.

The national notoriety of the swamp boom brought land sales and the drainage project to a virtual halt for nearly two decades. For some years after the scandal, the name "Everglades" had become almost a national synonym for "swindle." Thousands of investors later simply forfeited their land for taxes.

But the natural push of settlement in Southeast Florida, coupled with private developer drainage projects that were greatly aided by state and federal partic- ipation, gradually, over the years, brought much of the Okeechobee region and the southeastern Everglades into farmland. That rich dark muck today comprises one of the most productive winter vegetable gardens in the world.

Nevertheless, 70 years ago, a multitude of citizenry discovered that buying this farmland "by the gallon" was too much of a long bitter drink to swallow.

53.
Governor Gilchrist's Undulating Road

The governor was the first to create that illusory middle-of-the-road slogan, but he found it a difficult road to straddle.

The political catchphrase "middle of the road" has served many an office-seeker whose ambition was far more specific than his platform.

While the phrase suggests the would-be helmsman is a person of good sense who will guide the ship of state smoothly through crisis or controversy, it also serves to relieve the candidate of any obligation to disclose specific ideas of his own—if in fact he has any.

A model practitioner of this middle-of-the-road method was Florida Governor Albert W. Gilchrist, the state's chief executive from 1909 to 1913. His successful use of the phrase in his gubernatorial bid seems the more remarkable, coming under the shadow of his predecessor, Napoleon Bonaparte Broward, one of Florida's greatest leaders. As governor from 1905 to 1909, Broward ushered in an important era of progress and reform, championing the interests of farmers, small businesses, labor, and consumers against the burgeoning power of urban corporate interests. He fought for stronger regulation of railroads, utility companies, and trusts, a centralized state university system, the eight-hour day, better teacher salaries, strict child-labor laws, conservation, prison reform, pure-food laws, anti-gambling laws, and prohibition, to name a few. And he achieved many of these reforms despite opposition from most of the state's press. Broward died just before occupying the U.S. Senate seat to which he was elected in 1910.

Gilchrist, on the other hand, was not inclined to the cerebral efforts involved in formulating ideas or pondering complex issues. Aside from a long-nursed ambition to be governor someday, his only longstanding interest was in military matters.

Gilchrist grew up on his father's plantation in Quincy and attended Carolina

Military Academy in North Carolina, where he studied engineering. In 1878, at age 20, he entered the U.S. Military Academy at West Point, but in his third year a course in experimental philosophy so taxed him that he flunked the class, thereby forcing his withdrawal from the academy. This failure would rankle him for years.

Gilchrist returned to settle in Punta Gorda, in De Soto County, his lifelong residence. For a while he worked as a surveyor. But by buying up and speculating in tracts of land in the fast-growing De Soto area, he soon amassed enough income to give up surveying permanently. Later, he also served as Inspector General of Militia under Governors Edward A Perry and Francis P. Fleming, and in 1896 Governor Mitchell appointed him a militia brigadier general. This latter post enabled him to assuage somewhat his earlier humiliation by securing an appointment as a member of the Board of Visitors to West Point. He joined the Army during the Spanish-American War and was discharged as a captain.

It seemed in character that Gilchrist should designate himself the "middle-of-the-road" candidate when he announced his intent to run for governor in 1908. In a four-man contest, his most serious opponent was John N.C. Stockton, a Jacksonville banker and former legislator who ran on a strong Broward-type platform. Between the major city newspapers, who opposed Stockton as avidly as they had Broward, and the major corporate and railroad interests, the portrayal of Stockton as a "Broward machine" candidate met with a degree of success.

Gilchrist, however, was relatively unknown among the candidates, an obscurity that permitted him to project the image of an independent, unfettered by "faction, machine or ring." He deflected public scrutiny of his fence-straddling on issues by declaring that he wished to serve all groups equally. Thus, for example, he could make this vague assertion: "The corporation cannot do without the people, neither can the people do without the corporations. Capital is organized. Labor should organize. It has been said that the corporations are with me. Well, I'm glad of it. I want everybody to be with me, and if they will, I will be governor and will surely protect the interests of all classes." Gilchrist actually took a position on only one issue, prohibition, preferring local option by counties rather than a statewide referendum. In this he shrewdly eyed the substantial "wet" vote in the populous areas of Tampa and Jacksonville.

The philosophic depth of Gilchrist's style seems best perceived in a campaign gimmick he adopted: the Oriental motto depicted by three monkeys who "hear no evil, see no evil, speak no evil." He sent out postcard drawings of the monkeys with their hands covering ears, eyes, and mouth, respectively. Some boosters received porcelain figurines of the simians imported from Japan, prompting the pro-Gilchrist Tampa *Tribune* to enthuse over how "fortunate" were the recipients of this homiletic tour de force.

If newspapers like the *Tribune*, Jacksonville *Times-Union*, Ocala *Banner*, Miami *News-Record*, and Gainesville *Daily Sun* all supported Gilchrist, the latter, in turn, was almost fulsome in reciprocation. The press, he declared, "does more for the development of the state than all other agencies combined," adding, not unpointedly, it also "does much for the election of the successful candidates."

Press or no, the Punta Gordan's ambiguous platform was successful. In the first primary, Gilchrist topped Stockton 23,248 votes to 20,968 and in the runoff, 32,465 to 23,291; he went on to win in November.

The precise middle of the road seemed to have hazy markings under Gilchrist's administration. A pure-food bill and a uniform textbook law were passed, but the Legislature under him declined to approve either an income or an inheritance tax; it refused to pass a child-labor law or employer's liability bill; it took away control over telephone and telegraph rates and service from the cities; and when it did pass an act abolishing the state's notorious convict-leasing system, it refused to override the governor's veto of it.

The governor proved averse to almost any controversy. For example, he once proposed making Lincoln's birthday a state holiday but quickly dropped the idea when a lawmaker threatened his impeachment if such a law were enacted. When U.S. Representative Frank Clark labeled him "this little pin-headed governor" for failing to act against land company "sharks and bummers" selling Everglades "land by the gallon" to unwary out-of-state buyers, Gilchrist dismissed Clark as simply "a tool" for forces opposing the Glades' reclamation project. The scandal eventually drew a probe by the U.S. government. Another time, in Tampa, Gilchrist apparently "saw no evil," or at least as he said, "no undue violence," in an episode that drew national protest: During a cigar workers' organizing strike in 1910, citizen "vigilantes" employed mob actions, violent labor "goons," and two lynchings to break the labor action.

But the precise position of the middle of Gilchrist's road was more sharply defined during the presidential elections of 1912. Here the governor joined his state forces with the press and an unlikely Southern alliance of corporate interests and demagogic political leaders to support first Judson Harmon and then Oscar Underwood to oppose the Progressive Woodrow Wilson. But these Gilchrist forces had grossly underestimated Wilson's appeal in the state. Wilson won the nomination and then swept Florida with 70.2% of its vote in November.

By 1916, the voters had apparently determined that Gilchrist's vaunted "middle of the road" had a very uncertain center. The retired governor lost heavily behind two other candidates in his last bid for an office, the U.S. Senate. He died May 15, 1926. The metaphor seemed to ring true: the "middle" was as empty as it is on any public road.

54.
President Wilson's Miami Cable War

Wilson declared war on mighty Western Union in Miami's waters in efforts to break a foreign cable monopoly.

It was a strange little war against an improbable enemy, or so it seemed back in 1920 when the United States called out a Navy flotilla to stop Western Union Telegraph Company from landing a British-operated international cable at Miami.

"Just a tempest in a teapot," huffed the *Miami Herald* after President Woodrow Wilson had his secretary of state warn British authorities that it would be "extremely inadvisable" to attempt the cable landing. Wilson's language was veiled diplomatese for: "Try it and we'll blow you out of the water." And when later in the war Western Union officials tried to sneak the cable ashore anyway, the warning was punctuated, as the *Herald* bellowed in a front-page banner headline: "Sub Chaser Opens Fire On Cable Ship."

The *Herald*, of course, was an avid booster of this first direct, cable link between the United States and Brazil; it would make Miami one of the world's most important cable centers. Cables to the rich Brazilian markets then had to be sent via Europe or down the entire west coast of South America, thence to Argentina. Wilson's fears, the newspaper chided, were catalyzed by the "Red Scare" of that era, referring to a short-lived but intense nationwide hysteria over "foreign agents" and "Bolsheviks"—more imagined than real—who would exploit the country's post-World War I economic problems.

Ironically, however, it was not "reds" but "capitalists"—more specifically British monopolists—who had incurred Wilson's bellicosity. In fact, a staunch non-Bolshevik like U.S. Senator Frank B. Kellogg had begun hearings on a bill giving the president sole powers to grant or deny permits for any foreign-connected cable landings, direct or indirect, on U.S. soil. Kellogg was spurred by concern for the country's foreign trade interests amidst reports of a form of cable espionage affecting those interests.

Ever since Cyrus W. Field laid the first trans-Atlantic cable in 1866, the British enjoyed a virtual worldwide monopoly over this rich enterprise. Firms such as Western Union had cable links to Europe only via British cables and on British terms.

In March, 1920, Western Union applied for a U.S. permit to land a cable at Miami that would run some 2,000 miles to Barbados Island, then connect by automatic relay with Britain's Western Telegraph Company cable running to Brazil, where the British enjoyed exclusive cable rights. With Wilson's approval, the State Department denied the permit since Brazil barred landing of a competitive American cable. It cited the policy set by President U.S. Grant, who denied the French Cable Company a U.S. landing for similar reasons. Nevertheless, in July, 1920, Western Union, operating under a 20-year-old U.S. Army permit and acting upon British instructions, employed the British cable ship *Colonia* to connect line at a cable head buoyed just outside the three-mile limit off Miami Beach. Wilson promptly rushed four U.S. destroyers into Biscayne Bay and filed a protest at the British embassy. Within hours, U.S. Army officials and the British vice consul at Miami boarded the *Colonia*, and the cable operation was suspended. But Western Union then went into federal district court, claiming its right to lay the cable, and the court ruled for the firm. The U.S. appealed but lost again and went on to the U.S. Supreme Court, which would not hear the case until late spring 1921.

Meanwhile, the Kellogg hearings were producing disturbing revelations about British cable practices, dating from World War I and arising out of Britain's wartime censorship powers that remained in effect long after the war's end. Scandinavian and Dutch merchants had first raised vociferous complaints alleging that the British were delaying their business cables in order to give British merchants an unfair advantage over foreign rivals. Chairman Kellogg then heard Captain F.K. Mill, a former U.S. naval attache who had worked in the cable censor office in Brazil, testify that Brazilian and British authorities often delayed or turned over American cables to friendly local merchants. One "glaring" example, he cited, was the leaking of a cable bid by General Electric Company on a Brazilian firm's order for certain electrical goods. A British firm submitted a lower bid on an "identical list" of the same goods before GE even got a reply on its own. Another "astonishing" case was of a coffee firm executive who boasted to Mill that he could get coffee quotations from New York the same day while, for Mill, it would take two days to get the same quotations over the same British cable lines.

A more alarming disclosure came when Kellogg drew the admission from Western Union President Newcomb Carlton that American cables—transmitted by Western Union via British cable—were routinely turned over to the British naval intelligence bureau. Carlton hastily added that the cables were held "not more than a few hours," not long enough to decipher. Asserting that "there is no code that cannot be deciphered," Kellogg then pressed Carlton on "the major point," namely, were cables from U.S. military attaches or the ambassador or minister intercepted? First balking, Carlton "reluctantly" admitted they were. But, he added, Britain did this with all countries in efforts to learn of any pending domestic disorders such as could arise from "Irish unrest" or "Bolshevik propaganda." However, he expressed the belief that this practice had no adverse effect on any U.S. interests. Somewhat defiantly, he then declared that his company had "no obligation" to inform any government of the manner of British cable practices.

The hearings closed with a statement from a rival U.S. firm, All-America Cables, Inc., urging the committee to block the Miami cable landing until Brazil allowed free entry of American lines and arguing that America could not compete in world trade until it employed some of Britain's monopolistic methods of backing its commerce with legislative force. Congress apparently agreed; the Kellogg bill was passed overwhelmingly, and Wilson signed it before leaving office March 3, 1921.

A few days before, while visiting in Miami, Carlton, bolstered by his court victories, intimated to the *Herald* that he would soon try again to land his cable since he believed the new president, Warren Harding, would take a friendlier attitude toward Western Union. But though Wilson was out, the U.S. Navy was still on guard, and when, on March 5, Carlton sent his vessel *Robert Clowery* out to link line to the offshore cable head, a U.S. sub chaser sped out to the *Clowery* and hoisted warning signals. Either failing to see or simply ignoring the signals, the cable ship continued working and the chaser promptly fired a three-inch gun shell across the *Clowery's* bow. The cable ship quickly hove to and was then escorted to the Miami city dock, where its captain and crew were placed under arrest (but released later that night).

Despite the Kellogg bill—which Harding declined to invoke—the Supreme Court finally ruled in favor of Western Union. Nevertheless, the embarrassing Kellogg hearing disclosures had ignited an international imbroglio and some hasty diplomatic cabals between Britain and Brazil. In consequence, the British abandoned their monopolistic proviso, and the Brazilian president permitted the first American cable into his country.

And so the great Miami cable war had turned out to be a bit more than a teapot tempest; the U.S. had successfully challenged a powerful nation's virtual control of this worldwide system that had grated too long on the political and economic nerves of too many countries. And it stood ready to make Miami a battleground if that's what it took.

55.
Native Rebs Against the Rebels

*More than a few Florida natives called the Confederate cause
"a rich man's war" and rebelled against Jefferson Davis.*

"My men have taken an oath to stay in Taylor County," a Confederate deserter leader informed the rebel officer trying to woo him back. "They will not go into the war if you had as many men as dogs, for our title is Florida Royals, and, if we cannot get a furlough from Mr. Jeff Davis during the war, you will find our title right for awhile."

Thus spoke W.W. Strickland, a lanky Cracker farmer who headed Taylor County's "Independent Union Rangers" and who was, until his capture and execution in 1865, a symbol of one of the least popular (or mentioned) episodes in Florida's Civil War history: the widespread mini-civil war within the state's own borders.

At least 20 percent of adult whites in Florida during that tragic conflict became openly pro-Union, while thousands more, nominally loyal to "the cause," became indifferent or even hostile to its aims. And this disaffection was only compounded by gross official inequities and corruption, plus the near-famine and destitution of Florida's people. Nor were the "runaway rebels" simply those few who had opposed secession or Northerners still loyal to the United States. They were mostly frontier Cracker settlers who, like Strickland and his followers, organized into bands. However, after swearing allegiance to the United States, they turned and raided nearby plantations, seized provisions, freed slaves, and armed themselves. Sometimes they received food and arms from federal gunboats blockading offshore. Usually they hid out in the impenetrable swamps, riverlands, and forests of the region, often just a step ahead of Confederate cavalry and dogs.

These were men who had earlier migrated down from the Virginias and Carolinas, ruggedly independent, fundamentalist in religion, close-knit in community, whether at house-raisings or hog-killings. Most of them lived in sturdy one-room log cabins, with a few acres set out for cotton, produce, and livestock. Most of them could read and write passably well; their main books were the Bible and the McGuffey Readers. Taylor County was demographically typical. At the war's outbreak, the county's 1,384 citizens "seemed perfectly oblivious to the struggle in the offing," reports historian W.T. Cash. Yet they dutifully volunteered 250 men to Confederate ranks.

One distinctive difference between these settlers and the wealthy, slave-holding planter class was that most of the former neither owned slaves nor cultivated large plantations, a misalliance of interest that would more sharply define itself as the war progressed. Indeed, Taylor County became a major refuge and stronghold for deserter bands, while its citizens bitterly denounced "a rich man's war and a poor man's fight." Rebel General Joseph Finegan found their "disloyalty" widespread by 1864, and, he added, "They are not disposed to disguise their sentiments."

The distinction was real enough. Of the state's 78,000 white citizens, there were only 250 slaveholders with 50 or more slaves. Only seven counties—Gadsden, Jackson, Leon, Jefferson, Madison, Alachua, and Marion—held 40,000 of the state's 61,000 slaves, plus two-thirds, or $40 million, of the entire state's real and personal property wealth.

The South, and especially Florida, with its largely one-basket economy—cotton—was ill-prepared initially to begin a war. Thus, even as early as 1862, Florida families began facing shortages of the simplest food staples—corn, rice, meat, flour—as well as soap, clothes, and medicine. That same year, the Legislature was forced to distribute $20,000 worth of wool for cloth weaving to needy soldiers' families. As the destitution reached near-famine proportions in some counties in 1864, the lawmakers earmarked $1.2 million from 1862 to 1864 for statewide family relief, but only a fraction of this reached the families. Food fast became the most critical shortage looming over the war-torn state. Hundreds of soldiers deserted simply on learning of the severe destitution of their families. Strickland himself, who had served ably in the rebel ranks, deserted when his captain refused him leave to attend to his seriously ill wife.

Other factors served to aggravate the crisis. The rebel draft law of 1862 (the first in the country), was decried not only for its coercive features but for permitting wealthy family members to buy substitutes to serve in their place. Then came the controversial Impressment Act in 1863, enabling agents to seize food and property from home-front families, then pay for it at below-market prices with rapidly collapsing rebel currency. Many unscrupulous men posed as such agents, seizing food to be sold on the flourishing black market, sometimes taking a family's last cow or bushel of corn. Ironically, fervent pleas by Governor John Milton to secessionist planters to raise desperately needed food, instead of cash crops like cotton and tobacco, fell on deaf ears. And rebel General John Pemberton warned that "planter indifference to both the . . . war effort and the well-being of citizens has reached ominous proportions."

Meanwhile, war profiteers were driving prices out of sight for most families. Blockade-runners made fortunes, paying 17 cents a gallon in Havana for rum—indispensable for medical purposes—and selling it at $25 to $35 a gallon. The critically scarce preservative, salt, went from $3 to $20 a bushel. When the government gave draft exemptions to saltmakers, hundreds of able-bodied men flocked to the seashore to make salt—and much of this reached only the speculative market. Early in the war, South Florida cattlemen supplied the rebel army with beef, but later found the lure of Spanish gold in the best markets of Cuba a little stronger than rebel loyalty. The Tallahassee *Sentinel* would soon declare the "speculation and extortion [are] going to ruin us if anything does."

As widespread destitution accelerated, bitter disaffection increased. A rebel officer, noting that his men had no shoes, and the little beef they received was "so poor" as to be inedible, concluded that "the spirit of the army is in favor of peace." Union troops entering Apalachicola found people "near starvation" while a federal officer occupying Baldwin deplored the "appalling" destitution of its women and children. Wherever federal naval forces landed, another noted, "the inhabitants throng into our camp, asking for food."

Desertions and pro-Union sentiment rose sharply. Governor Milton termed most of West Florida "disloyal." A rebel guerilla leader reported three-fourths of the citizens along the St. Johns River "were aiding and abetting the enemy," while in South Florida, deserter "bushwhackers" raided those few cattle herds still being driven northward. But even Governor Milton had to condemn the "cruel violence" meted out by guerilla "regulators" against deserters and their families—home burnings, whippings, hangings—and warned that it served only to "increase the number of deserters."

But as Union victories mounted, and certain defeat loomed darkly for his once "glorious cause," Governor Milton bitterly surveyed the misery and desolation of his state. He had been helpless to alleviate that condition and unable to stem the profiteering and corruption that fed on it. And, finally, he gradually came to have on his hands what was tantamount to a mini-civil war within his own state.

Thus, on April 1, just eight days before General Lee's surrender, the heavy-hearted state leader drove home to his plantation, "Sylvania," near Marianna. And, while his wife and daughters prepared his "homecoming" dinner, he quietly went to his room, closed the door, and put a bullet through his head.

56.
The Historic Romance of Silver Springs

*The sparkling gem of Silver Springs boasts a romantic history
every bit as legendary as its pellucid waters.*

It is an anomaly of the 20th century. It is as if for centuries a portion of the Garden of Eden had been miraculously preserved and thus remained one of the hydrological wonders of the world—Silver Springs.

Set a few miles northeast of Ocala in jungle-like environs, the pristine beauty of the world's largest formation of artesian springs has enthralled and enchanted countless thousands over the years. Poets and writers have attempted in vain to describe the extravagance of its natural beauties.

"There is nothing on earth comparable to it," enthused Harriet Beecher Stowe more than 100 years ago. And even earlier, in 1826, a veteran Indian fighter, Captain George McCall, recalled how his heart "swelled with astonishment" as he canoed to the center of the springs' basin. The remarkable transparency of the water caused him to feel "suspended in mid-air," while the colorful array of fish and plant life more than 40 feet below seemed close enough to reach out and touch. He could only sit in spellbound awe and reflect on "the marvelous works of the Divine Maker."

The springs has been a "magic theater of nature" since earliest times. It was the stomping ground for the prehistoric mammoth and mastodon, whose chalky remains are still unearthed there today. The Indians called it Sua-ille-aha, "sunglinting waters," and generations of tribes worshipped it as a shrine to their water gods. In more modern times, millions glimpsed its primeval wonders via the adventures of Tarzan, as he bellowed and swung his way through the jungles of not Africa but Florida, fighting alligators under water more clear than the celluloid on which the movies were filmed.

The massive, powerful, silent upward boil of the springs has remained undiminished for centuries. The water enters from five major underground rivers and numerous smaller sources, all drawn from a vast network of underground reservoirs (aquifers).

The daily flow averages a half-billion gallons of water, enough to supply a city of several million. This in turn flows into the beautiful Silver Run River, turns eastward for seven miles, and then runs into the dark, murky, twisting Oklawaha River which is a tributary of the St. Johns.

The water of the springs is so pure (99.76%) that it makes ordinary city tap water seem almost polluted. Laboratory scientists have not yet been able to chemically produce such purity, which is created by the minute filtering process through numerous layers of pure limestone and sand. This contributes to the water's incredible transparency.

Yet for all its beauty, Silver Springs has been the scene of legend and violence, romance and war. Conquistadors Narvaez and, later, De Soto, paused here in their fruitless search for gold, slaughtering a few natives here and there. But the wary Ocali (Ocala) tribes, fearful lest their watery shrine be desecrated, craftily directed the treasure hunters to mythical "gold fields" northward where, later, both men found not gold but death.

Here also arose a tragic Indian legend of star-crossed lovers. Weenonah, beautiful daughter of King Okahumkee, fell in love with a rival young chieftain, Chuleotah, who lived at the springs. Enraged, the king waged war on and slew her lover, whereupon the princess, hoping to follow her beloved to "the flowery land," journeyed to the crystal pool one night and dove to its bottom, drowning herself. The long grassy filaments swaying on the spring's floor were said by Indians to be the loosened braids of Weenonah's long silken hair.

The great Osceola swam and fished here in his youth, and the Seminole Chief Arpeika made it his home until his eviction by the first white settler after the Second Seminole War. James Rogers bought the springs and 80 surrounding acres from the federal government for $1.25 an acre in 1845. At the same time, the county of Marion was created, and the small settlement of Ocala was made the county seat. These occurrences would mark the beginning of a new era for the springs.

Curious visitors by now were already coming in to the springs, among them the distinguished physician, archaeologist, and anthropologist Dr. Daniel G. Brinton, who in 1856 pole-barged his way through the "gloomy and amazing" forests of the Oklawaha. Emerging into the bright Silver Run and finally the springs where the deepest waters were bathed in brilliant sunlight, Brinton termed it "one of the most dramatic transitions from darkness to light that a traveler can make anywhere on the continent." Enraptured by the waters and the lush encircling forest, the doctor extended his stay and became the first modern scholar to study the nearby ancient Indian mounds.

But it was a Vermonter, Hubbard Hart, who was destined to put the springs on the world map. Hart settled at Palatka, on the St. Johns, in 1854, and operated a stagecoach line to the springs, Ocala, and Tampa. Inspired by the development potential of the springs and viewing the brisk steamboat traffic on the St. Johns, Hart wasted no time in acquiring a narrow, stern-paddled steamboat, the *James Burt*, labored for months clearing the Oklawaha of fallen trees and other obstacles, and made his first run with passengers and cargo to the springs.

The venture was successful beyond expectation. By word of mouth the first excited passengers exclaimed over the haunting jungle river trip, climaxed by the enchanting wondrous springs. Hart soon found his boat loaded to capacity; quickly he acquired another, the *Silver Spring*, for the two-night, one-day trip.

Despite the crude accommodations, and the incessant nuisance of mosquitoes and other insects, and the sharp cracks and scrapings of overhanging tree branches against cabins, sightseers experienced a vicarious excitement, even a sense of eerie mystery, as they passed through the heart of such wild primitive jungle where the forests of live oak, sweet bay, and towering cypress created a tunnel-like effect. Daylight was rarely glimpsed along the deep, dark, tortuously twisting river. The river's zigzag turns were often so sharp that heavy hawser lines on shore were needed to round them, due to the river's narrow width (50-80 feet).

The cacophonous chorus of exotic birds among the flowering vines, alligators lazing sleepily along the banks, and the occasional glimpse of a panther, deer, or bear all enhanced this effect of primeval mystery. And then, the climax on entering the crystal-bright springs' pool with its brilliant prismatic colors reflected from below like a fairy garden of awesome beauty.

These idyllic cruises were halted suddenly by the Civil War. Hart's boats were pressed into Confederate service, dodging federal patrols as supplies from east coast blockade runners were smuggled to the springs via the Oklawaha. The *James Burt* would be sunk before the war's end, and, after the war, Hart once more had to work for months to clear the river of trees felled or blasted by federals to obstruct the river traffic.

Postwar Florida tourism began to boom in the 1870s and 1880s, and within several years Hart had a fleet of steamboats. He built a plush hotel at Palatka to handle crowds and began advertising nationwide from an office in Boston. The springs by now was a leading national tourist attraction, drawing also the notable and famous. Robert E. Lee came and so did President-elect U.S. Grant, soon followed by widow Mary Todd Lincoln. Glowing reports of the springs appeared in northern newspapers as well as magazines like *Harper's* and *Scribner's*.

Typical was a report by a national writer called Rambler who noted that, after coming out of "the mysterious regions" of the Oklawaha, "we saw a sight which caused us to rub our eyes and gather up our senses to be certain we were positively awake." Later, canoeing over the pool, as his party looked over the side of the craft "we recoiled at the sensation of *floating in the air.*"

Scribner's exulted over "one of the wonders of the world," its environs "more luxuriantly beautiful than a poet's wildest dreams." As if in confirmation, poets William Cullen Bryant and Sidney Lanier both found themselves, for once, speechless to depict this beauty. England's noted Lady Duffus Hardy deeply regretted having to leave this "pool of wonders."

At first, Florida publicist Harriet Beecher Stowe balked at traveling on one of Hart's "gigantic coffins" but relented after persistent appeals by the captain. Later, in *Palmetto Leaves,* she wrote that her fellow passengers "had seen Europe, Italy, Naples, and the Blue Grotto, but never, never had they in their lives seen aught so entrancing as this. It was a spectacle weird, wondrous, magical—to be remembered as one of the things of a lifetime."

As captivated as they were by the view from above, these early sightseers could not then view the magic waters from 80 feet below, as recounted much later by veteran diver-photographer Bruce Mozert. He marveled at "the vivid coloring...the intensity of the sun's rays slanting down to the greatest depths and bathing everything in a golden glow. There is an unbelievable richness and a new dimension to these colors that cannot be described. It is like another world, a world so beautiful you feel you would like to stay there forever."

Above or below, this view includes more than 100 varieties of exotic marine plants, from long, silky bright green filaments of Angel Hair to the rich reds of the Water Primrose. And perhaps nowhere can one glimpse so natural an aquarium, containing every color and variety of fish; from giant three-foot-long catfish and huge 22-inch-long shrimp to vari-colored Sailfins, Red-breasted Sunfish, and Speckled Perch.

As the romantic and picturesque steamboat era drew to a close in the early 1900s, giving way to the faster modes of rail and auto travel, Silver Springs unaccountably settled into a long interlude of calm obscurity, drawing only occasional trickles of visitors. But the invention of another type of craft and the enterprising vision of two local men would once more restore the attraction's world fame.

The Glass Bottom Boat was invented by a local youth, Philip Morrell, in a crude rowboat. It would be perfected later by two area businessmen, Colonel W.M. Davidson and W.C. Ray, Sr., who in 1924 acquired a 50-year lease on the springs and set about on a national advertising promotion, mainly by highway signboards. Results were soon evident. From 11,000 in 1924, visitor figures began doubling each year, eventually to reach a half-million.

However, the greatest impetus to world renown was provided by the movie industry. Grantland Rice produced some underwater film shorts featuring two local young men, herpetologist Ross Allen and Newton Perry, fearlessly wrestling alligators and anacondas underwater. By 1932, major studios were scouting the area and, before long, millions thrilled to exciting underwater scenes of Tarzan (famed Olympic athlete Johnny Weismuller) fighting villains and alligators (with the aid of Ross and Perry) and swinging through the jungles along Silver Run.

Scores of major films would follow in later decades, among them Gary Cooper in *Distant Drums* and Robert Cummings in *Barefoot Mailman*. Howard Hughes brought his torrid discovery, Jane Russell, for a spectacular underwater world premier of *Underwater*, and a complete pioneer farm was built on the Silver Run banks for Gregory Peck in *The Yearling*. Television series like "Sea Hunt" were filmed here, along with countless other varieties of film features.

By 1962, when American Broadcasting Companies, Inc., acquired the springs and 3,900 acres along Silver Run, Davidson and Ray had acquainted millions with the grandeur of this wonder waterland. The new owners, likewise, have since dedicated themselves to preserving and enhancing its beauty.

The late journalist Ernie Pyle once exclaimed of the springs: "Fantastic beyond description...it just won't go into words." And because this pristine Eden has been preserved almost intact from its days as an Indian shrine, future generations can enjoy the artistic, sensual, and spiritual experience of this natural wonder.

Calamities and Social Turbulence

57.
The Stormy Reign
of a Mighty Mite

The lowly cow tick once created such a furor in the state that its effects embroiled a U.S. President and Congress.

The parasite known as the tick is a small, wingless, faceless, bloodsucking, often fever-laden mite hardly bigger than a corpulent flea.

But for nearly two decades in the first half of the century, the voracious appetites of this Draculan bug turned Florida and a major industry into turmoil with shootouts and dynamitings, state edicts and court fiats, feuds and protests, and Indians on the verge of a fourth Seminole war. The state of Georgia even strung its entire southern border with barbed wire to keep the mess from its doors. The melee worked its way right up to the nation's capital, dividing a cabinet and giving even the President a touch of tick fever.

The Texas fever tick was once a scourge of Southern cattle ranges in the United States, and in 1906 the U.S. Department of Agriculture set out to spend more than $50 million to eradicate it. By 1920, it had rendered some 15 states tick-free—all except Florida.

Florida's cattle industry, evolved from the scrawny, tough, semi-wild little vacos descended from early Spanish imports, took root in the early 1800s when early settlers began rounding up the vast free-roaming herds. The beef was free for the taking, and many cow kings waxed rich in marketing it, mainly in Cuba, from whence Spanish gold doubloons flowed copiously into Cracker saddlebags. But this golden bonanza ended with the Spanish-American War. Thereafter, beef marketing was tough, chiefly because the beef itself was tough, and Florida consumers chose to spend their coin on good Western grades rather than dentist bills. In their free-wheeling days, few cattle kings gave much thought to upgrading these herds, dubbed by some writers as "four-footed silhouettes" or "hidebound skeletons and walking jawbreakers." Nor did they think much of the USDA program of "dipping" cows in vats of an arsenic-tinctured solution to kill the ticks, since, as one of them derided, "Everyone knows that ticks come from inside the cows."

But they were rudely jolted up to date when vast numbers of cattle were virtually eaten alive by a near-epidemic of tick infestation. A second jolt came when Southeastern states slapped a quarantine on Florida beef; Georgia even strung two lines of four-strand barbed-wire fence, 15 feet apart, 200 miles long, from the Chattahoochee to the St. Mary's rivers, with a rider patrolling every 20 miles, to keep out Florida beef.

The chagrin of cattlemen turned to rage when, in 1923, Florida lawmakers passed a compulsory cattle-dipping law, under auspices of the Federal Bureau of Animal Industry, with a newly-created State Livestock Sanitary Board. The projected 10-year program began in Escambia County and gradually would work by zones eastward and then south. The program required biweekly dippings over about 14 months, at the cattlemen's expense for vats and roundup costs. Many cattlemen simply threw up their hands, sold their cows, and got out of the business. Others reacted violently. Vats in many zones were dynamited (15 in Escambia alone); federal range riders and cowhands shot it out; a federal marshal and a rancher were killed, and many on both sides were wounded.

But such rabid resistance gradually gave way to grudging cooperation as one county after another emerged tick-free. By 1927, the USDA reported 70,037 cattle approved for out-of-state shipment. By 1930, Georgia and other states lifted their quarantines. The State Livestock Sanitary Board also provided cowmen with 1,500 purebred bulls to try to upgrade their herds. Florida's tick woes were over—or so it seemed.

Then, as the tick program reached the southern half of the state, something happened. Repeated dippings in Orange County and points south failed to remove the ticks. By 1935, Georgia found ticks in three counties from cattle traced directly to Polk County and promptly renewed its quarantine. Federal "bugologists" scurried south to solve the mystery and, within months, identified a new villain, Boophilus annulatus, a variety of tropical tick hosted by the native white-tailed swamp deer and peculiar only to South Florida.

The only solution, they announced, was to kill all the deer. And so the state paid bounty hunters $80 a month to slay the deer. Hundreds were shot. But this solution was greeted with storms of protest from sportsmen, conservationists, and other citizens. The *Miami Herald* decried the policy as "brutal, pernicious and unjustified." A Deer Protective Association was formed and successfully sought an injunction from the Florida Supreme Court halting the extermination. But fuming cattlemen obtained a rehearing, and the injunction was lifted.

Outraged Seminole Indians on Big Cypress and Everglades reservations in Hendry and Collier counties warned they would use force to stop deer hunting in or about their lands. These areas were in fact under the protection of the U.S. Interior Department, and the Indians found friends in Interior Secretary Harold

Ickes and Indian agent John Collier.

Both men deemed it most important to protect Indian rights and preserve their unique wilderness culture—as well as the native deer—especially after the Indians exhibited 15 of their slain deer, showing them to be tick-free. Ickes banned further deer-killing in the two counties, leading him to repeated clashes first with USDA head Henry Wallace and, in 1940, with Wallace's successor, Claude Wickard. As he and Wickard wrangled over "conclusive proof" of tick-laden reservation deer, Florida Senator Claude Pepper was conferring with the cattlemen. In May, 1941, Pepper introduced a bill making it unlawful for the Interior Department to interfere with the program. "We're going after Brother Ickes," he announced. The bill's hearings dragged into 1942 as both Ickes and Wickard sought President Franklin D. Roosevelt's favor to oppose or support it, respectively.

The war-burdened President chided both men for not resolving the issue "without bothering me." With unsubtle sarcasm, FDR suggested they "put the whole thing off until we find out whether we are going to win this world war or not. If we don't win, ticks on animals and humans will doubtless take over the nation. If we do win the war, we can start a great national tick campaign for the unemployed."

Later, reflecting further, Roosevelt wrote to Wickard on March 20, 1942, that he did not "want any deer killed" in the two counties and warned he would impound funds for the program if Pepper's bill passed. With wry drollery, FDR added: "No one knows whether these unfortunate animals are host to the cattle tick or not," and he advised Wickard to tell the animal bureau that "they have never proved that human beings are not host to cattle ticks. I think some human beings I know are. But I do not shoot them on suspicion—though I would sorely like to." If he refused to cooperate with Ickes, FDR concluded, Wickard might have to "take it up eventually with Emperor Hirohito."

Wickard and Ickes finally agreed on a set number of deer to be examined; eventually 42 deer were killed and found tick-free. Meanwhile, Pepper's bill passed, and FDR promptly impounded the program's funds. Wickard finally capitulated and wrote Ickes that he was lifting the cattle quarantine on Hendry and Collier. This action was viewed as a victory for both Indians and preservationists. It also preserved the last seedstock for wild deer in Florida.

But the great tick war and the mite's sharp little spurs on cattle hide had also spurred the cattle industry out of its 19th century mindset, forcing it to upgrade herds and purebred sires—Hereford, Angus, and the Brahman—and to swap the tough prairie wiregrass for richer varieties such as Para, Bahia, and various clovers. And thus Florida's cow industry thrives today. But it took a tenacious little bug to rearrange it all.

58.
Carry Nation Dries Up Miami

The formidable lady with a hatchet laid her axe aside when she came to dry out sodden Miami.

She would walk right up to a knot of men smoking on a street and summarily slap the cigars from their mouths, or seize two bottles of whiskey from a saloon-keeper's shelf to use as "evidence," or rudely surprise some local denizen as he tippled and sported in a brothel.

Even at 61, even though she had hung up her fearsome hatchet in favor of the ballot box, the volatile fervor of Carry A. Nation, America's most militant scourge of demon rum, had lost none of its ardor when she came to Miami in March, 1908, to help the local temperance forces dry up and dry out the "wicked" little city. And in any tilt between the grapes of Bacchus and the grapes of wrath, it was, to Carry Nation, no contest.

Miami was born "dry" in 1896, thanks to its prohibitionist pioneer, Julia Tuttle, but upon her death in 1898, loopholes were wangled to bring saloons right into the city (they already flourished just outside town, in North Miami). But public drunkenness, violence, and other allied vices spawned a growing temperance force led by the Women's Christian Temperance Union (WCTU) and the Anti-Saloon League, and supported by the leading newspaper, the *Metropolis*. They managed to call a special "wet-dry" election for Dade County in October, 1907. The drys lost, but by so narrow a margin that their zeal was kindled to try again. They organized a campaign of rallies and speakers of which the star centerpiece would be the country's most famous—and controversial— prohibitionist.

Carry Nation had come a long way from the young girl of 19 who had watched her physician-husband, Charles Gloyd, drink himself to death in Belton, Missouri, leaving her with an infant daughter—her first tragic encounter with demon rum. A tall, physically strong, and not unattractive Carry later met and married a minister, David Nation, in 1877; they eventually settled in Medicine Lodge, Kansas. (Carry's chronic absence from home caused their divorce 25 years later.)

It was in Medicine Lodge that the fervently religious Carry and her WCTU sisters successfully clamored to close down the local saloons. Kansas was a dry state, but enforcement was lax at best. Saloons thrived. Thus, to Carry, more draconian measures seemed imperative. Then, reading scriptures one day, she sensed a "divine calling" to go out and tear up the "joints"—literally—although some aspects of her modus operandi seemed at times less the Lord's ideas than her own. Accordingly, she purchased a hatchet, threw in a few brickbats, and proceeded to blaze a fiery trail of splintered wood and shattered glass, first through Kansas and then across the country. Even rumors of her approach prompted salooners to bolt their doors and draw the shades. In New York, retired saloon-keeper and ex-boxing champ John L. Sullivan said he would "throw her down the sewer" if he saw her. But later, when Carry stopped at his place, demanding to see him, the great John L. shrieked: "Not on your life. Tell her I'm sick in bed."

When she wasn't in jail or nursing some bruising at the hands of irate "wets," or reducing joints to shards, she was on the lecture circuit from Chautauqua to town hall, attacking the evils of whiskey, tobacco, fraternal lodges, and illicit sex. Thousands followed her trail of "hatchetation," many wearing the mini-hatchet pins she often sold. Poems, cartoons, and editorials nationwide denounced or praised her. A sainted heroine to the drys, a lunatic and vandal to the wets, few of the latter escaped her caustic ire. To tippling California legislators she fumed: "This government, like a dead fish, stinks worse at the head." Even President McKinley was a "whey-faced tool of Republican thieves, rummies and devils"; Teddy Roosevelt was a "beer-guzzling Dutchman" who let his daughter, Alice, smoke cigarettes.

On arrival in Miami, Carry gave pep talks to enthused supporters in a tent pitched on Flagler Street across from the courthouse, reminding them that the same God who put a jawbone in Samson's hand and sling in David's had put a hatchet in hers. She has retired her hatchet, she explained, in order to go to the problem's "source," namely, Washington lawmakers. Applauding Carry's efforts, the *Metropolis* noted that those "who thought Mrs. Nation simply a sufferer from a certain form of dementia Americana . . . are daily changing their opinions."

When not lecturing, Carry and two of her WCTU hostesses made unannounced tours of the Miami vice scene, often sending gamblers scurrying for cover with cards and chips still in hand. In North Miami brothels, the ladies in "loose attire, smoking and using profane and vulgar language" were sternly berated while male patrons frantically sought less visibility. The tour convinced Mrs. Nation that there was "crime and corruption in plenty in Miami."

The charges moved County Solicitor H. Pierre Branning to subpoena the touring trio for information on such illegal activities. Hours after their talk, Carry addressed a crowd of over 2,000 (largest in Miami's history). Quoting copiously from the Bible on the baneful evils of drink, the crusader declared that local "official corruption" was responsible for Miami's wickedness. As she concluded, an excited and angry Solicitor Branning mounted the platform to denounce the allegations, challenging Carry to produce evidence of such crimes. From the folds of her long black skirt, Carry withdrew two bottles of whiskey, shouting: "These were purchased from North Miami on Sunday" (a state law violation). The audience erupted with cheers and laughter. As the tumult quieted, Branning began to speak on the "brutality of woman against man." But his words were soon muffled under the peals of an organ and the gustful chorus of the crowd singing "Onward Christian Soldiers."

If the *Metropolis* lauded Carry's "commonsense, logical talk," its rival, the *Morning News-Record,* denounced the "mountebank lecturer," claiming that her scriptural texts "had not the remotest connection with present day conditions" and that her charges were unsubstantiated. The journal's attacks were echoed as far away as the *Tampa Tribune,* which was surprised that "Miami seems to be taking Carrie [sic] Nation seriously with the aid of its disreputable daily, the *Metropolis."* When Florida's Governor Napoleon Broward, a prohibitionist, shared the platform with Carry one day, the *News-Record* disparaged his "fair imitation of the prohibition speech."

Also popular were Mrs. Nation's sex lectures, some talks segregated by sex, some not, in which she extolled the joys of the marital union while castigating the sinful and tragic effects of illicit sex.

At the end of Carry's visit, the *News-Record* affirmed: "People here will continue to be almost as good as ever—and no better." But Carry had made an impact. There was an unprecedented increase in arrests of liquor law violators and a new county civic association was organized to promote "good morals, good government [and] temperance." The city council enacted tough new laws: saloon closings at 10 p.m. weeknights, midnight Saturdays; no screens of frosted glass on saloon fronts obscuring the view of passersby; no women or children on bar premises; no liquor sale to intoxicated persons, and other strictures. Soon even the *News-Record* was urging citizens to "rid the city of vice" and "bad saloons." But it was not until 1913—six years before national prohibition—that the drys finally prevailed in an election and Dade County joined most other Florida counties.

Carry Nation and her legendary hatchet were history by then (she died in Kansas in 1911), but her crusade on behalf of "womanhood, family and home" had left many Miamians heartened, elated, and inspired, while others it simply left—exhausted.

59.
Massacre in Southeast Florida

*Fear and panic rippled through Florida's lower east coast
when a Fort Lauderdale family was massacred by Indians.*

Fort Lauderdale today is a sleek, bustling commercial and resort city, glossily swathed in ultramodern facades. So, it is hard to recall its sparsely settled wilderness scene of nearly a century and a half ago, or the tragic event—the Cooley Massacre—that led to the town's birth and its name.

In the late 1820s, when Dade County was little more than a lighthouse at Cape Florida, three families came to settle on the tranquil New River: the Howes, the Rigbys, and the Cooleys.

William Cooley arrived first in 1825 from Maryland, with his family and a business associate, David Williams. They settled on a 640-acre tract on the New River owned by a friend of Cooley, Richard Fitzpatrick. They were joined soon afterward by the Howes and Mary R. Rigby, a widow with two daughters and a son.

In the midst of jungle and swampland, their land was rich and arable. They successfully cultivated large vegetable patches, and the area abounded in seafood and wild game. In order to get hard cash to purchase livestock, the Cooley family turned to the lower Gold Coast's first and oldest industry—coontie starchmaking. Coontie, or comptic, once grew in abundance over the vast pinelands. The starch (arrowroot) in the tuberous root of the fernlike plant was processed, packed in 100-pound barrels, and shipped north, selling for eight cents a pound.

Cooley's starch mill soon flourished. In addition to acquiring livestock and building a large storehouse, he soon was able to complete construction of a comfortable cypress-log house with ceiling and floors, 20 x 55 feet and well furnished.

The families maintained friendly relations with the neighboring Seminole Indians who lived westward in the Everglades. When the Second Seminole War erupted in December, 1835, and the Dade Massacre near Bushnell occurred, the Cooleys still felt at ease with the area tribes. Cooley felt no qualms about leaving with his younger son and Williams for a trip to Key West for supplies the next month. His children's private tutor, Joseph Flinton, and two black servants stayed behind with the family.

It was a sunny Monday, January 6, 1836. Mrs. Rigby and her daughter had just returned from a visit to the Cooleys that morning. The Rigbys lived a quarter-mile away, across New River. Suddenly, around noon, the Rigbys heard gunfire, loud screams, and the yells of Indians. The Rigby boy ran up along the river bank and spotted the Indians attacking the Cooley family. He quickly returned and warned both his own family and the Howes, and the settlers fled southward where they obtained transportation for temporary refuge in Key West. Learning of the ambush the night before, a young Indian boy, Charley, had sneaked away to warn Mrs. Cooley, who had befriended the boy. The woman gently chided the boy in disbelief, but her disbelief soon changed to horror as she heard the first yells and gunfire. (The Indians punished the boy later, cropping his ears and sending him into exile. Many years later, people recalled an aged Indian, crop-eared and silent, walking the streets in rags.)

On his return several days later, Cooley stood stunned with shock and grief as he surveyed the grisly scene. The instructor, Flinton, had been mutilated with an ax and scalped. The elder son and daughter each had been shot through the heart, their study books still in hand. His wife, still clutching the infant, lay nearby, both fatally shot. For some unknown reason, the Indians had spared the family itself the indignity of scalping. The two black servants had been carried off but would later escape and return to Cooley. The house was burned to the ground. Large stores of beef, pork, coffee, wine, $480 in silver, dry goods, lead and powder, 80 hogs, five sheep, three horses, and numerous fowl had been carried away or destroyed. Nevertheless, the stricken Cooley remained in the area and gradually rebuilt his homestead.

The Cooley Massacre sparked such an outcry that U.S. War Secretary Joel Poinsett moved quickly to set up an army post in Southeast Florida, a difficult task in a war that was going so badly elsewhere. But within a year he received an unexpected "troop bonus," largely at the behest of former President Andrew Jackson, who persuaded veteran Indian fighter Major William Lauderdale to lead a 500-man battalion of Tennessee mounted infantry volunteers to Florida. By March, 1838, the unit had reached New River and quickly erected a fort on the river's north bank close to Cooley's farm; Poinsett officially named it Fort Lauderdale. By conducting a series of offensive forays, Lauderdale was able to keep the tribes permanently dispersed and away from coastal settlers.

Most troops withdrew at the war's end in 1842, and the area remained only sparsely settled until almost 1900. But the nucleus of the town had been permanently established within the original 640 acres of the Fitzpatrick tract on which the three pioneer families had lived. The town's name remained, too—the name brought at such a terrible cost to one of those families.

Thus came the bloody baptism of Fort Lauderdale, the swampy scrubland wilderness that grew into a gleaming city on a river—one of Florida's most thriving cities.

60.
The "Arrest" of Henry Flagler

Governor Mitchell viewed it as technical duty when he signed an arrest warrant for the rail mogul, but it was politically fatal.

Gov. Henry L. Mitchell

It was an act that seemed out of character for the governor, a man of blandly conservative temperament, one whose administration, in retrospect, was somewhat less than distinctive.

But Florida Governor Henry L. Mitchell (1892-96), having once served some years as a judge, was keenly attuned to what he construed as his lawful duty. And so he sat down one day and routinely approved papers ordering the arrest and extradition to Texas of Florida's then most renowned developer, Standard Oil mogul Henry Morrison Flagler.

The governor might just as well have flipped a lit cigar into one of Standard's open oil tanks; the statewide furor he ignited was as instant as it was explosive.

Flagler, the oil, hotel, and railroad magnate who, in the late 19th century, opened up the state's entire east coast wilderness to unprecedented commercial and social development, was revered by many Floridians as both savior and benefactor, the Yankee prince who awakened the slumbering Florida maiden to her destiny. But even his detractors—and he had a few—reeled slightly at the prospect of the titan's arrest.

And thus ensued a maelstrom of sound and fury unlike anything in Florida's past. It generated a political heat so intense that the governor finally fled the kitchen; had he postponed his exit just briefly, he might have emerged from the cauldron politically unscathed. But he didn't, and he was scarred permanently.

The requisition papers to extradite Flagler were sent to Mitchell in late December, 1894, by Texas Governor James S. Hogg, the legendary Populist of that state who had long been fighting the corporate giants in banking, oil, and railroads in Texas, contending that they were on the verge of completely controlling state government. This was also the era of national outcry against

228

the abuses, real and alleged, by giant trusts, monopolies, and "robber barons" generally, against the public interest. Across the country sweeping reforms spawned numerous progressive and populist movements, symbolized in 1896 by the presidential candidacy of Populist William Jennings Bryan. In Florida, the advocates of reform to throw off "the yoke of Bourbonism" were led by such stalwarts as Wilkinson Call, Duncan Fletcher, and Napoleon B. Broward, the latter eventually becoming a reform governor.

Numerous congressional investigations, especially focused on the monolithic Standard Oil Trust, led to the enactment in 1890 of the Sherman Anti-Trust Act. A conflict arising from Standard Oil interests in Texas prompted Governor Hogg, claiming a violation of the state anti-trust laws, to seek the arrest of every Standard Oil official he could find. The fact that Flagler, still a director of the oil trust, was also a railroader only enhanced his villainy in Hogg's eyes. Flagler was charged with violating both Texas's and the Sherman Act's anti-trust laws.

In his own state, Mitchell had given lip service to some of this reformist ardor. But, basically, his temperament was quiescently conservative. Or, as his biographer, George B. Church, notes, Mitchell "had enough of the Bourbon political characteristics to gain the support of conservative Floridians and the [state's] corporate . . . interests."

Consequently, Mitchell's decision to arrest and extradite Flagler left his political peers stunned and confounded. The governor was at home in Tampa when he was informed of Hogg's request. Determining that the requisition papers were in proper legal order, he routinely approved them, all within a matter of hours.

The decision had no sooner been announced than controversy rocked the state. Friends of Flagler frantically rushed from around the state to see the governor personally. Within days, the chief executive's office was flooded with letters and telegrams from bankers, growers, developers, merchants, and just ordinary citizens, the bulk of them pleading with Mitchell to reconsider. Many attributed Hogg's request to a sinister plot concocted by Texas "anarchists" and "socialists." Others direly warned that Flagler's extradition might seriously wreck, or doom, the state's economic development.

Of course, the flurry of outburst was not totally one-sided. Jacksonville's *Florida Times-Union* supported the governor, declaring that Mitchell was a man who "knew no difference in pauper and millionaire where the law was concerned." Other editorialists agreed. But perhaps the most vitriolic criticism ever uttered against Flagler came from Mitchell's home town paper, the *Tampa Tribune*, on January 5, 1895.

The writer asserted that it was no question of law, but solely "the arrest of Mr. Flagler that raises the howl...the man whose magic wand touched the barren wastes of the east coast and made it blossom as the rose. That he should be arrested and made subject to the law of the land...has so fired the imaginations of his pimps they have gone into spasms and are striking at everything in sight. Who is Mr. Flagler? Is he greater than other mortals that he may trample constitutional law under his feet? Granted that he has done much for Florida and that he has vast possessions here, did he do these things as a matter of charity for the state, or for his own personal aggrandizement as a shrewd businessman? ... H.M. Flagler is no fool."

The writer concluded that Mitchell "has done his duty, nothing more, and if Mr. Flagler, as a member of the Standard Oil Trust, has violated the laws of ... Texas, he should be held amenable to them."

But by this time Mitchell was already wavering. The pleas and entreaties from Flagler supporters had taken a different turn; now they were threats, veiled and unveiled, of political reprisals. Intense conservative pressures painfully reminded the governor that, while there may be "no difference in pauper and millionaire" under law, there were formidable differences in the political leverage of either. And so, a few days after the *Tribune* blast, the governor rescinded the extradition order.

The *Times-Union* pointedly remarked that Mitchell's switch came when he realized that his political life might be "seriously damaged." The governor later went to great pains—unsuccessfully—to deny he had ever considered political pressures.

Had Mitchell earlier paid heed to a commentary in the Pensacola *Daily News* of January 1, 1895, he not only could have changed his decision but done so with honorable political face. The *News* set forth a simple legal requisite that, as a lawyer and former judge, Mitchell should have known, namely, that Flagler had never even been to Texas and, therefore, could not possibly be a fugitive from justice in that state. Later, somewhat desperately, Mitchell tried to use this fact as the real reason for his decision switch. He even produced an affidavit submitted to him by Flagler (but one made days after the reversal) swearing that he, Flagler, had never been to Texas. It was of little use; it only compounded the governor's image problems.

The overall consequence was that, by the time his term of office ended, Mitchell's political capital had declined to a point near total depletion. But, fortunately, he had a little of it left in his own hometown, otherwise he might have faced a destitute retirement. He was elected Hillsborough County Circuit Court Clerk and later County Treasurer. He served in those capacities until his death on October 14, 1903.

61.
When Dunnellon Was Wild and Woolly

No boomtown of the Old West could rival Dunnellon for turmoil after phosphate was discovered in the area.

Peaceful, quiet Dunnellon in Marion County, known today mainly for its nearby beautiful Rainbow Springs, was once a "roaring camp" gold-rush type of town in the 1890s that rivaled even the great Alaskan Klondike scene.

The only difference was that the "strike" that transformed a tiny obscure health resort into a bustling mining camp that drew worldwide attention was phosphate instead of gold.

But even the wild California Forty-Niners had nothing on Dunnellon, as prospectors poured in by foot, train, horseback, and wagon. She was authentic boomtown, complete with riotous saloons, bawdy bar girls, honky-tonk pianos, gamblers, conmen, gunmen, and Saturday paydays accompanied by fighting and shooting that made Monday morning a regular "clean-up" day of victims.

It was to last only a turbulent decade, but, in that time, the town became the phosphate center of the Western world.

It all began on a fine spring day, May 1, 1889, as one Albertus Vogt was sinking a well at his Dunnellon home on the Withlacoochee River. In the process, he became excited on uncovering enormous quantities of rock and fossils. He hurried to Ocala banker John F. Dunn who, a few years earlier, had founded Dunnellon as a health resort. After prospecting the area himself, Dunn found not only Vogt's place but also the entire surrounding area saturated with the mineral. After having many samples analyzed by a number of nationally known chemists—all of whom confirmed that it was the richest of hardrock phosphate—Dunn purchased that summer a half-interest in Vogt's 10 acres, along with large adjoining land tracts. After buying 8,000 acres, Dunn was joined by two Ocalans, Frank A. and Samuel W. Teague, who secured interest in another 5,000 acres. Dunn then persuaded a Captain John L. Inglis, of North Florida, to invest in mining operations. By October, The Dunnellon Phosphate Company was organized with $1,200,000 in capital stock. In total, the company would control some 90,000 acres.

The industry developed quickly as investors from other states and Europe rushed to Florida and formed numerous mining operations—41 such by the following year, and more due. Within this period, the Dunnellon company constructed a shipping basin at the mouth of the Withlacoochee—Port Inglis— and vessels would soon carry the rock to every country in Europe, while a railroad later shunted huge quantities to ports at Tampa and Jacksonville for domestic shipments. Port Inglis no longer exists today, but at its peak, it once led the world in phosphate shipments.

The boom began in Gold Rush style as speculators poured in and tracts of land were sold on every side; newspapers and magazines carried lavish ads and stories; millions were plunked down for land and plants; and railroads competed heavily for lucrative rights-of-way to choice mine sites. Prospectors poured in by the hundreds, living in the woods, sleeping under blankets, wagons, or ragged tarps, or throwing up flimsy shanties. They crisscrossed the county and adjoining counties with their own "analysts" and sounding rods, puncturing the sandy soil like a pin cushion. Scrub soil hardly worth a dollar an acre zoomed up a hundredfold in value. A poor Cracker farmer who had rarely jingled more than 10 cents cash in his pocket at one time might find himself suddenly addressed as "Colonel" by some speculator who casually took a fancy to some prehistoric bone substance on the man's land. A greatly impoverished area would get a mammoth economic booster shot. Widows and illiterate dirt farmers who went to bed at night hungry from a diet of grits, grease, and gravy often arose next morning to find themselves wealthy in phosphate land. More than a few canny Crackers, having shrewdly scattered lumps of phosphate rock about their fields the day before, would out-slick the slickest speculator who came to visit them by innocently inquiring about all this "fossofat" business they had been hearing about. By nightfall they would be headed for the border, rich; the speculator, stuck. Wiser souls refused to sell their land and reaped fortunes. They would simply lease the property and collect a royalty per ton. After so many years, they might then sell the land for a handsome profit.

Dunnellon itself boomed with giddy excitement as lumber mills moved in and shacks and buildings sprouted up to house the land dealers and investors who would buy and sell often on hearsay alone. A man's land might be bought on no more than the examination of a white rock in his pocket. Companies were formed around the clock, while paper stock floated like confetti over the area. Merchants quickly moved in to do a rush business supplying the hordes. Labor was scarce for the mines, and chartered "labor trains" fanned out over Georgia and Alabama to bring in hundreds of sharecroppers and field hands glad to exchange their wretched poverty for at least a token amount of hard cash as miners.

But no old Wild West town was ever so wild and woolly. As one scribe reported: "Everyone toted a gun and the Justice of the Peace held coroner's inquests and Justice's Court every Monday morning over the victims and culprits of the Saturday night and Sunday festivities. Court was held under an oak tree with a bacon box for a desk, a nail keg for a bench, and a heavily armed constable near for emergencies." Nor did these woolly boys ever want for fuel to keep these "festivities" at fever flush. There were almost as many saloons as there were houses, and they were usually packed. The favorite drink in town was the "phosphate cocktail," a lethal bit of white lightning. The town's streets could, indeed, be hazardous to your health—and often were.

Compounding this problem was the fact that nearly all the mining companies in and around the area paid their labor on Saturday afternoons; the stores and saloons remained open around the clock until midnight Sunday. Paynights sounded like the Fourth of July with the incessant crack of gunfire competing with the raucous roars of rage or laughter and the shrieks and squeals of brothel or bar girls. Decent folk found weekends a wise time to visit a distant relative or else bolt the doors, douse the lamps, and stay inside. If a wayward slug caught some innocent visitor, he would merely be collected with other victims in the street or alley in the regular Monday morning "pickup."

Merchants enjoyed such brisk business that they often ran out of stock before supplies arrived. Typical was a Hernando merchant, E.C. May. May had earlier been warned by Dunnellon merchants not to open a competitive store there or they would band together and "put me out of business." He opened anyway, and his business thrived; he often found on closing his store Sunday that "there was not $50 worth of anything left" in it. When the miners, armed with their 16-shot Winchester rifles, made too much racket with their shooting, May would tell them to keep it off until they got home. Then "they laughingly piled into the store and stacked their rifles along the wall by the dozen." Business was so heavy that the miners often would sleep on the floor until it was their turn to be waited on.

When the need for larger quarters forced May to move to the "wrong side of the bicycle track" (the south side of Pennsylvania Avenue where most of the saloons, brothels, and shanties were), he was warned that he would get no "respectable" business, especially from the town's housewives. But he reconverted one of "the town's worst dives" and prospered, even hiring the first woman clerk to tend the needs of—the town's housewives.

As an organized city government, the town fared little better. Guns often spoke louder than law. No streets were paved, and sanitary measures were nil. Tax assessments were rarely equitable, and tax fees collected were disbursed invariably under a cloud of suspicion. Assessments on new businesses were far higher than those on entrenched establishments, since the owners of the latter were in sole control of the city council and all taxing matters.

Although half the population of Dunnellon was black, they shared little if any voice in its affairs, even while contributing greatly to its prosperity. They toiled long hours in the mines at subsistence wages—always lower than a white man's—and had to live in the flimsiest of shacks.

Physically, the city was an open running sore. There were no water or sewer systems, and outhouses proliferated. With no drainage, during heavy rains the open wells used by many people for water were thoroughly polluted. Hogs and cattle roamed the streets unmolested, breeding beneath houses and leaving wastes everywhere. Wagons groaned and jolted over the rutted sand roads, millions of flies, gnats, and insects feasted on the animal and human waste heaps, and children played in the midst of it all. It was no wonder that malaria and typhoid fever were fairly common ailments, and the town was hit with a smallpox epidemic in 1899 that killed more than 100 persons.

It was not for lack of funds that such conditions prevailed, for the town's investors, landowners, merchants, mine operators, and so on were among the wealthiest people in the country. It was simply that those who profited so greatly from the richest of booms did not feel any obligation to their city or its inhabitants.

Lynching episodes involving "suspects" (usually black) began increasing to such an extent that blacks secretly formed an "Anti-Mob Lynchlaw Society" and came close to seizing a widely known racist marshal of the town. They were repelled, but racist attitudes increased so much that many black families simply packed up and left.

The Panic of 1897 and resultant depression wiped out many of the mining companies, especially the "skinpole plants"—those based mainly on "paper stock"—while hundreds of men were laid off; stockholders took staggering losses when a flooded market slumped tonnage prices to less than one-fifth their value.

But the brief depression seemed to have a stabilizing effect on the whole industry, with increased competition among fewer but more efficient companies. The boom continued for a while into the new century, but the decline was steady, and World War I would see its virtually total demise. The more easily mined pebble phosphate of Polk and Hillsborough counties would make them the phosphate center in Florida thereafter.

But the bloody barbaric days of Dunnellon's golden boomtime Nineties, when she was the phosphate center of the world, would foster tales of fact, myth, and legend, retold yet today in a more peaceful modern setting.

62.
A Rail Union's Dream Town—Venice

Railroad workers hoped to build a dream retirement haven, but a busted boom and mismanagement left the town deserted.

It was a dream city, the little town of Venice, one that might make its Italian namesake look slightly slummish. It promised to be the most perfect community ever laid out in Florida.

And therefore, the day it suddenly died and became a ghost town, the few people still around were stunned and bewildered. Virtually overnight, it seemed, clumps of choking weeds filled streets that led to nowhere, and the vacant hollow buildings echoed only a distant surf.

Of course, what happened to Venice had happened the year before to all of Florida during the great land boom bust in 1926. Beautiful archway entrances to scores of Paradise Manors and Golden Rancheros now led to pine trees and palmetto thickets. Fortunes made overnight were lost as quickly, banks toppled, and the great exodus to Florida was turned off like a giant spigot.

But up to that time, Venice had been different. Here were none of the gaudy promotions and grand-scale speculations, the frantic buying, selling, and re-selling of lots, the "binder boys" and "bird dogs" that swarmed like locusts over other cities like St. Petersburg, Tampa, and especially the Gold Coast to Miami. Indeed, Venice promised to stand out like a rock of stability in the state's often turbulent, feverish land madness.

Venice was distinctive, too, in that its builders were not the usual real estate tycoons, bankers, dabbling millionaires, or corporate developers. No, the architects of Venice were union members of the Brotherhood of Locomotive Engineers, one of the older and more conservative unions in America.

The B of LE wanted to build a model city-farm community for their retired members, where others would be welcome as well. A burst of local enthusiasm greeted their plans; between 1925 and 1927 the engineers organized several corporations and ultimately plowed over $16 million into the creation of this prototype city. They purchased more than 30,000 acres, reserving 2,000 acres for a town site, and called in one of America's most eminent city planners, John M. Nolen, of Boston, to lay it out.

Stressing the aesthetics of space, form, and Mediterranean architecture, Nolan plotted straight, broad boulevards, spacious parks, and distinctly buffered zones for residential, business, and industrial districts. The rest of the land was drained and carved into small farms. Roads were built, and a demonstration farm-dairy was set up. By 1926, a peak force of 2,000 workmen had constructed three large hotels, numerous apartment buildings, four blocks of shops, and 300 residences.

That same year, the legislature officially incorporated the thriving little city of Venice, population 4,000. The governor appointed the first mayor, Edward L. Worthington, and three councilmen, Charles S. Brearley, R.L. Welliver, and H.N. Wimmer. The first city meeting was held December 9, 1926.

And then, the following year, with startling abruptness, all work ceased on the development. The engineers found themselves broke, and, in the boom-busted economy around them, there were few if any conventional means of paying debts. Homes and apartments were vacated as people moved away.

The city's financial resources had also been exhausted. To protect stock-holders, the engineers permitted an orderly liquidation of its interests. Even with this measure it had to levy an assessment on union members just to meet fixed charges and pay nearly $300,000 annually for several years. In fact, the B of LE was on the verge of bankruptcy.

Venice had been luring settlers with its natural attractions for decades before the B of LE influx. In the 1860s, Venice and the Nokomis area on its north boundary was a beautiful tropic setting of land, wildlife, and water. To the Reverend and Mrs. Jesse Knight, its first settlers, it looked to be the perfect homesite. With eight girls, seven boys, and 300 head of cattle in tow, they moved to the area in November, 1868. Knight (called "Reverend" because of his staunch Methodism), moved from what is today Knight's Station, north of Tampa.

Earlier he had discovered the rich grazing lands of the lush Myakka River region, and he staked out this area for a 300-square-mile cattle range. His herd flourished, growing from 300 to 20,000 head. The Knights prospered and, over the next half-century, became one of the Gulf Coast's leading families.

Venice was then called by the odd name Horse and Chaise, because to passing fishermen two clumps of forests on its coast closely resembled the outline of a horse and carriage. The name Venice came from a later settler, chemist Frank Higel, who thought the area's network of bayous and creeks suggested the ancient city. This name was adopted with the arrival of its first post office in 1888. Other settlers began to trickle in, and by 1897 there were 18 families in Venice.

But the area's development lagged behind Sarasota, its growing neighbor 15 miles northward, for lack of a railroad or even a passable road. Even so, the beauty of the area prompted a major Sarasota land buyer, Joseph H. Lord, to buy up 1,394 acres of Venice for $1,000. Lord would gradually buy some 70,000 acres in both the Venice and Sarasota areas at similar prices.

A spur of the Seaboard railroad came to the Venice area in 1911, mainly at the initiative of Mrs. Potter Palmer of Sarasota. Mrs. Palmer once considered developing Venice into a west coast "Palm Beach" resort, but the cost estimates proved too high for her, so she dropped the plan.

For a while before World War I, promoter Mike Evans succeeded in luring a number of prominent northerners to a small resort at Eagle Point on Roberts Bay for winter sports and fishing activities. But it was not until 1916 that the town got its first street—a nine-foot-wide asphalt road, running south to Englewood and north to Sarasota.

In 1920 Dr. Fred H. Albee, a well-known bone surgeon, moved to Venice. With land still relatively inexpensive, Dr. Albee began buying up large tracts in the Venice-Nokomis area and, the following year, erected the Pollyanna Inn.

The region remained largely undeveloped until the arrival of the Brotherhood of Locomotive Engineers in 1924. The union was searching for "an ideal site" in Florida and found what they sought in Venice. Along with the sea and climate, the attractive contours of the land made them vote for the area on the spot.

Needless to say, the entire county became excited over the proposed "new city of Venice." Area citizens eagerly helped promote the project, and some of them became actively involved as officers or stockholders in the corporate groups organized by the B of LE. A flurry of construction commenced, and new residents began to flock into the town as fast as homes and apartments were built. The town would have 4,000 citizens by 1926, and these were solid settlers. Venice appeared to be the shining exception, a solid achievement in a manic boom that had almost literally busted the rest of the state.

A major cause of the project's demise was the huge amount of funds the B of LE had to pay for the land itself, funds that might otherwise have sustained the development to a successful stabilization. Between September 28, 1925, and March 28, 1927, the brotherhood had purchased 30,511 acres of land at a total cost of $4,043,092, roughly more than $130 an acre. Even by boom standards— and such a solid project was hardly in this category—this was an unusually high price. Not many years before, land in this area bought in tracts of far less size had gone for as low as 80 cents an acre. Moreover, much of it was undeveloped land, requiring extensive, costly drainage. Development and sales expenditures totaled another $12 million, which brought the total cost of Venice to the B of LE to more than $16 million.

Two years after the project collapsed, Stanton Ennes, former general manager of the development, charged in a story in the *Sarasota Herald* that huge sums were paid for the property in excess of its value. He also charged that contracts for improvements were let in "an extravagant and wasteful" manner and that costly blunders by boards of interlocking directors, who were financially inept, caused serious damages to the development. Nor did he spare the B of LE, some of whose officers, he asserted, lent tacit or explicit approval to these practices and thus came close to bankrupting the union. Later, the *Herald* confirmed that none of these charges were ever disputed.

And so the ghost of Venice limped into the Great Depression. However, a well-planned community in such an excellent location was not destined to lie dormant for long. In 1932, the Kentucky Military Institute acquired two hotels— the Venice and San Marco—as a location for its winter classes. Then, in November 1933, Dr. Albee (who in the Depression had acquired a large part of the B of LE's former holdings) established the Florida Medical Center in the Park View Hotel, to which he brought his patients each winter. The government later used the center as a hospital to serve the Venice Air Base during World War II.

Venice's revival would not really begin until June, 1945, when a syndicate of St. Petersburg businessmen, headed by Robert S. Baynard, purchased most of the B of LE's former holdings from Dr. Albee's widow. It was reported that 14,000 acres were acquired for $400,000, or roughly $28 an acre. This purchase included most of the city of Venice and 12,000 acres of adjacent farmland.

From here on, the city took on flesh and life, and the ghost of a dream was resurrected. So the Brotherhood of Locomotive Engineers may not have failed so badly after all, having left "an ideal framework" on which to build the prosperous bustling community that is Venice today.

63.
Baiting and Switching on Sarasota Bay

Scotch colonists, lured by promises of balmy seaside "estates,"
suffer a winter of discontent upon arrival.

The story might be called: "The Scottish colonists and the case of the missing town"; or, "Who said you couldn't con a Scotsman?"

It happened about 100 years ago when Sarasota County was a sparsely settled frontier wilderness, waiting to bloom with people and cities. Meanwhile, across the ocean, Great Britain was suffering severe depression. True, the sun had never set on her empire, but it had certainly set on her economy as a result of the lavish costs of maintaining that empire. And Scotland was hardest hit of all; her natives were desperate for relief. But it was not long before a number of them began spelling relief, S-A-R-A-S-O-T-A.

"A wonderful new town on Sarasota Bay," exclaimed the promotional newspaper article being read by John B. Browning, a lumber miller of Paisley, Scotland. His interest mounted as he read on. Colonists were needed to settle this tropical "paradise" where a man "does not have to work too hard for a living." In the richly fertile soil and year-round warm climate, citrus and vegetables could be grown at little expense, commanding premium market prices. Fish and game were also abundant, and the people already there lived "an idyllic existence," the article noted. For the sum of 100 pounds sterling, each colonist would receive a 40-acre "estate," plus a town lot.

To Browning and his brother-in-law, John Lawrie, it all sounded like "a bonny wee bit of heaven." Both men and their families became enthusiastic over the prospect. Any doubts were easily quenched by the prestigious names associated with the promoting firm, the Florida Mortgage & Investment Company, headed by Sir John Gillespie, a Scottish nobleman. The story was written by land agent Selven Tate, nephew of England's Archbishop of Canterbury, one of FMIC's directors along with the Lord Dean of Guild of Edinburgh. No doubt it was the real thing, and soon both families were on their way to Glasgow, having sold their properties and purchased their "estates." At Glasgow they joined 21 other families (68 persons in all), called themselves the Ormiston colony, and, on November 25, 1885, sailed for New York.

Arriving in New York December 10, where they were met by agent Tate, they then took another boat to Fernandina, Florida, and journeyed from there by rail to Cedar Key. In this village, they had their first disquieting moments when Tate suddenly informed them they would have to wait there a while until lumber reached Sarasota for the erection of some housing. Tate then took off for Sarasota, purportedly to "hurry things up." Having been led to believe housing already existed and with no word from Tate even after Christmas, the impatient colonists chartered a side-wheel steamer and sailed into Sarasota Bay on December 28.

As the steamer moved in, the excited colonists crowded the rail, peering anxiously up and down the junglelike coastline, eager for a glimpse of the new "model town." But they looked in vain. There was not a town in sight. Excitement soon changed to consternation as the vessel finally anchored 100 yards off shore. The only structure in view was an abandoned fish oil plant that housed the FMIC's company store, plus a dilapidated shack further inland. The colonists gathered at the store, where they were met by A.C. Acton, FMIC's local agent. Acton explained that they had arrived "earlier than expected." The town was only in the "blueprint stage," but he assured them that with the "millions behind the project . . . it would soon be the finest city in Florida."

The colonists' anger and concern were at least partially mollified by Acton's glowing explanation of the area's future. By this time, some of the native settlers—Whitakers, Abbes, Crockers, Tatums, Tuckers—had come in to greet them and offered to take a few of them into their homes temporarily. Since there was little food available in the store except hard crackers, Whitaker and a few others went mullet-casting in the bay and soon returned with enough for a gigantic fish fry. On New Year's Day, settlers provided game meat, fowl, pan bread, and more fish for an all-day welcoming feast.

But this gathering was brief enough. The hard reality of their situation was setting in fast. The year-round warmth turned unusually cold, and most colonists were without adequate shelter, making do with hastily built crude log structures or lean-tos, while room was made to bed the children in the store. But the biggest disappointment came when they went to search for their "estates." Most of these were several miles back in the dense woods and overgrowth, and some took days to locate; none was even near the waterfront as the new colonists had been led to expect. By now their resentment over "gross misrepresentation" was churning in anger. As Browning recalled: "A few of the hotheads decided to call on Tate with a shotgun, but he [Tate] got wind of it and disappeared. He never returned."

Food supplies were dwindling, and the mostly urban-bred colonists were inept at game-hunting. Then, on January 9, the temperature dipped so low that it began to snow, a phenomenon that even locals had never seen. The severe cold forced all work to cease as families gathered around tree stump fires to keep warm. To most of them now, their "wonderful new town" was rapidly becoming a grim and nightmarish caricature.

The progression of their disillusion was perhaps summed up with thoughts in the diary of colonist Dan McKinlay: December 29, "We are occupying a little log hut. It's a queer experience; I can't describe it. I am going to light my pipe for I am very sad"; January 11, "The night was awfully cold, we could not keep out of the cold . . . not at all like 'sunny' Florida"; January 25, "The talk is all of leaving [Sarasota]"; by February 4, the Lawries and several other families had left, and the diary noted: "Prospects here are so bad...in fact, it means starvation if we stay"; February 15, "Start today for Tampa."

And thus the Ormiston colony soon became a colossal failure. By May 1, 1886, almost all of the colonists had left; Browning was one of the few to remain. Having left their homeland with the highest hopes, many of the Scots were now almost penniless, having spent all their "estate" on the long trip's expenses. Most had to borrow money to get to Northern states to find work or aid.

Sir John Gillespie himself had never seen the 49,431-acre tract in Sarasota that his FMIC syndicate had purchased for speculation from Hamilton Disston at $1 an acre. The tract was part of four million acres in Florida that Disston had bought from the state for 25 cents an acre. A year after the colonists had left, Gillespie's son, John Hamilton, came to Sarasota and made an attempt to develop a settlement after building a small tourist hotel and several other structures. But his efforts failed; not until 1903, when the Seaboard Railroad ran a branch to the townsite, would Sarasota begin its growth.

But the unfortunate Scots could perhaps be considered "pioneers" of sorts—the pioneer prototypes of victims recurrently peculiar to Florida's later boom years, when more sophisticated modern versions of "a bonny wee bit of heaven" lured many into dubious or disastrous land investments—a lure that proved too much for a colony of shrewd and canny Scotsmen.

64.
The Toll of a "Killer" Inlet

*The Ponce de Leon Inlet seemed cursed with freakish waters
after exacting a chronic toll of shipwrecks and lives.*

Shipwrecks off the Florida Keys are legendary, but few Floridians are aware of a small inlet on the state's Atlantic coast that, by the end of the 19th century, had acquired almost a "devil's triangle" reputation for marine calamities.

Indeed, the Ponce de Leon Inlet, slicing barely a mile's width through nearly 40 miles of the barrier beaches of Daytona and New Smyrna, was responsible for such a steady toll of shipwrecks that area settlers came to dub it the "Killer Inlet." Its deadly and mysterious combination of tidal currents, wind patterns, and ever-shifting sandy sea bottoms have crushed, splintered, and gutted a host of the stoutest hulls ever since Ponce de Leon discovered the inlet in 1513. It was also the site of one of the state's greatest maritime disasters: the wreck of the *Vera Cruz* in 1880, which claimed the lives of 71 men, women, and children.

Early Spanish explorers called it Mosquito Inlet (and also made navigational note of its treacherous, capricious waters), until beach land promoters in the 1920s Florida Boom had that slightly forbidding name changed to Ponce de Leon Inlet. It was the only entrance to the salt lagoon waterways called Indian River North, south of the inlet, and the Halifax River running north.

Aside from the hazardous shifting bar that lay at the inlet entrance, the erratic cross-currents and winds extended far offshore into the Atlantic. All of this combined with one of the most tremendously pounding surfs known to any shore; its cement-tight packing of Daytona Beach would make it world-famous for auto racing.

Sparsely settled until the late 19th century, not many records of shipwrecks in the inlet area were ever kept, but mariners through generations passed down tales of many a hardy ship that met a watery doom in or off the inlet.

One of the earliest noted was on November 15, 1837, when the steamer *John McLain*, carrying troops, muskets, and ammunition to a New Smyrna campsite during the Seminole Indian War, was skewered and smashed trying to cross the inlet bar. All lives were saved, but the cargo was a total loss. In the 1840s, the steamship *Narragansett* sank just near the inlet, but she was not discovered until later when a portion of her hull floated into the Halifax River; area settlers salvaged several hundred pounds of valuable copper sheathing and ship bolts. In this same period, the *Roxanna* was spun about and smashed in tricky currents just north of the inlet, while the *Ocean*, making it across the inlet bar, grounded on a shifting sandbar where a hammering surf gutted her insides. All lives were saved on both wrecks, but the cargoes were lost, except for a remnant washed up later and salvaged.

Records were kept of three calamities in and after the Civil War period. The steamship *Luella* had just delivered some machinery to a mainland settler and then attempted to race a falling tide out of the inlet in a light wind; she smashed head-on into a roaring surf and splintered apart. Wind and cross-currents capsized the sloop *Martha* just off the inlet; two of her crew drowned, but her cargo of barrels of salted mullet was salvaged. Four miles southeast of the inlet, a shifting sandbar caught and held fast the schooner *Wilton*. Anchors heaved out to make her steady were no match for the powerful winds and waves which snapped the anchor cables and broke up the vessel. The crew survived, but her cargo floated to sea.

On June 28, 1877, an early Volusia County settler, Captain Charles Fozzard, tried to outrun a violent Atlantic storm in his schooner, *Frank E. Stone*. Lacking enough ballast, he still tried to cross the inlet bar and reach the mainland. But the rolling waters within the inlet hurled the vessel over on her side, her masts and sails dragging. While passengers and crew clung for life to the ship's keel, the daring captain swam almost a mile to shore, acquired a boat, and, with great effort, returned to the wreck and rescued the victims, except for three who lost their grip on the keel and drowned almost immediately.

During the stormy period in September, 1878, beach and mainland settlers grated and oven-dried the white meat of most of 125,000 coconuts that spewed from the hold of a Central American schooner, wrecked five miles from the inlet. This delicacy kept indefinitely and was used long after for cakes and cornbread. Two settlers salvaged a valuable load of mahogany from a wrecked Norwegian bark and later earned a handsome profit from it. Several other ships, though badly damaged, were towed and salvaged by their captains, but the *S.S. Agnes* was less fortunate. She was totally wrecked near the inlet, and her hull settled diagonally across the *Narragansett*; both wrecks had to be dynamited out 30 years later.

One of the worst disasters was the *City of Vera Cruz*, carrying 82 passengers and crew from New York to Havana, in August, 1880. Caught in a storm some distance from the inlet, she grounded. Frantic attempts to dump her cargo failed, and a near-tidal wave smashed her apart, sweeping men, women, and children into the furious swells. Some bodies washed ashore as far as Cape Canaveral south and St. Augustine north; only three passengers and eight crewmen reached shore alive. A few settlers organized to guard the bodies from jewelry looters and rooting wild hogs, but finally they were forced to bury 67 bodies in one large pit behind the sand dunes.

The shipwrecks brought huge quantities and varieties of supplies to early Volusia settlers—large containers of flour, lard, bacon, wine, liquor, bolts of calico, silk, and lace, furniture, hardware, shoes, clothing, and other items. Often, exhausted salvagers would place planks across their bounty and sleep on them, whereupon other "wreckers" would come along, gently lift both planks and settlers aside, and do some re-salvaging. U.S. Customs captain Charles Coe reported that settlers often threatened, or beat up, collectors attempting to impound salvage goods.

After the *Vera Cruz* disaster, a public outcry brought construction of a new lighthouse on the north side of the inlet, a 168-foot brick tower. Finished in 1887, the *Halifax Herald* ironically reported that five of the "8 or 10" schooners used in the project were wrecked in the inlet, with six men drowned. Nor did the tower prevent the breaking up of the *Nathan Cobb* in 1896; it finally washed up on a bar 1,000 feet from Ormond Beach. The ship's mate and steward both drowned, and a settler, Ford Waterhouse, was fatally swept under in a heroic effort to run the breakers and secure a rescue line to the vessel.

Even into the 20th century, wrecks in the inlet area continued, with an average of six lives lost a year, according to one historian. Finally, in 1941, a new Inlet and Port District enabled the government to bring the inlet area up to a measurable standard of navigational safety.

But older residents still call it the "Killer Inlet," the high-mark symbol of a sprawling underwater cemetery where, over centuries, the timbers and bleached bones of hardy ships and able men lay scattered for miles in briny unmarked graves.

65.
The "Miracle" Execution

It was possibly Florida's first official execution, but when the doomed man survived, it was hailed as a "miracle."

The executioner was a professional, but his final touch may have been too professional; consequently the "dead" man survived his own execution in perhaps the only such instance in Florida history.

Franciscan friars assembled around the execution platform hailed it as "a miracle." They then rushed the unconscious body to their convent, resisting even the threats of an angry governor who demanded the prisoner's return for re-execution. Townspeople were awed and, long afterward, would recall it as "the miracle of the noose." It was certainly a singular episode in the history of America's oldest city, St. Augustine, 300 years ago.

In the 17th century, St. Augustine was a small military outpost of about 1,000—soldiers, churchmen, tradesmen, women, and children. It served not only to protect Spain's Florida colony but also was watchguard for the treasure plate fleet that sailed each year through the Bahama Channel. Over years, the town had been subject to numerous attacks, even sackings and burnings, by pirates—French, English, Dutch—who roamed the Spanish Main preying on the silver and gold Spain drew from her American colonies. The town's "pirate-phobia" finally prompted construction of the enormous Castillo de San Marcos in 1672. (The fort, which took 30 years to complete, still stands today.)

Then one day, in 1684, a Spanish warship from Havana raided the port of New Providence, in the British Bahamas, which it suspected of harboring a pirate ship. In retaliation, the Bahamian governor authorized a Captain Thomas Jingle to raid St. Augustine. Jingle set out with 11 vessels but postponed the attack after rough storms caused the loss of five ships. Instead, he sailed north and anchored near the St. Johns River, hoping to forage for badly-needed food and water. Among the crew on one ship was an English seafarer, Andrew Ranson, who had signed on as a ship's steward. Ranson had come to the West Indies, married, and operated a small merchant vessel among Caribbean ports before settling in New Providence. Sometimes, in the custom of those days, he carried contraband items, an act that once cost him a brief hitch in a Havana jail.

On arriving at the St. Johns, Ranson was ordered to take a half-dozen men ashore to hunt for wild cattle, game, and water. But Spanish sentinels near the river had spotted the ships and sent word to St. Augustine. Soon after, 50 Spanish soldiers arrived on the scene and captured Ranson's party. Discovering what had happened, Jingle sailed away. The prisoners were marched to St. Augustine.

In town, Governor Juan Marques Cabrera ordered the prisoners to the rack. Under torture, the crewmen quickly revealed Jingle's attack plans. Hoping to elude further torture, they also agreed to name Ranson as their "leader." On the rack, Ranson insisted he was not a pirate, but only a ship's steward searching for food at the time, and knew nothing of Jingle's plans. But one soldier present, who had recalled seeing Ranson in the Havana jail on the contraband charge, accused him of being a pirate. The governor then ordered Ranson, as "ring-leader," to be executed by garroting for piracy; the others were given 10 years at hard labor on the fort.

Awaiting execution in the fort's chapel, Ranson, a Catholic, continued to protest his innocence to the town's head chaplain, the Franciscan Father Perez de la Mota. La Mota came to believe Ranson's story that he was not a pirate, but, at the time, the prelate could only console the prisoner and give him a rosary.

Ranson was clutching this rosary as he was led to the execution platform in late October. Flanked by six guards on either side, he was placed with his back to a pole. The executioner then pushed a loop of the garroting rope through a hole in the pole, fitting it firmly around the prisoner's neck. Then, behind the pole, he began to slowly turn the wooden handle secured to the noose. After the sixth such turn, the writhing body finally slumped motionless. At this, a group of friars in the crowd began to chant a requiem, and church bells tolled for the departed soul. The executioner, although satisfied that the job was done, took both hands to exert one more turn of the garrote; the rope snapped, the limp body falling forward.

After hurrying up onto the platform, Father la Mota discovered that the "dead" man was still breathing. "A miracle," he cried, and before the guards were aware of what had happened, la Mota and some friars picked up the body and rushed it to their convent. La Mota also retrieved, and took with him, the broken noose. The crowd of spectators began murmuring excitedly, one of them shouting "a la iglesia" (to the church); another echoed la Mota: "A miracle."

As Ranson slowly revived, his throat sore and head throbbing, he stared about the convent room with a trance-like expression of disbelief. Then tears began to stream down his face, and he eased off his bed and knelt in prayer. The guards, meanwhile, gathered outside the convent and demanded the prisoner, but la Mota refused them entry. The priest was convinced that his and the friars' prayers had invoked a miraculous act of God's will. When an angry Governor

Cabrera sent his personal envoy to demand Ranson's return, an equally angry la Mota claimed "ecclesiastical immunity" for the prisoner and even threatened the governor with excommunication if the convent's immunity were violated. The dispute set off a long and acrimonious debate between the two men as both appealed to authorities in Spain. La Mota insisted on official recognition of a church miracle; Cabrera demanded the re-execution of "a pirate." The controversy continued until 1687, at which time Cabrera was transferred to another post. Ranson, himself convinced of a divine deliverance that had vindicated his innocence, remained safely in the convent.

The new governor, Don Diego Losada, discussed the matter with la Mota and, upon learning that Ranson had skills in carpentry and engineering, agreed to grant the prisoner safe conduct if he would live and work at the new fort. The prisoner gratefully accepted the offer.

Father la Mota was finally summoned to Madrid in 1692 to present arguments for the claimed "miracle." In an eloquent appeal, la Mota even exhibited the "strong, sound" garroting rope he had kept. But the higher authorities remained unconvinced that the rope was "divinely severed." However, they did commute Ranson's standing death sentence.

Many theories were offered to account for this "miracle." Historian J.L. Wright, Jr., believes that the rope may have had a concealed defect. But the known evidence indicated that, even when exhibited eight years later, the cord was of "strong, sound" weaving. A physiological theory suggests that Ranson's neck muscles constricted in such manner as to only temporarily squeeze shut the vital arteries, but not for a period sufficient (up to four minutes usually) to induce brain death. Thus, when the rope snapped from the sheer strength of the final twist, the blood rushed forth and revived the victim in time. Of course, to those who truly believed in "a miracle," including la Mota and Ranson, no other explanation could suffice.

In 1702, when war broke out between Spain and England, another new governor, Don Jose Zuniga, offered all prisoners freedom if they would help defend the undermanned fort as it underwent siege from the invading English colonial Governor Moore, of Charleston. Ranson, now in his fifties, volunteered his services and became a free man when the siege was finally broken two months later.

At this point, Ranson's name fades out of historical record. It is probable, however, that he remained in St. Augustine, in view of his service against England, and may or may not have summoned his wife to join him. At all events, it is certain that he never forgot the rarest of experiences: surviving his own execution with little more than a tender soreness about the throat and a splitting headache.

66.
The Burning of
Old St. Augustine

*Sir Francis Drake almost wiped away any trace of the oldest
city when he raided and torched it.*

The night they burned the old town down nearly 400 years ago, St. Augustine narrowly missed extinction as the oldest and one of the most historic cities in America.

Spain was ready to scrap the settlement forever after the devastating raid in June, 1586, by England's daring corsair, Sir Francis Drake. He had just returned from "singeing the beard" of King Philip II by sacking his finest Caribbean cities—Santo Domingo and Cartagena. St. Augustine then served both as the capital of "La Florida" and "Gibraltar" to protect Spain's treasure-laden galleon fleets. But Philip's court advisers termed the military base "indefensible" and were prepared to relegate its smoldering ashes to ghost-town status.

Drake himself was on his way home after a modestly successful pillaging of key Spanish Caribbean ports. In fact, he would have passed on by the little town had he not spied its rickety watchtower on Anastasia Island at the entrance to the city's harbor. Piracy in those days was legitimate big business (euphemistically referred to as "privateering"), and Queen Elizabeth I was the major shareholder in the joint-stock company that had financed Drake's recent venture. Drake had won fame earlier for circumnavigating the globe (between 1577 and 1580), a voyage from which he also brought the Queen loot valued at a half-million pounds sterling. The covetous Queen was so delighted with this booty she knighted the renegade corsair on the spot—Sir Francis.

Drake's Caribbean raids had an enormous political and psychological impact on England and Europe while King Philip seethed in humiliation. But Drake's actual loot was not much more than the 60,000 pounds sterling his backers put up for the trip, enough to return each "stockholder" about 15 shillings on the pound. He had also just missed—by 12 hours, he cursed—one of Spain's richest silver-plate convoys, and he had lost 750 of his 2,300-man contingent, mostly to yellow fever, during the voyage. Therefore, he was surprised to discover perhaps a little "bonus" money to pick up on the way home. Upon sighting Drake's fleet, the lookout sentinels canoed hastily back across the Matanzas River inlet to give warning to St. Augustine and its inhabitants.

The town, which was being commanded by Pedro Menendez Marquez, the nephew of Pedro Menendez de Aviles, St. Augustine's founder who died in 1574, was a sitting target. Several months before, Menendez had learned of similar raids and had begun construction of a fort which had not been completed. The town had only 340 inhabitants, including 150 soldiers, their wives and children, the clergy, and a few slaves. The town grid of eight large city blocks contained a church, a council house, several stores and buildings, and homes built of wood with palmetto-thatched roofs. One large and several smaller orange groves, along with corn fields and a produce garden, adjoined the town's main area. The fort itself, San Juan de los Pinos, was built simply of thick palmetto tree trunks driven into the ground. Its platforms, holding 14 brass cannons, were made of pine-tree trunks laid horizontally and packed with earth.

After landing a force on Anastasia Island, Drake reconnoitered and decided the fort could be easily taken, but a small advance contingent he sent across the

*St. Augustine survived Drake's fiery assault in 1586. It is shown here
85 years later as a prospering town. (FLORIDA TREND)*

river was quickly repelled by cannon fire. His deep-draft ships were unable to enter the shallow water in the harbor, so the admiral brought up heavy reinforcements for an all-out assault. In full view of his foe on the mainland, Drake lined his men in formal ranks, to the beat of martial music, and hoisted six red flags, which meant that "no ransom would be accepted and no quarter given" the defenders of the town. He then fired several cannons, and the ball of one even toppled the fort's flag mast.

By this time, Menendez had evacuated all the women and children to a remote, friendly Indian village deep in the woods, and that night he sent a surprise raiding party of soldiers and Indians against Drake, inflicting numerous casualties before withdrawing. He also harassed them all night with gunfire to keep them awake. But realizing he was hopelessly outnumbered, he finally abandoned the fort to take refuge in the Indian village.

Gathering for the assault next morning, the English were suddenly gripped with silence at the sound of a fife playing a song, an anti-Spanish tune familiar to every Protestant in Europe, the "Prince of Orange" March. The musician was Nicholas Borgoignon, a French prisoner captured at French Fort Caroline in 1565. During the night's melee, he had escaped, and now informed Drake of the abandonment of the Menendez Fort. The invaders immediately sailed in pinnaces for the mainland. The outpost had been stripped clean, but in their haste to leave, the Spanish had left behind their pay chest of 10,000 ducats, their entire annual Royal support subsidy and payroll. An Indian also located the 14 cannons which the Spanish had tried to bury. Later, combing the residences for loot, the English found that a hostile Indian tribe further south had beat them to other spoils. Drake decided to remain in the area to rest for a few days while his men traded copper pieces for valuable articles with some of the Indian looters camping nearby.

But the respite was fatefully marred when Drake's trusted sergeant-major, Anthony Powell, found a stray horse and decided to take an exploratory ride in the area, unaware that the horse's owner, a Spanish sniper, was waiting behind a bush with a well-aimed arquebus. With one fatal shot to the head, he felled Powell, and fled.

Beset with grief and anger, Drake ordered his men to set fire to the fort and every home and building in the town. He then had them chop down every orange tree, burn the corn fields, and tear up the gardens.

As Menendez emerged from the woods in time to see the last topsail of the invader's fleet slip over the horizon, he was aghast at the desolate scene, which was made all the more painful by the reminder of his negligence in leaving the pay chest behind. The cannons were also a critical loss, since Spain had not yet acquired the art of cannon-making and had to either import them from Italy or smuggle them out of England. He quickly sent messengers on an urgent request to Havana for food and farm tools, noting that he had "only six barrels of flour to feed 340 people." The supplies soon arrived, but not before 30 hungry and desperate men set out overland to Mexico; only eight survived the harsh journey.

King Philip seemed now determined to abandon St. Augustine as an Atlantic base and use Santa Elena (Port Royal Sound), South Carolina, instead. Spain's prestige had been severely damaged throughout the world. A year later, Philip would send his great Armada to invade England, only to have it routed and defeated. But Menendez was joined by other naval and military figures in a fervent plea to spare the settlement, noting its strategic position. After much heated debate, a last-minute reprieve ensued, and the King chose to abandon Santa Elena instead.

It would take many years for St. Augustine to recover from the disastrous raid. Not until the huge and impregnable fort of Castillo de San Marcos was completed in 1696 (it still stands today) would St. Augustine truly become a "Gibraltar," easily withstanding successive British assaults in the following century.

Thus the settlement, which barely missed a fiery extinction, survived to become one of the most historic cities in the nation—and the oldest of them all.

67.
The Case of the Reluctant Bridegroom

Adelantado Menendez's marriage of convenience to an Indian chieftain's sister may have drastically altered state history.

The Spanish official tugged at his royal collar and sweated uneasily. He had faced death often in the past with coolness, but now he felt awkwardly incompetent as he glanced at the tall, poised Indian maiden before him.

Yet the settlement of all South Florida, the future course of the Spanish empire, even his own prestige and royal favor might hang on his decision. The question itself was very simple: To take this brown heathen woman as his wife, on the spot, or not to take her?

But how could he? He was a zealously devout Christian, devoted to a loving wife and family back home in Spain. It would be bigamous—or worse—he lamented inwardly. But if he refused her? The likely consequences chilled his thoughts.

And thus unfolds the tale of the reluctant bridegroom; or, more importantly, how a star-crossed honeymoon may have delayed South Florida's settlement by white men for more than two and a half centuries.

In all of Spain's wealthy empire of that day, there was no more formidable, brilliant, honest, or loyal a figure than the captain-general of the Spanish fleet, Pedro Menendez de Aviles. At age 14, his career began with an astounding defeat of the fleet of the notorious pirate Jean Alphonse; for years after, he continued to be the scourge of free-booting corsairs who preyed on Spain's treasure-filled galleons, until his traits of daring and leadership prompted King Philip II to appoint him, in 1554, as captain-general of the royal fleet in charge of all New World commerce. In 1565, after driving French colonists out of North Florida (notably in the infamous massacre of French Huguenots at Matanzas), he was named adelantado (governor) of Florida, and he persuaded the King of the peninsula's critical value as a citadel to protect Spanish galleons from French and English marauders, especially in the southern Florida straits.

Thus South Florida became his next colonizing venture. In February, 1566, he dropped anchor in the vicinity of Charlotte Harbor. He was surprised to be greeted by a Spanish shipwreck survivor—now an Indian slave—who led him to the village of King Carlos, ruler of the Calusa tribes who controlled most of South Florida from the Keys to the great Lake Mayaimi (Okeechobee). After distributing many gifts among Carlos's braves—knives, bells, mirrors, scissors, and other baubles, for which the astonished soldiers received in turn bars of silver and gold which the Indians had retrieved from shipwrecks—Menendez set out a banquet to honor the chief.

Carlos was about 25 years old, unusually tall, with an intelligent face, yet his eyes held an expression of truculence and cunning. The two leaders parried politely, suspiciously, for a while, until Menendez won agreement from the cacique to release eight Spanish Christians, five women and three men, shipwreck survivors who had been Indian slaves for almost 20 years. They had escaped the fate of some 200 other survivors who were periodically killed in sacrificial rites held by this fierce tribe.

Warmed by the adelantado's hospitality—and anxious to secure more gifts—Carlos invited Menendez and his soldiers next day to a great village feast. But soon after the festivities began, the chief brought forth his favorite sister and insisted to Menendez that, to bind their friendship, the Spaniard must take her for his wife. The woman was very tall, like her brother, with a sober and plain face, unlike the attractive, smaller young girls in her attendance. Aside from various necklaces, all of these women were garbed only in brief skirts made of Spanish moss.

To conceal his anxiety over this dubious "gift" of friendship, Menendez said nothing, and proceeded to busy himself by presenting the women with gifts of chemises and gowns with which, with amused delight, they clothed themselves.

The banquet of roasted fish and oysters, Spanish wine, biscuits, and honey was quickly consumed. Meanwhile, Menendez thought to himself: *He can't be serious.* But as the adelantado sought to take leave of the chief and return to the ships, Carlos's stern, narrow gaze fixed him. The chief insisted that they remain and that Menendez take his new wife to an adjoining room and rest with her. He darkly explained that his people would be insulted and scandalized if they were not united in wedlock that very day.

Although much perturbed and anxious, Menendez drew himself up and, through his interpreter, explained to the chief that Christian men could not sleep with women who were not Christians. No problem, Carlos replied. His sister and he and his people were already Christians since he, Carlos, had taken the adelantado as an elder brother. It was not so simple, Menendez said, as he began to summarize what one must do to become a Christian. Carlos replied that he

had come to see how Spanish customs, food, music, and religion were better
than his own, and so he would adopt the Spaniard's religion. But he insisted that
Menendez give her baptism that evening and unite with her, before taking his
new wife and her maidens with him when he sailed.

And so Menendez, his men, the sister, and her female entourage went down
to the beach, erecting tents and preparing a big dinner, while Menendez
anxiously counseled with his captains as to any means by which he could
extricate himself from this conjugal dilemma. The presence of his brother-in-
law, Gonzalo Solis de Meras (who later wrote of these events) hardly relieved
his discomfort. But the understanding Solis conveyed only sympathy for whatever choice his commander made. If Menendez refused the woman, his captains
advised, he would endanger settlement of all South Florida, he would be unable
to Christianize these people, he would endanger the welfare of his own men,
and he might lose further royal support for his colonizing ventures.

Menendez sighed heavily and nodded; he really had no choice. And so, that
night, he baptized Carlos's sister, giving her the name Dona Antonia (hoping this
might vaguely appease his favorite Saint Anthony). Then, after a rollicking wedding
feast of music and dancing, the adelantado retired with his new "bride" to their beach
tent, while his soldier captains, professing to honor the nuptials, also retired with
the bride's maidens. In the morning, Antonia emerged from the tent "very joyful";
she was truly in love with her new husband, Solis reported.

But Menendez's mind was elsewhere. He had learned by courier of attacks
from the Aix Indians on settlements near Cape Canaveral, and he made plans
to return there at once. He first erected a huge cross in Carlos's village which,
he explained to the chief, his people should worship each morning in his
absence. The devious Carlos was not about to give up his tribal idols, but he
suavely persuaded Menendez to let his sister be instructed in Havana in her new
religion so that, upon her return to the village, she could teach him and his people
what they must learn. Even though now skeptical of the chief's designs,
Menendez agreed. He instructed his captains to return to Havana with Antonia
and her court, while he sailed alone in a fast brigantine to the east coast.

Upon his return to Havana, Antonia joyously greeted her new husband, but
the reluctant bridegroom stalled her by telling her that his religious order, the
Knights of Santiago, forbade members from sleeping with their wives until eight
days after putting into port. An eager bride sadly accepted this excuse. But later
that night, she changed her mind and, by a pretext, entered his lodgings. A
surprised adelantado awoke to find her sitting on the corner of his bed, and he
earnestly reminded her of her promise. But she answered that her brother would
be greatly angered, and their people might even rise up against him, if they

learned that the pair had not had a proper "honeymoon." Menendez relented for that night, but only after winning her agreement to wait out the remaining time of the eight days.

But, learning of severe logistic and morale problems at St. Augustine and Fort San Mateo, Menendez left early to return Antonia and her court to Carlos's village, leaving her there and telling Carlos to prepare to become a Christian and "go to a land of Christians [Spain]" with him, when he returned from the east coast. Carlos had other plans, however, so he told Menendez that his people might rise against him if he forced them to become Christians now, but, when the adelantado returned some nine months hence, he, Carlos, would have time to persuade them in the new faith. The chief in fact hoped to later maneuver Menendez into helping him attack and destroy the Tocobaga tribe northward, on Tampa Bay, and thereby extend his rule into all of the central west coast.

Months later, when Menendez returned, Carlos finally confided his war plans to the adelantado, but the latter informed him that, as Christians, they must make peace between the tribes. He persuaded Carlos to go with him to visit the Tocobagan chief. This formidable but peaceful tribe gladly consented to a peace treaty. Carlos, inwardly fuming, reluctantly agreed also, but on the return voyage to Carlos's village, the cacique argued heatedly with Menendez; one of the latter's men even overheard the chief vow to kill all the priests and soldiers now encamped near his village. On arrival, Menendez learned that his new wife shared her brother's hostile feeling toward him for not attacking the Tocobagans; this ill feeling had already been enhanced after Carlos learned of their less than ardent honeymoon in Havana and the absence in later months of any fruitful sign of their union—the bride remained barren. She lashed out at the adelantado for having "two hearts," one for himself and the other for the Tocobaga, and none for her or her brother.

This was the end of it, Menendez finally concluded. The treacherous Carlos could no longer be trusted, and the grand plan to control and settle South Florida for the Spanish crown was now aborted. He had loved neither wisely nor well enough, it seemed, and so now he would return to put his other Florida settlements in order and then sail home to Spain.

In later years, he would suffer to know that, while the church had absolved him for his rage of momentary madness in the slaying at Matanzas, it would never forgive him for his bigamous lapse of behavior at Charlotte Harbor. Furthermore, while he had succeeded in settling the oldest town in America at St. Augustine and, later on, most of North Florida, his sacrificial marriage of convenience not only failed but very probably delayed any settlement of South Florida for the next 250 years, at least.

BIBLIOGRAPHY

Numbers at left refer to chapter numbers.

1. Leslie, Stuart W. *Boss Kettering*. New York, Columbia University Press, 1983.

   Boyd, Thomas A. *Professional Amateur: the Biography of Charles F. Kettering*. New York, Arno Press, 1972.

2. Gilliland, Marion Spjut. *Key Marco's Buried Treasure*. Gainesville, University of Florida Press, 1989.

   Wardle, H. Newell. "The Pile Dwellers of Key Marco," *Archaeology* 4(1951):181-186.

3. DuBois, Bessie Wilson. *A History of Juno Beach and Juno, Florida*. Bessie W. DuBois, 1978.

   Shappee, Nathan D. "The Celestial Railroad to Juno." *Florida Historical Quarterly* 40(1962):329-349.

4. Strickland, Alice. *The Valiant Pioneers*. Miami, University of Miami Press, 1963.

   Hinkley, Ada G. *The Colonization of Ormond, Florida*. Deland, E.O. Painter Printing Co., 1931.

5. Straub, W.L. *History of Pinellas County, Florida*. St. Augustine, The Record Co., 1929.

   Grismer, Karl A. *The Story of St. Petersburg*. St. Petersburg, P.K. Smith & Co., 1948.

6. Straight, William M. "The Frontier Physician of Dade County." *Journal of the Florida Medical Association* 52(1965):479-485.

7. Fairchild, David G. *The World Grows Round My Door*. New York, Charles Scribner's Sons, 1947.

   ————. *The World Was My Garden*. New York, Charles Scribner's Sons, 1938.

8. Nelson, Richard Alan. *Lights! Camera! Florida!: Ninety Years of Moviemaking and Television Production in the Sunshine State*. Tampa, Florida Endowment for the Humanities, 1987.

9. Blakey, Arch. "The Florida Phosphate Industry, 1888-1918." Master's thesis, Florida State University, 1964.

10. Will, Lawrence E. *A Cracker History of Okeechobee*. St. Petersburg, Great Outdoors Publishing Co., 1964.

    Hanna, A.J. and Kathryn Abbey. *Lake Okeechobee*. New York, Bobbs-Merrill Co., 1948.

11. MacDowell, Claire L. *Chronological History of Winter Park*. Winter Park, MacDowell, C.L., 1950.

12. Burnett, Gene M. Personal interviews of Dick Pope and associates, 1982.

257

13. Burghard, August. *Mrs. Frank Stranahan, Pioneer.* Fort Lauderdale, Fort Lauderdale Historical Society, 1968.

    Ogle, Boyd and Wally Korb. *Stranahan's People.* Fort Lauderdale, Stranahan High School, 1975.

14. McKay, D.B. *Pioneer Florida.* Tampa, Southern Publishing Co., 1959.

    Straight, William M. "Odett Philippe: Friend of Napoleon, Naval Surgeon, and Pinellas Pioneer." *Journal of the Florida Medical Association* 53(1966):704-708.

    Proby, Kathryn Hall. *Audubon in Florida.* Coral Gables, University of Miami Press, 1974.

16. Roseberry, Cecil R. *Glenn Curtiss: Pioneer of Flight.* Garden City, N.Y., Doubleday, 1972.

17. Johnson, James Weldon. *Along This Way.* New York, Viking Press, 1933.

    Levy, Eugene D. *James Weldon Johnson: Black Leader, Black Voice.* Chicago, University of Chicago Press, 1973.

18. Mowat, Charles L. "The Tribulations of Denys Rolle." *Florida Historical Quarterly* 23(1944):1-14.

    Corse, Carita Doggett. "Denys Rolle and Rollestown, a Pioneer for Utopia." *Florida Historical Quarterly* 7(1928):115-134.

19. Karpis, Alvin. *The Alvin Karpis Story, with Bill Trent.* New York, Coward, McCann, Geoghegan, 1971.

20. Hanna, A.J. and Kathryn Abbey. *Lake Okeechobee.* New York, Bobbs-Merrill Co., 1948.

    Akerman, Joe A. *Florida Cowman, a History of Florida Cattle Raising.* Kissimmee, Florida Cattlemen's Association, 1976.

21. Matthews, Janet Snyder. *Edge of Wilderness.* Sarasota, Coastal Press, 1983.

    Grismer, Karl A. *The Story of Sarasota.* Tampa, Florida Grower Press, 1946.

22. May, Ellis C. *From Dawn to Sunset.* Tampa, Florida Grower Press, 1955.

23. Hanna, A.J. and Kathryn A. *Florida's Golden Sands.* New York, Bobbs-Merrill Co., 1950.

    Clark, Mabel K. *Titusville: An Illustrated History.* Cambridge, Md., Western Publishing Co., 1976.

24. Gilpin, Vincent. "Bradish W. Johnson, Master Wrecker, 1846-1914." *Tequesta* 1(March 1941)21.

25. Hecht, Ben. *A Child of the Century.* New York, Simon and Schuster, 1954.

26. Davis, W.W. *The Civil War and Reconstruction in Florida.* 1913 edition, Gainesville, University of Florida Press, 1964.

    Brown, C.K. "The Florida Investment of George W. Swepson." *North Carolina Historical Review* 5(1928):275-288.

27. Will, Lawrence E. "King of the Crackers (Jake Summerlin)," *Tequesta* 26(1966):31-38.

Hetherington, M.F. *History of Polk County*. St. Augustine, The Record Co., 1928.

28. Hammond, E.A. "Wreckers and Wrecking on the Florida Reef." *Florida Historical Quarterly* 41(1963):239-273.

Browne, Jefferson. *Key West, the Old and the New*. 1912 edition, Gainesville, University of Florida Press, 1973.

29. Grismer, Karl A. *Tampa: A History*. St. Petersburg, St. Petersburg Printing Co., 1950.

30. Washington, Booker T. *The Story of my Life and Work*. New York, Negro Universities Press, 1969.

White, Arthur O. "Booker T. Washington's Florida Incident." *Florida Historical Quarterly* 51(1972):227-249.

31. Hitchcock, Ethan Allen. *Fifty Years In Camp and Field*. New York, G.P. Putnam Sons, 1909.

Davis, Frederick. "Milly Francis and Duncan McKrimmon, an Authentic Pocahontas." *Florida Historical Quarterly* 21(1943):254-265.

32. Carper, N. Gordon. "Martin Tabert: Martyr of an Era." *Florida Historical Quarterly* 52(1973)115-131.

Shofner, Jerrell H. "Postscript to the Martin Tabert Case: Peonage as Usual in the Florida Turpentine Camps." *Florida Historical Quarterly* 60(1981):161-173.

33. Dickinson, Jonathan. *Journal, or, God's Protecting Providence*. 1699 edition, New Haven, Conn., Yale University Press, 1961.

34. Patrick, Rembert W. *Florida Fiasco*. Athens, Ga., University of Georgia Press, 1954.

35. Groene, Bertram H. *Ante Bellum Tallahassee*. Tallahassee, Rose Printing Co., 1971.

Eppes, Mrs. Nicholas Ware. "Francis Eppes (1801-1881), Pioneer of Florida." *Florida Historical Quarterly* 5(1926):94-102.

36. Ross, Ishbel. *Silhouette in Diamonds*. New York, Harper, 1960.

37. Drake, Samuel G. *Tragedies of the Wilderness*. Boston, Antiquarian Bookstore and Institute, 1844.

38. Patrick, Rembert W. *Florida Fiasco*. Athens, Ga., University of Georgia Press, 1954.

Smith, Joseph B. *The Plot to Steal Florida*. New York, Arbor House, 1983.

39. Mormino, Gary R. and George E. Pozetta. *The Immigrant World of Ybor City*. Chicago, University of Illinois Press, 1987.

Hersey, John. *Men on Bataan*. New York, A.A. Knopf, 1942.

40. Burnett, Gene M. *Florida's Past: People and Events that Shaped the State, Vol.1.* Englewood, Pineapple Press, 1986.

————. *Florida's Past: People and Events that Shaped the State, Vol.II.* Sarasota, Pineapple Press, 1988.

41. Arnade, Charles W. "Tristan de Luna and Ochuse (Pensacola Bay) 1559." *Florida Historical Quarterly* 37(1959):201-222.

Kenney, Michael. *The Romance of the Floridas*. New York, The Bence Publishing Co., 1934.

42. DuPont, C.H. "History of the Introduction and Culture of Cuban Tobacco in Florida." *Florida Historical Quarterly* 6(1928):149-155.

LaDunca, Charles E. "A Preliminary Study of the Tobacco Industry in Gadsden County, Florida." Master's thesis, Florida State University, 1949.

43. Beach, R.E. *The Miracle of Coral Gables*. New York, Currier & Harford, 1926.

44. Yulee, C.W. "Senator Yulee." *Florida Historical Quarterly* 2(1909):3-22, 26-43.

Lord, Mills M. Jr. "David Levy Yulee: Statesman and Railroad Builder." Master's thesis, University of Florida, 1940.

45. Manucy, Albert C. "The Gibraltar of the Gulf of Mexico." *Florida Historical Quarterly* 21(1943):303-331.

46. McCall, George. *Letters from the Frontiers*. Philadelphia, L.B. Lippincott, 1868.

47. Covington, James W. *The Billy Bowlegs War*. Chuluota, Fla., The Mickler House Publishers, 1982.

Gifford, John C. *Billy Bowlegs and the Seminole War*. Coconut Grove, Fla., Triangle Co., 1925.

48. Proctor, Samuel. "William Jennings Bryan and the University of Florida." *Florida Historical Quarterly* 39(1960):1-15.

49. Gibson, Charles Dana. *Boca Grande*. St. Petersburg, Great Outdoors Publishing Co., 1982.

Kerr, John Law. *The Legend of Useppa*. No publisher, no date..

50. Blackman, William F. *History of Orange County, Florida*. Chuluota, Fla., The Mickler House Publishers, 1973.

51. Mahon, John K. *History of the Second Seminole War, 1835-1842*. Gainesville, University of Florida Press, 1967.

Hamilton, Holman. *Zachary Taylor*. Hamden, Conn., Archer Books, 1966.

52. McIver, Stuart B. *Fort Lauderdale and Broward County*. Woodland Hills, Calif., Windsor Publications, Inc., 1983.

Hanna, A.J. and Kathryn Abbey. *Florida's Golden Sands*. New York, Bobbs-Merrill Co., 1950.

53. Staid, Mary E. "Albert Walter Gilchrist: Florida's Middle of the Road Governor." Ph.D. dissertation, University of Florida, 1950.

54. Schreiner, George Abel. *Cables and Wireless*. Boston, The Stratford Co., 1924.

55. Reiger, John F. "Deprivation, Disaffection and Desertion in Confederate Florida." *Florida Historical Quarterly* 48(1969):273-298.

56. Martin, Richard A. *Eternal Spring: Man's 10,000 Years of History at Florida's Silver Springs.* St. Petersburg, Great Outdoors Publishing Co., 1966.

57. Akerman, Joe A. *Florida Cowman: A History of Florida Cattle Raising.* Kissimmee, Florida Cattlemen's Association, 1976.

    Dacy, George H. *Four Centuries of Florida Ranching.* St. Louis, Britt Printing Co., 1940.

58. Asbury, Herbert. *Carry Nation.* New York, A.A. Knopf, 1929.

    Taylor, Robert Lewis. *Vessel of Wrath: The Life and Times of Carry Nation.* New York, New American Library, 1966.

59. Collver, Leon L.W. *The Pocket History of Fort Lauderdale.* Fort Lauderdale, Tropical Press, 1940.

60. Church, George B. Jr. *The Life of Henry Laurens Mitchell.* New York, Vantage Press, 1978.

    Weilding, Philip J. and August Burghard. *Checkered Sunshine: The Story of Fort Lauderdale 1793-1955.* Gainesville, University of Florida Press, 1966.

61. Dinkins, J. Lester. *Dunnellon: Boomtown of the 1890s.* St. Petersburg, Great Outdoors Publishing Co., 1969.

62. Grismer, Karl. *The Story of Sarasota.* Tampa, Florida Grower Press, 1946.

63. Matthews, Janet Snyder. *Edge of Wilderness.* Sarasota, Coastal Press, 1983.

    Grismer, Karl. *The Story of Sarasota.* Tampa, Florida Grower Press, 1946.

64. Strickland, Alice. *The Valiant Pioneers.* Miami, Center Printing Co., 1963.

    ———. "Ponce de Leon Inlet." *Florida Historical Quarterly* 43(1966):244-261.

65. Arnade, Charles W. *The Siege of St. Augustine.* Gainesville, University of Florida Press, 1964.

    DeCoste, Frederick. *True Tales of Old St. Augustine.* St. Petersburg, Great Outdoors Publishing Co., 1966.

66. Covington, James W. "Drake Destroys St. Augustine, 1586." *Florida Historical Quarterly* 44(1965):81-93.

    Luther, Edith A. "Sir Francis Drake's Raid on St. Augustine, 1586." Master's thesis, University of Florida, 1957.

67. Solis de Meras, Gonzalo. *Pedro Menendez de Aviles: A Memorial.* Gainesville, University of Florida Press, 1964.

261

Index